Completely Fragmented:

Nigel Pearce.

29/03/19.

Nigel Pearce

chipmunkapublishing
the mental health publisher

All rights reserved, no part of this publication may be reproduced by any means, electronic, mechanical photocopying, documentary, film or in any other format without prior written permission of the publisher.

>Published by
>Chipmunkapublishing
>United Kingdom

http://www.chipmunkapublishing.com

Copyright © 2019 Nigel Pearce

ISBN   978-1-78382-474-8

CONTENTS

Fiction.

1) Two disciples of Nietzsche (a short-story from the 'counter-culture').

2) The night becomes darker: being 17 and in difficulties.

3) Petra daughter of the revolution. A tale about the Socialist Patients Collective (S.P.K.).

4) A Naming of the Unnamed One.

5) Musing of a Majoun Eater.

6) George Orwell's '1984': revisited.

7) The Prank.

8) A modern psychomachy.

9) The Swallow.

10) Two men and a mermaid.

11) Janet, you were on my mind.

Drama.

12) Electra Unbound: A Modern Tragicomedy.

Life-Writing.

13) Why Elise Cowen?

Non-Fiction.

14) William Shakespeare & Bertolt Brecht *Coriolanus*

15) Lord Byron's and John Clare's Don Juan: a question of class.

16) On Milton and Blake.

17) On Defoe and the colonial encounter.

18) On Literature,

19) On creativity, exorcism and recovery.
20) The Situationist International: then and now.
21) On the revolutionary poetry of Bertolt Brecht.
22) On dialectics and Marxism: a philosophy for today.
23) On Allen Ginsberg, '*Howl*' and Trotsky.
24) This thing of darkness I acknowledge mine": Jungian analysis of *The Tempest* (Prospero and Caliban).
25) An encounter between Virginia Woolf and some Poets.
26)   Miscellaneous Poetry ...

'A non-writing writer, is a monster courting insanity

Franz Kafka,

He who controls the past controls the future, and he who controls the present controls the past?

-

George Orwell.

'The social revolution cannot take its poetry from the past, but only the future.'

- Karl Marx.

In my writing I am acting as a map maker, an explorer of psychic areas, a cosmonaut of inner space, and I see no point in exploring areas that have already been thoroughly surveyed.

-

William S. Burroughs

W. H. Auden on socialism and poetry:
'In such a society it, and, in such alone, will it be possible for the poet, without sacrificing any of the subtleties or his integrity, to write poetry which is simple, clear and gay. For poetry which is at the same time light and adult can only be written in a society which is both integrated and free

- W.H. Auden

The 'Turn' to academia.

1986 and I was returning to the Earth's orbit after a year rotating around the moon and was being nursed by an excellent ward Sister K' and a consultant Doctor C'.Sister K' was the driving force with Dr. C overseeing the whole scheme. The cleaning ladies bucket room was turned into a room which became known as Nigel's study, it was locked with a table and chair and study materials from and relating to The Open University. G.M., an inspiring lecturer, visited me in the hospital twice a week for gradually longer and more demanding sessions. Eventually I left the hospital and went to live in a 24-hour staffed pre-discharge unit in the community. Here I worked with less support, but systematically. I would become ill without the stimulus of any illicit drug and on occasion Dr. would enforce a 'no-study period' or admit me to the new hospital. Sometimes I would be advised to take a year 'out.' but this was becoming, with my creative writing, a life-line.

Two years in this unit, then a group home for five years, another uninduced florid episode and Dr. wants to put me in long term residential care. I persuade him to give me a chance in another group home. My drug problems resolved by the Drug Misuse Team, principally J'. Rayner and then into Rehab for the *delirium tremens*. I came to live in my flat in 1999. It is great, books and writing and study materials as well as and music, particularly J. S. Bach the year after I finally graduated when. Dad said

'This is the greatest day of my life.'

Dad had taken an interest in my degree and we were finally reconciled, thank goodness during his life.

The 'turn' to Chipmunkapublishing.

This will be my eleventh book with Chipmunkapublishing. A nurse named Nancy T' noticed an article about Jason Pegler and his company Chipmunkapublishing. She knew I wrote and had bits and pieces published and gave me the article. This 'turn' which has enhanced my being in the same fashion The Open University did and does. So I now have a second degree B.A. (Hons) Humanities with Creative Writing and have completed a M.A. English with Merit. This is a consequence of writing for and being published by Chipmunkapublishing and I was very pleased to become one of five Chipmunka Classics authors.

**Two disciples of Nietzsche
(a short-story from the 'counter-culture').**

1969 is buzzing like a swarm of bees and its lovers are dissolving into an orange mist. A stereo is spewing the music of the fashionably lost. Mick Jagger's voice is licking 'The Mid-Night Rambler' from speakers which are pulsating. The dust seems to leap off them in synchronized beats with the bass line, it jumps into this room. Jeremiah, his body emaciated by the sea of speed which had frothed through his veins that are now hardened and ulcerated by the pricks of needles, smiles. He had spent many nights dancing on the periphery of nebulae and diving into the solar circle of sacrificial rite.

Jagger sings: 'I'm talking 'bout the mid-night rambler, 'bout the mid-night gambler.'

Jeremiah whispers from eyes ablaze with love and then remembers to connect with his vocal cords, then with the muscles around his mouth:
'Hey Icarus, dig that chick, man we're talking Electra here, she just shot that ½ gram.'

Icarus ponders as the membrane within his consciousness twangs with the image of her body; it is gradually etched into his mind:
'She seemed fairly cool to me man.' Icarus wraps his long arms around his knees which seem to protrude from their sockets, rolls his mind into a ball and places it in a dusty corner of the room. Here his dream machine, the plastic syringe, lies mourning the last fix. His body suddenly jerks alert:
'Jeremiah, do you mind if I change the sounds, perhaps the Bartok, those String Quartets, just want to tune into some lunar stuff like Blake, dig.'

From somewhere deep within the recesses of his mind, Jeremiah replies: 'Cool man, I'm easy.'

Rigid structures had formed in Icarus' mind; they were clearly defined by lines of white light contrasted against a black background. Now struck with wonder he remembers reading that Allen Ginsberg had a vision of Blake. Ponders if he will have a similar experience, it brands his mind. The chains are being loosened…

A light-bulb hangs by a frayed cord from the ceiling which stares back with a yellowish pallor. It seems naked, vulnerable, emitting light, but this glow is from the grid's energy. Icarus turns to his companion and says:

'Man, the white-coated one's shoot that stuff through the brains of revolutionaries.'

Jeremiah replies 'What stuff?'

Icarus hums: 'Electricity, they wire you up to the grid and zap, there goes the class consciousness.'

Jeremiah sighs: 'Heavy man, really heavy. Be cool just bring the whole stinking system to its knees and start again.'

'What I'm saying is, like, they the oppressors burn the brains of the innocents.'

   'You seen the 'works'   man, we're beginning to come down.'

'No way man, we're really buzzing now, connecting about some important stuff. I noticed you've scribbled more notes on Nietzsche in the book of the dead, that writing pad you keep stashed away.'

Jeremiah begins to crumple, but then regains his mental balance and his body relaxes into a stream of energy:

'Yea man, the book of the dead, that's the book of the living, true immolation, cool disintegration whilst embracing our separation from what Nietzsche called 'the herd', I mean the 'straights', dig, they're the blind.'

Icarus continues:

           'Us, those who speed through time and space, man, we're a new evolutionary stage, apple blossom flowering on their dead wood, man we're wired tonight, last night, tomorrow, it just emerges into one Hegelian…'

'… 'Absolute Idea', right, that's incarnate in us baby, need a fix?'

A swarm of bee's swirls again like the dust whipped up by a desert storm, this torment which can only assuaged by the prick of a needle, but the sting remains in an arm, in our minds. The woman, who'd mainlined a ½ gram of amphetamine, had left behind a token of her love, a small square of tin foil. She'd smiled, tossed back her head and said:
'When it's cool, do this gear and remember me.'
Her beatitude of night is beginning to caress into curves the oblong structure of this haunted room. She will never be threatened by the banality of day as the integrity of oblivion will never be threatened by the rising of sun. She is the high priestess who will celebrate the beatification of night; it is her Last Supper which Jeremiah and Icarus will share. Her name is ancient; she is Isis and has returned at these End Times to save her children from the Patriarch and his wrath which could never be quenched. She lives in the 'counter-culture'.
Jeremiah muses: 'That God stuff man, it's all finished,
Nietzsche said: 'God is dead', dig.'
Icarus agrees: 'Yea, I dig, like the shrinks say you can't believe in God if there wasn't a cool bond with your father.'
'Yea, so right man.'
Icarus ponders: 'Those 'straights' are weird, really crazy.'

 A haze begins to encircle them, the desire to transcend this world and embrace an essence, something the 'elders' did not possess, ignites within them again. They're two outcasts of the system, but within them burnt a love of the 'Idea'. Both choose to live in the 'counter-culture' which is the body of Isis when she is pregnant with the 'Word'. A prophet of this tribe named Timothy Leary had said 'L.S.D. creates an ontological awaking.', but he hadn't intended that it should be taken intravenously!! Electra cruised back later; the sacrament had lain silently in a sea of shadows, solitary in its wrapping of tin foil, awaiting an awakening, its benediction.

She is, also, the goddess Isis and welcomes Jeremiah and Icarus to her mass, it is here she will celebrate the 'Word', the creative energy of the universe which comes from the lunar muse, the feminine. She gently unwraps the square of tin foil with long pale fingers and holds the four green micro- dots in her hands, raises them above her forehead and says:

'This is my body, take it and eat, you will be sustained by its vibrations and given a glimpse of infinity.'

Jeremiah and Icarus genuflect before her Host and Isis places two tabs of acid on each of their palms, they then prostrate their bodies before her alter. She smiles and whispers:

'Have a good trip, never forget me.'

They were dizzy with anticipation when Isis left and quickly found their dream machine, prepared the L.S.D. for a fix and located the mainline…

Wwwwhhhhhhhmmmmmm without any fear of flying this room is left dancing. A specter of William Blake appears in its corner reciting:

  Hear the voice of the bard!
Who Present, Past & Future, sees; Whose ears have heard. The Holy Word That walk'd among the ancient trees.'

Tangerine lights are merging into purple clocks which climb the walls, their disembodied smiles swirl into seas of lemon, lime green flowers melt and kiss the skin, and then the mind dissolves into a pool of turquoise which weeps back into the ceiling, from the stereo Jimi Hendrix's lyrics caress:

'Purple haze is in my mind, nothing don't seem the same, excuse me while I kiss the sky.'

Eight hours later the ambulance men found Jeremiah's body rigid, his eyes staring and the blood congealing in a syringe which hung limply from his arm. They found Icarus an hour later in a near-by park curled into a ball, he was repeating a mantra:
'"My name Is Oedipus, my name is Oedipus, my name is Oedipus….'

He'd flown close to the sun often, this time his mind had melted, his friend had died, and Electra/Isis had fled, forced to go underground because the 'heat' was closing-in.

The night becomes darker: being 17 and in difficulties.

This child had been expelled from a womb, aged 7, during the "summer of love". The place, where he had lived was without love, a place of darkness, a matrix of oppression. In this place the glare of intimidation was the god and the angels lived in fear of another deluge of threats. These places, they are called families, are dark places. He does not know why, perhaps it is just in the nature of these places? Ten years had passed in a whirl of tempest and fear. He had sought sanctuary in the company of souls who did not yell at him, his new companions did not have the strut of oppression and welcomed this outsider into the company of dreamers, in this place he felt safe, these people where not branded with the iron of hypocrisy. They kissed him with potions, wondrous white powders which beckoned him into a world of meaning and caring.

Initiating him into a world of compassion and the poetry of oblivion, they prepared his fix. The pristine white powder floats into a spoon, a lighter ignites, a wait until the liquid begins to bubble with significance, cotton wool is placed, with the zeal of the mystic, into the magic liquid, the plastic syringe sighs as the plunger is drawn up, hell will cease now, heaven's dance begins again caressing the verse in the mind of the poet.

Those shackles will float away again, the needle fits snugly onto the syringe, the singer of dreams smacks his arm, the tube becomes swollen, and the spike pierces the purple vein, deliverance from the world. As the plunger draws upwards a serpent of blood dances into the cloudy liquid, thank god, a hit the first time, the plunger pushes this chemical dream out of the syringe into his arm, he trembles ahrrrrr...he warmth radiates up the arm rushing into the catacombs which were his mind....this heat begins to permeate the entirety of his body, he is blessed into the Kingdom, the stigmata on his arm are aching with knowledge now: peace dawns with lilies floating in a pool of violet...this is the innocence denied him as a child.

A crisp autumn wind caresses brown and blood-red leaves into a frenzy of swirls. The psychiatric hospital sits alone in the platitudes of the rustic. It is a place where light is reciprocated between the damned, on occasion. The outsiders, ostracized by a world of squares which cannot accept circles, seek sanctuary in this place of shadows, a place of vibrations. The ambulance cruises through a bleak, but welcoming afternoon; he hopes that the hospital will be like a monastery, a convent where the anguished will be saturated with love?

What strikes him when the nurses help him undress is the crisp institutional nature of this place. The bed has white sheets, they feel like there've been bleached. The nurses wear uniform, the women are dressed as nurses in a general hospital, the men in identical hospital suits. A doctor, in a white coat, drifts onto the ward; he smiles:

'Nurse will give you an injection. You are safe here. I'll see you soon. Rest the mind and build-up your body.'

'Thank-you. I'm quite interested in Jung's work.' 'We will talk about many things, but rest now.'

Two nurses puzzle towards the poet, lost in a dance of the tragic and ego which pervades these places. They carry a grey cardboard tray, its edges raised to prevent any deviance from the task allotted by the god in a white coat, on it are a plastic syringe, same model as used by the dreamers, a brown glass ampoule which rests in supplication, in this place the drugs are checked before administration, cotton wool and a pink plaster which cannot hide the wounds given in Eden. They smile, he lies with the fear of the finite resounding around this howling labyrinth of unquiet spirits, and the exorcism begins.

Words drip like droplets of sweat from their tight mouths:
'Now we can do this the easy way, or you can make it difficult.'
The dreamer is metamorphosed into a patient, he lies resistant, but he recognizes in their eyes something of the priest draped in black, preparing to utter words of absolution. The needle is eased into hard muscle, it is painful, a largactal daze strikes his body like the thud of thunder in a prison cell, the mind does not begin to relax, there is nothing vaguely opiate about this chemical, rather it is like being struck by a truncheon, battered by the blows of mediocrity.
Twelve hours pass in a void without a flicker of consciousness. He begins to re-surface; the vision is blurred, but intact. At the foot of his bed sit two nurses, his sight focuses on them, but he becomes aware of other beds, two lines of iron bed-frames on which are mattresses with alternate orange and lime green covers. On these ships of dreams, within the house of whispers, sit these mystics of the psyche.
Ten days on and he can wander around the ward, the watchful gaze of the uniformed ones observe his tracks of body and mind. The voice of the ward's patriarch booms through the ward:
Medication time, come and get your pills everyone.'
Those shackles are about to be locked into place again as an orderly queue forms. The poet ponders that this may be a form of victim hood? But who are the victims: patients or nurses? The rigid frame of the clinic's entrance anticipates the medication, it is blocked by a steel trolley, behind which stand two nurses, on its top lie ordered rows of medicine tots awaiting the sticky brown syrup: chlorpromazine. The taste is foul and the odor unpleasant, it slips down the throat like swallowing the Sulphur of Hades. However, this young man feels an empathy with the flowers of the night, he becomes aware that he has found his home; the asylum.

Gradually the poet learns the rules and mores of this place, he grasps the nature of
the hierarchies, the maneuvering of staff and patient, the look of fear which registers in the eyes of some when approached by a certain nurse, the life of this organism resounds through his mind, he can resist actively or passively, on occasion to defy the authority of this place, other times to play the role of submission, to appear broken, it's all part of living in these places, it's the way you learn to survive. But his mind is never subordinated before their high alters of absurdity with those candles which burn like acid in the soul. Of course, there are caring staff; he learns to seek them out, other outsiders who also seek sanctuary in the hospital, but on the other side of the fence, sometimes the boundaries become rather confused when we live in this place and some of the nurses sing a similar song. It is 1977 and the world still inhales the breath of revolution, we are dizzy with vision, each other and ourselves. However, the revolution has its enemies in these places.

As evening caresses this tormented place, the poet decides that the revolution should be alive in this palace of dreams. He resists with his body; his body is like a weapon which cannot be soothed with the language of oppression. This resistance is the poetry of darkness; it is the drama of the physical, so he begins to refuse food, a week later and he becomes accustomed to the ache of hunger in his stomach, and the verse which is his defiance. The retreat into the damp cell of the body becomes a reason for existence and his sigh to the night has become a song with all the oppressed. The situation begins to tighten like an elastic band which is gradually stretched until its tension winds up to make a doll dance.

The nurses are not detached from the drama, they are part of this whole scene, and the atmosphere begins to become heightened as his refusal of food enters its fourth week. The white- coated ones come to check his blood-pressure on the hour and he is

transferred to the disturbed unit. Here electricity
buzzes every breakfast between the poet and the
nurses, they want him to eat the greasy bacon and
beans which is shuffled before him. The struggle
reaches intensity again at lunch and returns like a rat
invested plague as tea-time approaches, but his
poetry still flows with the ink of memory and the frost
of autumn in these places.

Venus also lives on the disturbed unit, she is 18, has
shoulder length ginger hair, crimson cheeks and a
ribbon of freckles across her nose, she wears faded
blue denim jeans and an orange tee-shirt. Venus is
huddled in a wheel-chair, the poet wonders who she
is, is she "cool", perhaps she's a real human-being?
Venus and the poet are like flowers in a wasteland of
twisted iron. They soon become aware of a
reciprocal vibration:

The bastards, I jumped, wanted to fly and die, know
what I mean?' she aches.

'Yes, yes, I do, I want to bring this rotten edifice
crashing down with me. They're the living dead, you
know Jesus said: "Let the dead bury their dead".

"My name is Venus: I take acid and speed, do you?'

'Yea I do'.

Venus smiles and says: 'Let's trip in the bin'.

Their conversation is the dialogue of dreams in the
dream-factory, the asylum, but these visions can be
aborted. The staff have taken away her wheelchair
and hidden it somewhere on the ward. They say she
can walk, but Venus's legs are smashed, and the
nurses know this. They don't like young people with
a vision which defies a world which has its stone
grinding lives into the flour of platitudes. The nurses
are sitting on cheaply upholstered wine-red chairs at
random points around a white-washed room. They
stare with eyes which burrow into your most hidden
being, there is no escape here. One method of
control is to take the patients cigarettes and issue
them hourly, the hours begin to revolve around the
next cigarette, this becomes the accepted form of
communication in these places, and all other forms

of human contact are frowned upon on this unit. In this place, when you're 17 or 18, resistance becomes the ideology of despair and this gradually becomes the only hope, the dream. It is Sunday and as usual the porters bring the meal trolley. It is a steel box with draws which contains dinner, then beneath pudding; on each corner is a castor with a black rudder tyre. The nurses plug it into a socket, already the tension begins to rise. Venus needs a cigarette, she must drag herself across the floor to the charge-nurse's office, and she understands the process of subordination on this ward:
'Please nurse, may I have a cigarette.'
A snapped reply: 'You know there aren't any.'
We all know that Venus's mum brought in 20 at visiting time the evening before:
'Please nurse, a smoke.'
'Clear off.' Is the response. 'I only want a smoke.'
'If you carry on there's an injection, you don't want that, do you?'
Venus pulls her broken body across the carpet; tears are washing the pain from her face, she sobs silently. These places could be like interminable night.
The poet sits at a white vinyl covered dining table, he feels dizzy. A nurse pushes a plate of cabbage, sprouts, roast potatoes, beef and gravy before his trembling face:
'You will eat today, you will eat this.'
His silence has more resonance than any shout. The ward-sister slams a food liquidizer on the table, it has a brown square base, about 4x4 inches, on top of this is a cone shaped container, his dinner is slopped into this, the lid is snapped into place, a button pushed, there is a whirling noise, the product is thick green liquid, the lid is removed, and the contents poured into a beaker:
'You will drink this, now!'
'I'm not drinking that slime.'
Lightning between patient and nurse's sizzles and sparks. They surround him, one gives him a poke in the ribs, their loud voices sting his mind; this seems,

to him, like a manifestation of Dante's worst dreams. The torment continues, eventually he agrees to drink their potion and swallows the green slime. His stomach contracts and expels the liquid, he spews uncontrollably. Before the poet lies a pool of yellow vomit and green bile.
They demand: 'Clean that up immediately.'
This sounds, to the poet, like an expulsion of the Fallen from heaven; he is cast into an abyss of fear where the flames of their anger lick his soul and body in frenzy of domination:
I'm not cleaning that up; you made me drink the stuff.'
He was 17 and the night had become very dark. It will be over a year before he will see the outside of the hospital and the doctors never did discuss Jung with him. The only comfort, for this poet, was to scribe the voices of other outsiders in his verse.

Petra daughter of the revolution.
A tale about the Socialist Patients Collective (S.P.K.).

The dark allurement of revolution and sweet aroma of introspection are intertwining like phantoms in this squat in 1975. Petra, a small round woman of 19 is sitting in the smog of contemplation. Her hair is brown, untidy and short, it sits on her head like the crown of a recently resurrected Rosa Luxemburg. A brown tee-shirt with embroidered flowers around the neck emphases her plump physic and faded tight black jeans combine to say that she is a goddess of the underground and nymph of primordial night. Smiling vaguely at a middle-aged man who looks like he comes out of some 19th century Russian novel, perhaps he keeps a chronicle of the demise of his shrink into madness, she suppresses a smile: 'Comrade...but let's just cut the shit baby, what kind of crap are you lying down'.

Peter slowly strokes a long ginger beard which seems temporarily, to Petra, to be creeping across the roach littered floor boards like a startled lizard. He mumbles:

'It's like the movement needs a push to tip the balance, the proletariat are in the mood for poetry, we have to become their calligraphers, you dig'.

She sighs: 'O I dig man, I really dig, know what I mean'

The rapid rattle of a typewriter sends waves of disturbance through their awareness, it's like an automatic rifle firing into a black chasm of zero, like the relentless march of the masses into nirvana, muses Petra. In her mind there are images like water forming into vapor, into clouds which sometimes obscure the sun, now they spill their seed upon soil in a shower or in a deluge, either to fertilize seed or to wash it away in a torrent. Peter is pondering whether he should scatter a little fertilizer in this garden, the Garden of Love, where iconoclasts are welcome and encouraged to participate in its rites. But he decides, with a jolt from the intellect, that everything is subordinated to the

struggle. He wonders what the dynamic of the armed struggle is, some of its shadows were illuminated and a solution had surfaced during those group therapy sessions with the professor, now imprisoned himself for activities against the State and Capital, where they had discussed the dialectics of liberation. They had discovered that for them, those especially damaged by capitalism, that their situation was more complex than for their comrades without psychiatric problems, their liberation from illness was directly linked to active participation in the emancipation of all the oppressed, it must be an attempt to grasp the full implications of the "death of God", but more than that, it was to be an active assassination of God, of the patriarch and of all his oppressive relationships and the, consequent, rebirth of the child. He murmurs to Petra:
'The struggle, all of it, is about regaining innocence lost when we were children.'
A shadow passes across Petra's face:
'Yea man, you're talking 'bout the armed struggle, call it just cool baby, self-realization, just getting rid of all the shit they put in the head.'
Peter says: '"Have you read the poetry of Sylvia Plath?'
'Of course, 'Daddy'…that's hot poetry, it's really groovy."
'Sylvia had grasped something of the essence when she wrote that line: "Daddy I had to kill you"'.
Petra becomes animated; a crimson flush was rising in her face: 'She wrote those lines, there're like furrows in my mind, yea know, "Daddy, daddy, you bastard, I'm through" that's just real man, wow, so real. I've something to tell you, I'm Lady Lazarus, yea know, like in the poem'.
Peter's gaze tightens; he looks intently at this young woman: 'You attempted suicide?'
'Yea, I guess I did'.
'Do you have a name comrade?' 'They call me Petra.'

The incessant bashing on the typewriter continues without relief, it is thumping through the wall and invading Petra and Peter's consciousness. This is the remorseless beating of History:
I have a name, it is Peter. Take my hand daughter, daughter of the revolution'
A loud explosion, a blaze of orange light flashes into the room, black smoke billows and then their disembodied screams reverberate in the chaos:
'Shit, man this is heavy!!'
Hard and sharpened steel voices jab them like poisoned spear heads:
'Freeze it's the police… don't move, down, get down you scum'.
Petra and Peter are thrown against the floor, then heaved up and pinned to the wall:
Peter shouts: 'Resist them.'
Petra yells: 'Defy them baby, I love you.'

A Naming of the Unnamed One.

Dawn anticipated twilight and the wisdom of night. He rolled up a rather tatty blue sleeping-bag knowing that today would herald his Naming, a gaining of an essence in meaningless existence. He would dance into those rivers of darkness which are within the self and sink into the shadow of the black oceans which bubble within all people. On this journey he will embrace those he meets, who, like him, are driven by ideas and deep passions. This Unnamed One will find a home within the rippling chaos of reality. With worn green denim jeans, a pink tee-shirt with flowers lovingly sown into whirls of love and a multi-coloured shoulder bag this young man could have been any hippie embarking on 'the quest'. Long brown hair complimented by an olive skin suggested a middle-eastern nature. Tall and slim, his bangles rattled with the sweep of a languid gait. A thirst haunted his mouth and an indefinable hunger drove him to a working-man's café. The tables stood like sentinels with their squeeze bottles of red and brown sauces standing with an ease of habit on each table. The smell of fried food appealed, but he assuaged the hunger with a slender glass of milk. Here the worker bees, the drone crew, glanced at the Unnamed One with the suspicion of medieval peasants anticipating the next witch-hunt. Now the wind belonged not to those bees, but to those who dreamt beyond the hive of History. But his destiny would unravel amongst this stream of workers buzzing their way to work. He believed that work had become an opiate and was a manifestation of an estrangement separating people from their essence. It seemed like a vortex whose dance is the allurement of a drama that had dissolved. A play in which the lines had been forgotten and the theatre burnt to the ground by those who would make a cathedral for the proletariat. The Unnamed One wept with those tears that bleed down a dreamer's face. These are like the flames which have always burnt heretics, those who are crazed and caressed by flames. Our bodies are left like a burnt offering tied to the stake of oppression. The smog around him was choking and he saw a giant black heart pulsating, pumping men and women ceaselessly through a giant body which was ravaged by the pursuit of emptiness. This beat of darkness seemed to be possessed by involuntary tremors which reminded him of a leaf blown across a frozen field that cried with the cold.

Walking without purpose he eventually glided into the city's park. It was vibrating with rumors of an insurrection, but this was silenced by the wailing of discarded syringes. Those accessories to bliss and death stared into his eyes and he trembled before their spectrum which was without colours. It could only provide the constant buzz of white noise which is a distraction from the silence of the void. He thought that the fear was not of the void itself, but the act of throwing oneself over the precipice. That was the anguish, the dread that one may leap into nothingness without making a conscious decision to do so. The Unnamed One looked at the desolation in this place and wondered if this ocean of unfulfilled dreams would begin to dream again if that black pulsing heart stopped its beating, its mindless pumping, stopped the thumping of people through the arteries of a corpse. Ideas wounded his body like a scythe cutting through wheat fields which has become ripe for the harvesting. Now he began to realize that the act of flinging oneself off the cliff of reason into a sea of expectations and drowning in the delights of imagination beckoned him like a poet welcomes the opium dreams. The Unnamed One became aware, it was like a message from desert hermit who had tuned into his wavelength, that absurdity and zero can only be transcended by a journey that builds icons. It must then place them on an alter which is draped in the cloth of self, genuflect before them in the night and smash the images with the passion of an iconoclast. A feeling of release overcame his temple of broken mirrors and now visions transcended introspection. Suddenly like a jolt of E.C.T. without anesthetic, the consequences of realization dawned; this storm is to be navigated. Drowning only bought a morning without the dew and it is that dew which nourishes writing. For now, the desire to record this odyssey had intoxicated this young man.

In the mid-morning this Nameless One drifted with the crowd's motion. A woman with a full black face roses before him like the sun dancing. She wore flowing robes of white cotton. She was surrounded, almost engulfed, by a mass of black, white, brown and yellow faces. It was a gathering of the enlightened who believed they were the damned. The Unnamed One skimmed the fringes of this flock. The woman, who was possessed by the primal gene, was speaking animatedly.

She beseeched her flock to: 'Wait no longer for the Second Coming of the Lord.'

She shaped them into a chalice to be filled with the wine of her belief.

They must: 'Prepare yourselves to wash your bodies with the Blood of the Lamb.'

She began to sigh and moan like a summer evening breeze, her words like her breathing were gaining intensity slowly, then faster, deeper and now whipped like a typhoon which reached its peak in a rush:

'We must cast-off the soiled carcass of the World.'

Most of her flock stood in a daze, their eyes glazed with lack of understanding. They began to filter away, deaf to any song which had been sung before Eden. However, a number began to chant with that primal rhythm. They became like a willow caressed, first, by a breeze, then kissed by a tempest which howls:

'We are the Saved, we are the loved, and love is the night, come Lord Jesus awake the dead.'

The priestess spoke quietly now, her voice like nectar touching gossamer:

'Have no fear, for fear is death, love one another.'

The Unnamed One listened with the tenderness of pain, he could see an icon of fire and love, but he

knew that it was an image which reflected an absurdity, the cosmic nothingness in which people attempt to drown themselves. The priestess stood alone, she was enfolded in the profundity of solitude. He approached her and asked: 'Do you believe that Jesus was Divine.'
She replied: 'Yes, he is my Lover. Have you read the bible brother?'
He sighed: Yes, but one or two questions remain, for me, unanswered. Firstly; New Testament eschatology is quite clear that the 'Second Coming' was imminent. Jesus and the early church believed that the New Jerusalem would be heralded in and the sufferings of the 'faithful' would reach their conclusion within a generation.'
She smiled with the certainty of eternity: 'The End is close my friend.'
'The Nameless One whispered: 'You are denying the teaching of your own Sacred Text. It is better to tune into your primal gene and vibrate with an ancient song.'
He sensed the icon was disintegrating and with compassion his mind fell upon it like the hammer of History:
'Your scripture records Jesus saying: 'Father, Father why have you forsaken me' as he was experiencing a lingering and brutal death.
Surely the Son of God could not be so alienated from his Father.'
The Unnamed One saw the icon crumble and its fragments blown into infinity like the dust of the dead. He felt a deep sorrow but knew that icons must be smashed on this quest. The sorrow of those dispossessed of their icons was like a steel spike which pierced his heart.
She spat: 'Get behind me Satan.'
Leaving this stratum, the Unnamed One entered the labyrinthine sub-city of electric neon. Here the death bell of work did not abuse the bodies of proletarians, for here there wasn't that ethic of labour or, for that matter, the availability of work. There was a shared feel which was distinctive; a 'bee-bop' scene for

those who claimed asylum with Burroughs' ghost or the defiance of thudding bass beats and the rapping of voices of the young energized by cheap cocaine and its variants. It was in this maze of heightened inactivity that the Nameless One glimpsed a few young woman and men selling a badly printed paper with its title emblazoned in red letters: 'Struggle'. The Unnamed One approached one of the young men and spoke with tenderness:
'Comrade, how many papers have you sold today?'
He replied: 'About four, but you addressed me as 'comrade', are you a Marxist?'
'My interest is in dialectical materialism?'
The young man's eyes shone like a lighthouse beam cutting through a foggy night:
'Yes, of course, would you like to talk?'
A fire was burning in the Unnamed One's mind, he seized the moment with the embers glowing like an awaking. Speaking as if animated by tides whose motion vibrates in the night encircling the moon he began:
'Marx and Engels described religion as the 'sigh of the oppressed', but this is a concept contradicted by their atheism. A conflict between these two opposites is resolved by a 'dialectical leap'. This will, itself, produce a 'synthesis' which is the fulfillment of our human condition. But comrade, I'm sorry, it's Hegelian dialectics which are the key to this, not Marx's critique of Hegel. Do you see? It is not the triumph of matter that is in the past. Now we need the ascendancy of the 'Idea', the rise of the imagination. Its home is in Hegel.'
Tears ached grooves in his face, for a belief had become enshrouded. A dream had evaporated into clouds whose rain burnt like acid.
The young man replied: 'But, the struggle of the proletariat, that's my life.'
He had lost his rudder in an ocean of absurdity and would drift into a vortex, spiraling into the Void.

The Unnamed One continued: 'Icons will vaporize into a rite without boundaries, humans will transcend them, and love shall chant her forgotten mantra.'
The young man asked: 'Who are you?'
'I am nameless.'
The Nameless One slipped from the city into its surrounding countryside. It beckoned with an allurement which was ancient like a memory of birth before he was curled in the womb of his mother. Finding a river, he sat on the bank; a ballet of water whispered away those icons which had haunted his mind. The sun and moon shone into the river's darkness. He became aware of their motion, a metamorphosis of Light and Dark reflected from their depths. The Nameless One got to his feet and stroked himself into the water; he is Named, a child of Alpha and Omega, which is the ebb and flow of infinity. The water gulped his limps and they moved in slow motion. It was as if they were being sucked into and then suspended in a solution of syrup:
'My God, that kid has just walked into the river. Help, quick help me, he's gone under.'
'Okay mate, let's dive down and pull…come on get in.'
Two men in their forties waded into the river and braced themselves. They ripped off their jackets and dived. But this river had torrents no one other than the Named One could see. Their minds became confused and colours rushed before their eyes. Skulls seemed to rise from the river bed beckoning them with the seduction of death. A vortex had swallowed the bile of a soul lost in the pitch of an abyss. Others on the shore pulled them free. They lay exhausted on the grassy bank. A group of laborers had gathered; some were shouting, some were silent, others asked questions:
'Who was he?' 'Why did he do it?'
'I think he came from the mental home.'
'No, he was a wanderer.'

Musing of a Majoun Eater.
During a lull in the Intifada a young man whose brown face contrasts with billowing pristine white robes strode towards a group of Israeli soldiers. They were young men, conscripted and spiced with a taste of Zionist venom. They eyed him with disquiet, a distrust of the outsider.
One yelped: 'Stop, no nearer.'
'I come from Africa with the wisdom of a Primal Gene and that infinity of the Serpent. The true essence of Jesus of Nazareth is held in these scrolls I carry.'
One of the soldiers addressed his confederates: 'Another one who thinks he's Jesus.'
'Come back to save us all.' replied his mate.
A soldier crunched towards him:
'If you're so high and mighty stop this.' A rifle butt crashed across his back:
'How about that. Still think you're Jesus?' 'A real nutter'
A sergeant intervened: 'Now lads...better get him to the loony bin.'
And sand blew across the soldiers' check point and their eyes were smarted.
At the hospital Dr. Rue sat down in a small white-washed room. He was rotund with
whispery blond hair, which was so fine it appeared to be gossamer in nature.
'Well you nearly got yourself shot. Those soldiers are trained to shoot fast first, and no questions asked.'
'I am the bearer of wisdom.'
'Yes. Is it esoteric?'
'It can only be disseminated to the few and then must be preached globally.'
'And whom...?'
'The burden of truth upon me is so much.'
'What's in your bag?'
'The Truth is in the scrolls.'
'I am a spiritual man, do you think I could, under your supervision, read the scrolls?'

'There is a yoke of burden upon my shoulders, it is the weight of enlightenment.'

The room hummed with expectation as the psychiatrist prepared for the usual Majoun delusions. Was the young man just another Majoun Eater?

He began: 'I was handed these scrolls by a young woman, she wore rags and had a certain presence, a charisma about her. She named me much to my astonishment and told me to head for Jerusalem. There I should gather a group of those who are spiritually and socially illegitimate. She gave me these scrolls and strolled into the distance without another word. A sense of mission enfolded my body with comforting warmth, my spirit was exalted. So that is how I achieved enlightenment, a brief encounter with an effervescent girl whose eyes were like purple light.'

He took the scrolls from his bag and began to speak the text which they contained:

'This is the truth about Jesus of Nazareth. Three wandering teachers in a quest for illumination were travelling through Africa in search for its ancient knowledge, Africa being the cradle of civilization and a land of fertility. As the sun rose and awoke these mystics, they perceived a golden matrix. Slowly they approached and became aware of dancing purple lights. They had stumbled or been led to the Oracle who spoke of her sister the Primal Gene which is the source of humanity. Having located the precise spot, they unearthed an urn shrouded in a golden fleece. The oracle then caressed them with the wisdom to carry the urn to its appointed place and the knowledge of the precise moment to break the seals. It directed them to Palestine.

Mary, a quiet girl of 13, had spent the sun beamed day looking after a moderate sized flock of lazy sheep. Running home, she felt warmth of weariness and settled down to rest on straw in a barn. Three itinerant mystics, hungry and thirsty, saw purple light drifting around the barn. The lights were intense and confronted the teachers. It became immediately clear that at location they should break employ the

ancient law and break the bejeweled jar. They entered the barn and while Mary was asleep, they carefully broke the seals on the urn and then gently fertilized her with the Primal Gene. This was in accordance with he wishes of the Oracle, that ancient law. She awoke with a sense of unutterable tranquility.
As the months passed it became clear that she was pregnant. Joseph, her boy-friend, decided to marry Mary to remove any social stain which others would besmirch them with. The boy child was born in a shower of purple droplets. Jesus was illegitimate having been conceived outside marriage. Jesus was a reticent and pensive child who preferred solitude to the games of other children. As a youth he was bullied by other boys because he was illegitimate. On one occasion Jesus saw flashing purple lights and these animated with an authority as old as Africa and he said:
'I am the illegitimate One who draws everyone who is also illegitimate in any way to his side, I take you into my heart'.
The others thought this weird, but some regarded him as enigmatic and stopped the bullying.
Mary understood her son's serpent. The serpent swallows itself eternally and therefore creates an infinite circle where it consumes itself: good and evil consume each other for infinity. But Jesus realized these concepts were all rooted in the material, he realized there was a bio-chemical basis for these phenomena. Upon this epiphany Jesus was Transfigured, the primal gene within exploded and he was wrapped in a cloak of purple. His body and mind were vibrating with an explosive ecstasy. Surrounded by veils of purple he began to teach. He spoke in parables and with an intensity which captivated his congregations. Banished from the synagogue, he wandered with a core of disciples. He said: 'I am the primal gene, the alpha of humanity.' And again, my gene is your gene, I am within you.'

Once he said: 'I am you and you are me.'
He taught: 'As my heart beats so does yours.'
Jesus made his journey complete by travelling to Jerusalem. Banishing his disciples, he entered the Garden of Gethsemane, the Garden of History and was alone except for his purple lights for company. He prepared to discover the quintessential nature of his destiny, the primal genes sparked within. His contemplation, a barbed introspection became so intense he sweated blood.
He sighed: 'I am wisdom incarnate and it is stroking every strand of my hair. I am the illegitimate one and I bring socio-political illegitimacy to its fruition.'
Jesus now knew is destiny, he would become a sacrifice for the Zealots who were revolutionaries opposing both the Jewish establishment and the Roman occupiers.
The Jewish ruling class with the notable exception of Joseph of Arimathea had conspired to put Jesus on trial and have him executed by the Roman colonial power. Jesus was subsequently arrested and found guilty of sedition. But as he was being handed over to Pilot, the Roman Governor, a purple splinter cut into his mind and he drew out a dagger from his cloak and assassinated Pilot shouting:
'I am history, History will vindicate me.'
While in the dock for the murder of Pilot he said:
'The trail of the illegitimate one is the trail of the Zealots and consequently you will deal with the people. I am he people incarnate. My wisdom is their Wisdom. I leave the people in tumult but weep not for true revelation is incarnate in my chosen Zealots. Their path is immaculate struggle'.
Jesus is taken to a quiet place and nailed to a cross. Hanging he ejaculates: 'In leaving I remain, I am the DNA of the masses, in this illegitimacy I gather all those who weep in my heart.'
Dr Rue inhaled:
'Fascinating.'
The reply: 'Do you believe?'
Dr Rue whispers:

'You have the Divine Madness, go in peace Majoun Eater.'

George Orwell's '1984': revisited.

Winston Smith and Julia had been banished by Big Brother to a sandy and wind-swept wilderness. Here their flesh was burnt by the relentless sun and their hunger only assuaged by a love which transcended the abysmal curse of the 'Thought-Police'. Bodies almost too raw to touch, they made love with a deep and dark energy which came from a liberated libidinal drive. They had penetrated deep into the Id and like a hurricane that came from their essences banished all banality, intoxicating with interacting unconsciousness'. Other exiles had struggled and heaved their way across the shifting desert and torn themselves on its obscured rocks. Their feet were cut and bruised as they climbed into incrustations which provided temporary shelter from the blazing sun. These exiles had been drawn from the various strata of the 'Outer Party'. Some accused of tarnishing the purity of 'Newspeak'. Others cast-out for sexual activity which was banned for them and, yet, others for keeping clandestine journals.

Big Brother had cast these outsiders into this harsh terrain from where there was no apparent return only after they had been 'de-cultured' and professed their love for Big Bother. Torture had been used until they 'confessed' to their crimes; Electro Convulsive Therapy had been employed as one method to extract these so-called revelations. Then processed in the 'Ministry of Love' they had been accessed as being rehabilitated and therefore needed no further treatment and where cast, apparently broken, into the wilderness. Gradually they had melted into the night like roaming pariahs, but they left sighs like all scavengers and they began to locate each other and form into little bands, almost packs. These groups moved in every reducing circle until they began to coalesce. When this jell had formed it was inevitable

that Winston and Julia would become a beacon, because of their intellectual and erotic challenge to Big Brother and his apparatus the 'Thought Police'. They would guide their comrades through the bitter nights of wilderness and isolation. But passivity began to pervade the group, choking it like a hangman's noose.
Winston and Julia left the group saying:
'We may be gone a little while, its important ideological work, remember love and solidarity '
They wandered into the wilderness guided by the anti-Father, the antithesis of Big Brother who was the collective memory of Goldstein. They were drawn to a ragged cliff and climbed until exhausted they had reached a crevice hidden by brush. Within lay pure white tablets of stone about the size of a volume of Marx/Engels 'Selected Works', delving into the aperture they found three, a trinity. On their return other members of the group or as they were now calling themselves: 'Revolutionary Proletarian Cell', for Winston had said long ago:
'If there is hope it lies in the proles.'
Upon these stones Winston and Julia, employing the instruments devised by their brothers and sisters, their comrades, began to give tangible form to their abstract thoughts and their physical experiences. It read, indeed proclaimed:
'1) Only the proletariat can overthrow the Party and Big Brother. This is the product of our objective analysis and is our goal.
2) We do not know what the subjective conditions are within the proletarian zones, by that we mean there is no awareness of the consciousness of the proletariat; their class consciousness.
3) Consequently the 'Cell' must adopt the tactic of infiltration into the proletarian zones. The zones of the lost, who by their own activity shall, be found as a class.
4) Any means necessary is, ultimately, justified by the achievement of the ends.'

After many forages across the wasteland to the workers ghettos, they obtained essential items such as worker's clothes. Gradually they accumulated a collection of items, bits and pieces and like a circling eagle reconnoitered the terrain before swooping on its prey, but the masses weren't the prey, they were the instrument to be employed against the prey. Like the dawn wipes the tyranny of night from the world the 'Cell' began what they believed and had interpreted from Engels as their:
'World historic mission.'
As twilight began to dissolve the colours of day they penetrated the worker's zone; then were confronted with an ink black smog which was almost Dickensian and the neglected tower-blocks where the masses existed with the horrors of a life separated from its meaning, its essence, but the 'Cell' would help create this essence even if it required destroying the existential to allow the essence to have a vehicle to articulate itself, allowing the masses to emancipate themselves. Winston and Julia now rested from the 'Cell's period of wandering, assumed the everyday running of their group. Everywhere the belching of factories and the preparations for yet more wars in which the workers would be sacrificed to the insane logic of Big Brother created a terrain of ideological anemia as well as poverty. The people seemed to walk bent over under the yoke of alienation and be shackled to the hopeless grind of their lives. Their intellectual and cultural diet, force-feed, was a combination of sentimentality and pornography which, in totality, had led to a soporific and subservient proletariat.
Winston was despondent: 'How can we organize or ignite these people it's like the task of Sisyphus. All is lost.'
Julia replied: 'Let us travel beyond appearance into essence, we may be surprised what we may discover and find.'
The 'Cell' conducted a collective analysis after all had reported back to Winston and Julia their

experiences of the 'class' atomized and suffering from state sponsored Banalism and the 'line' was agreed. Julia and Winston would emerge into the masses and try and find some, any, tool of disrupting the sickness of the proletariat. The others would behave as invisible revolutionaries awaiting the call to action.

The moved, almost staggered through the proletarian zones only to be met with blank smiles or vacuous grimaces. Days heaved into weeks and it was becoming like a razor-blade before a suicide attempt. It appeared that the labouring masses were, to all intents and purposes dead, certainly unresponsive to anything than the 'Party's' constant stream of platitudes and patriotism. Eventually they entered the central areas; here there were just shacks, dismal hovels. Julia suddenly smiled and said:

'It is here that the wound is at its most rancid. It is here where the depths of the oppressed are to be found.'

With a trembling sense of trepidation and expectation Julia and Winston approached one of the hovels. They knocked on the flimsy but heavily chained door. A head, well a skull with deep blackened sockets peered around the edge:

'What yer want...best smack we got, ten quid a bag... blow yer away.'

Julia answered in the language she had learnt in an 'Outer Party' manual of 'prolespeak.' 'Cool, we can score here.'

'Yea baby...got any works.'

An emaciated figure unshackled the door and said: 'Best shooting gallery in town man.' Winston and Julia entered this palace of despair, quivering.

A man, the 'Man', sat in a haze of tangerine; his eyes seemed like amber jewels glaring like furnaces in the gloom of the shooting gallery. He hovered out of the door leaving the two revolutionaries and the skeletal worker.

He groaned: 'Do you up for that other ten quid bag.

Just do my business first.'
Julia and Winston looked in horror as he slithered up his shirt-sleeve, arms covered in needle marks, bruises and seeping abscesses. He searched pathetically for a vein that wasn't just an inflamed track:
Got a hit...far out man... ahhrrr cool stuff.'
The junkie was how in a haze and flushing blood and water in and out of his syringe, sucking it and out then squirting it into cracked white mug. Immediately with the force of a passion released from the unconscious by a lover Julia and Winston became aware that this polluted blood with its dream serum was the agent of social transformation. The 'Cell' gathered in the depths of the inner zones and a new line was, this time, enforced by the revolutionary couple on their comrades:
'We had believed that only through the rise in class consciousness and a consequent proletarian revolution could Big Brother, or to be more accurate comrades Big Daddy, can be removed. However, it has become apparent it is only through the dissemination of decadence and hedonism particularly through i.e. drug use that the system can be undermined, if not overthrown. This pollution must happen from the base to the pinnacle...only in this way can the next generation be cleansed and emancipated. You remember the ends justify the means by any necessary praxis.'
Julia continued: 'Hence decadence contains the apotheosis of the masses.'
Winston concluded: 'It is necessary to spread an immorality, almost a plague, it will eventually consume the Party in its entirety and Big Brother Himself. And from these ruins will raise proto-communism.'
During the next day/nights the 'Cell' fueled by what was becoming a contorted, almost distorted, zeal, they spread hard drugs and whatever other encouragement was necessary to propagate the new line. Making money and then investing,

reinvesting; wasn't this a little like the cycle of Capital accumulation discovered by Marx? However, workers became too ill to work regularly and the Gross Domestic Product began to fall, the destruction of the masses was being used for the emancipation of the masses: to destroy 'double-think', well that's what the 'Cell' had come to believe. They had been in the wilderness so long they had lost touch of their own philosophical concepts; these had become hopeless abstractions without a base in the material experience of the masses. But Big Brother's war-drive finally collapsed and with it the dynamic of His system.

Intravenous heroin use became endemic within the 'Inner Party' which was already disintegrating because of factional struggles. Suddenly with the combination of economic failure and a structural crisis in the leadership in the ruling class the 'Cell' (they hadn't made any attempt to recruit members to their group) saw their strategy had proven successful. The problem was though they had destroyed the structure of the system they had also weakened the only force that could replace it; the proletariat. Mistakenly they had believed that an almost sacrificial plague, the immolation of and by the masses through the spreading of dissolute habits and practices was the solution, but it was not.

One morning Julia and Winston stumbled upon a building where the 'tele-screen' was still working, but only just...it was a grey blurred haze with a figure that seemed spectral.

They realized it was a dim image of Big Brother. He said solemnly and in a measured tone:

'This is the final analysis. We have reached Omega; therefore, the Inner Party has dissolved itself. History and hence Reason or sanity has been concluded. The only option for me is...'

He slowly eased a revolver from the desk he was sitting behind:

'Too create my own myth.'

He placed the revolver in his mouth and the 'tele-screen' panged into darkness.

As the next few years past a semblance of order returned to society. Methods for treating the previous socio-cultural problems were successfully created and implemented.

Julia mused: 'Could Humanity really taste its essence in these conditions, isn't the freedom for self-destruction a much deeper drive than socio-economic drives.'

She realized Big Brother, Big Daddy was just an image from her unconscious, and she had destroyed the symbol of the father from whom she never received love. She grasped a kitchen- knife and in a deliberate and potent act stabbed herself in the heart.

But rumors were now beginning to spread. Had Big Brother really committed suicide for the 'tele- screen' had blanked out at the vital moment? Had Big Brother really fled with some close 'Inner Party' comrades into the wilderness as Winston and Julia had years before? Did all this really happen or was it a ghastly delusion projected by some expelled members of the 'Inner Party' which had led to Julia's suicide? Only you can decide.

The Prank.

The student bar was jumping with youthful drunkenness. Ian enjoyed this apparently harmless pleasure. However, as he walked a little unsteadily to the bar, Jake, who was known for his ability or vocation to obtain mind-altering drugs, slipped a crunched micro-dot of LSD into Ian's beer.

Jake muttered: 'This will give him God

I should explain that Ian was reading 19th century History and had discovered that strain of dissent to the march of industrial Capital called 'Evangelism'. While he didn't practice he was aware and had spoken of the intense spiritual experiences claimed by that while being converted. It was late, and Ian had begun to feel a little peculiar. He noticed a vibration inside his skull. Focusing on reaching his room and with a great grey mist hovering above managed to close the door to his room with huge relief. Time and space seemed to be melting into the walls. He could hear colours, surely this was madness. Then an exquisite beam of lime light shone room a gulping mouth in the ceiling. As this humming beam of joy approached Ian felt the most unutterable peace that penetrated his head, the most sublime ecstasy. This could only be a conversion experience he thought, it was like the accounts he'd read on the History module. A Bible on his bookshelf became alight with 'tongues of fire', indeed he appeared able to be speaking tongues, was this the 'gift of the Holy Spirit.'. About six hours later as the L.S.D. wore off Ian became convinced he'd had a profound religious experience. You must remember he was unaware that his beer had been adulterated with L.S.D.

Dawn rose, and its tentacles strangled the last of the hallucinations and Ian who felt purged slipped into his bed and dozed. As the sleep caressed his inner most depths the idea of his mission began to congeal in Ian's mind. He spent the morning with a sense of being purged and became convinced he must evangelize. He realized his transformation in him would be recognized by other students but didn't think they would be any adverse consequences; he was a man of vision and they were blind he believed. During the next weeks Ian's desire for food diminished, he paced the campus with eyes like fire and most shrunk away and avoided him. Ian believed this was a natural reaction to his elevated state of awareness, for isn't a prophet always shunned by his contemporaries. A young woman named Anna, unlike most others, wondered how such a transformation could have overtaken Ian. She was drawn by his intensity and his increasingly ragged appearance intrigued her; she was curious. Over the next three weeks their conversations became more and more intense.

Anna finally said:

'How you suddenly changed, you were such a diligent student, I'm not sure who you are?' You seem to wrap me in the warmth that I only remember as a small child, being held by my parents. You ease my emotions, being different, not like one of the other students. I feel made whole by you, are you, please don't misunderstand me but I came from a Christian background, but are you the Chosen One...?'

She blushed and fell inside, had she revealed too much of herself. Ian sat like a crumbling statue, he was unshaven and brown hair hung helplessly in a mass of greasy sprigs.

Trembling he replied:

'I am the prophet and you are the prophetess. You are an incarnation of the 19th century prophetess Joanna Southall. We are together, our souls and bodies will intertwine in a frenzy of divine love. Our child, he or she will lead those who are of the Light to their kingdom of God... this will be in the New Jerusalem which is to be established on earth.'

They held each other in a sparking aura of orange mist, the child was conceived, and their sighs seem to pulse with the beat of nature. Exhausted they slept in each in each other's arms, but once madness is fanned it can become a raging blaze. The gossip began to wind its way through campus like a vine of ivy. Jake thought: 'What have I done? It was a prank, a joke but now he's insane. It is my fault.'

Jake was brimming with remorse. In his box of tricks from which he had conjured the L.S.D. that had spiked Ian's drink there was a syringe and several grams of amphetamine. He cooked-up and with a steady hand and wrote:

'I am full of remorse, so sorry to have ruined Ian's life and that of his weird girlfriend. Put some drugs in his drink. Can't live with the guilt. Mum and dad, am so sorry.'

By the time Jake had committed suicide Ian and Anna were living in a tent and roaming the countryside. They lived a nomadic life until Anna went into premature labour. Between them they managed to persuade a very wary person to drive them to the nearest hospital. The nurses were shocked at their disheveled appearance; their dirty hair and clothes. The labour was intense but the baby was stillborn. Anna was to be kept in hospital for several days while Ian was given a shower and a solid meal. He was in a state of shock and then wondered:

'Why, why? Our child was to a beacon which would banish darkness and now he is dead, my God, dead.'

He was devastated, and a tidal wave began to destroy any rational analysis that might have remained since his 'trip' and involvement with Anna, the floods of worthlessness followed by dark whirling pools of self-hatred, a mental crucifixion of his mind followed. If she had been provided with the proper care during the last few months the child might have lived. He would rather have died than the child should have been born dead. Ian left, then roamed until he found a pub where he could buy drugs, the language of the 'scene' was becoming to have an assonance with him, he had 'scored'. He emerged from the pub with an assortment of 'downers' for oblivion seekers. Ian was functioning on automatic now. He bought a large bottle of lemonade and walked from the town into the countryside. His one perceived aim – self destruction. This he thought in a distorted ay would compensate the World for the 'sacrifice' of their child who they believed would have been Divine. Totally focused on the child's death and his failings...Anna was outside the orbit of his awareness. He sat with his back to a hedgerow and began o stuff handfuls of tranquilizers into his mouth and washed them down with lemonade. An hour later he was unconscious and drifting towards death. Fortune intervened, and a farm worker stumbled upon Ian, he was close to death.

Ian had no recollection of his stomach being pumped and the days in an Intensive Care Unit. Slowly he gained wakefulness and became aware of the numerous tubes and pipes in and around his body. As day followed day Ian left the Intense Care ward. Within a week his strength was returning as a sponge draws in liquid and gradually he began to ponder the future. Then one day a doctor appeared who was not dressed in a white coat unlike the other doctors:

'Hello Ian' he said in a tranquil voice. 'How are you feeling?'

Ian replied   'Stronger.'

'Do you have any thoughts or ideas about your unique spiritual nature?'

'How do you know anything about my beliefs?'

The doctor smiled: 'We've spoken to your girlfriend.'

'Ann, she would not say that she is a prophetess.

'We're enlightened parents of a child who would take people from darkness to light.'

The psychiatrist replied: 'Okay, have you ever taken LSD?'

'No, no absolutely not.'

You had a friend called Jake, I'm afraid to say he died, but in a note admitted to spiking your beer with L.S.D.'

Ian exploded: 'I don't believe that, I was chosen by God, not some drug dealer.'

Dr. Guy replied: 'Right, I'm going to give you some medicine.'

Ian shouted: 'You fool, I don't want your potions, I'm leaving hospital soon anyway'.

Dr. Guy smiled again and walked briskly away. Ian thought there could be trouble here. Soon a pack of nurses arrived with a cardboard plate with a brown ampoule and a plastic syringe. Ian panicked and screamed;

'What are you going to do to me?' The male nurse coldly replied:

'Just something to make you feel comfortable, Oh, by the way, if you're thinking of refusing treatment don't, you've been detained under the Mental Health Act. You are going to be given compulsory medication, don't resist.'

Ian cried aloud: You are the forces of darkness...'

'Now, we don't want any tantrums, do we? You can have it the simple or the hard way and you will remember that for a long time.'

Four nurses held Ian on the bed. Struggling was useless now. One said: 'There's a good lad.'

And he jammed the needle into Ian's leg.

'Just what the doctor ordered, Ian.'

Ian soon felt a chemical drowsiness and plunged, like diving into an ocean of pitch black, into a deep sleep. When he awoke here were two male nurses sitting on chairs at the bottom of his bed. One spoke: 'Oh, God's woken up.'

The other said menacingly: 'You're coming up the Hill with us.'

Ian realized that is was a reference to a mental hospital. Still in hospital issue pajamas and dressing gown, a drowsy Ian was bundled into an ambulance with the nurses.

He moaned: 'I hought police'.

The response: 'Quiet, now you don't want to be a difficult lad, do you?'
Ian stuttered: 'You have not experienced the Sublime.'

'Look Ian, you can either make this stay easy or we can teach you a lesson, it's up to you. And we don't want any more of this prophet business. We can make your life easy or tough, it's your choice.'

He was heavily sedated for several weeks, his memory weak, his thoughts paralyzed, and he felt generally leaden. In fact, he spent most of this early part of his admission asleep.

Nurse would say: 'No trouble now, just some syrup to make you feel your old self.'

Ian's medication was gradually reduced. He began to wonder what his 'old self' had been. Bewildered he wandered the corridors of Ward 10, with its floors of regimented tiled floors and cream walls.

The ward sister said: The next step is for you to go on a ten-minute escorted walk around the grounds. Clare will be with you. Remember, no antics, you're still on a section and we don't want any performances, do we Ian.'

Ian quietly consented.

As the next few weeks went by Ian's walks with Clare became longer and longer. Having explored the undulating grassy lawns, walked around the ivory clad long-stay wards and the many trees which seemed like old and reassuring friends in the grounds, they began to set out for the cornfields and beyond. Clare would talk about the nature of religious experience. Ian was cautious about and resistant to these conversations.

But as the months travelled into autumn he began to understand that his drink had been spiked. Clare went step by step through Ian's experiences on that fateful night. She compared LSD experiences and drug induced psychosis with spiritual experiences. Gradually she showed him that it was possible to re-build his life. Dr. Guy was busy, cancelling Ian's twelve-month section and putting him on a cocktail of less sedating drugs. With the encouragement of Clare Ian was banishing, coming out of his psychosis. He began to feel warmth in her presence and noticed her brown hair, always a little untidy but this attracted him. Her aura seemed to him to be one of compassion and wisdom. He was falling in love. As the illness was evaporated by her sun, that same sun kindled his desire.

It was now winter, and Ian was to be returned to the community and hopefully to university for the next academic year. Clare and Ian, as part of the rehabilitation program, had been buying clothes and books. They were sitting in a café with two hot mugs of tea in their hands, Ian slid is hand, so his fingertips brushed Clare's. He then began lightly stroking her blushing cheeks:

'I love you with all my heart, my feelings whirl around me when we are close. You are my life, my love sweet Clare.'

She began to weep softly:

'Ian, I am sorry, but there is something you must know. I was a nun. I took vows of obedience, poverty and, poor Ian, chastity. I broke the vow of obedience by leaving the convent but have maintained the other two vows. We could never have a relationship other than friendship. You will return to everyday life, fall for a girl, and fall in love. I am sorry...'

She dried her eyes:

'That is not my path.'

Ian felt numb 'I suppose to quote Lawrence 'we are crucified by desire.'

Clare replied: 'It need not be like that Ian...'

A modern psychomachy[1]

A troubled and largely sleepless night and Peter the priest scuttles like a frightened beetle out of his shell of reverie. His dreams are becoming a little too intense and seem to merge into wakefulness. The priest slumps beside the bed and prays:
'Holy Mother of God, the habit is returning, I beg you Blessed Virgin, I've got to give it up'.
His skin is no longer young, not a fresh page on which to scribe poetry to the grandeur of God who had been his fountainhead in the early years. Alternatively, it is not the wrinkled crisscrossed dried parchment of an old man awaiting his wake. His prayers seek solace in the Christ of the sacrament he celebrated at Mass daily.
'Jesus of the Holy Blood I need a hit of you like that first time I celebrated the Holy Mass, what joy, unadulterated beauty. '
It had been over three years ago when he read Goethe aloud at an evening with some close priest friends from those spring sweet scented blossom seminar days. Father Liam had played a jig or two on his battered and scratchy violin. Those notes had pieced Peter's side like a knife and he had bled poetry:
'Two souls, alas, are housed within my breast, and each will wrestle for the mastery there'.
'Yes, Father Peter, Goethe again, very good and all well when we were novices, but we're ordained priests.'
'I had noticed that Father Pious.'
'Come come, poetry and Father Pious' sherry.' smiled Father Liam.

---

[1] The term psychomachy comes from a Latin poem 'Psychomarcia' (c400BC) by Prudentitrus about the battle for a person's soul. In the Medieval period they were dramatized as 'morality plays.'

He knew the others had looked-up to him in those days, but they were so staid except for Liam, not of the 'Kingdom of God'. But something snapped that night, a 'dark night of the soul' had engulfed Peter. His understanding of what was meant by the immaculate had been transformed; indeed, body and soul were transmogrified almost like that quivering melody which caressed him from Liam's violin. Immaculate blood had meant only in the silver chalice he raised with extreme care to a line above his forehead for his meagre bunch of communicates to genuflect before. His parish had been mainly hypocrites and deceivers, a real bunch of Pharisees. One or two he had high hopes for like 'madman John':

No reason you cannot fulfil your vocation to the ideals of Saint Francis of Assisi.' John had begun shoplifting and giving away stolen-goods to those street-addicts in the poor quarter.

Yes, that was a place for a priest to minister, but not to have their brown and white powders and those hellish off-white crystals administered to madman John or anyone else. He'd genuinely believed then the flock at Mass were different to those skeletal, emaciated creatures with taunt yellowing shin pulled around sunken eyes, those deep black hollows, those empty eyes, my God.

Peter quickly pulls on his baggy black priestly uniform which covers and gives some volume to a meagre frame, the rest he explains by his devotion to fasting. But then the cold burrows, almost bites, like a pulsating, squirming pile of purple worms and claws, eats into his body which would whiplash into sweat that seemed like a tropical fever. He knew that the mainline to the Divine is not the one recommended by his spiritual director, who he assiduously avoids, but the immaculate track which is marked by those stigmata which were nothing but regular neat lines of needle marks. Mass was at six fifteen, he needs to straighten-out for that, but he could not celebrate that Mass for those who attended so early where the real zealots and had the suspicions of your average drug-squad officer. What was the remedy? He knew only too well, it smashed through his skull into that tormented brain, of course there was nothing to worry about; he had stashed a little 'brown' away and with a couple or three tablets of diazepam he would be fit again, perhaps not to celebrate the Mass, but manage automated performance without his fingers becoming appendages of his hands fiddling feebly and trembling in a fumble out from his vestments. He rummages under the sink, thank God, here's the stash.

Unravel the brown paper in a flurry of hands, yes here's all that's required, praise be to whom, he wonders to God or to the 'man'? Suddenly Peter is disorientated no need to worry about 'madman John' he'll get through okay. Disengaging from the surroundings the priest thought he'd fall back into the tedium of the business at hand and it will be soon be Easter. Peter, with the precision of a locksmith, smoothed the silver paper, maneuvers with the assistance of a razorblade a line of brown powder that within a minute or two will sooth the creases from his mind. The 'line' of brown powder is straight down the middle of the foil which he holds left handed. A cone had   been inserted into his quivering lips, constructed of silver foil, lovingly three years ago. It is now fashioned by his claw like fingers into a utensil of pleasure no more than an instrument of necessity. In his right hand is an orange plastic lighter. He raises the left hand which holds the foil to within about four centimeters of the cone, ignites the lighter, a click, and with the swift yet careful cigarette...warmth engulfs his mind, then a womb-like peace enshrouds him. Finally, he exhales stumbles and sits down.

'Not the mainline to the divine, but it will be adequate until later.' Peter sighs aloud. The tumbler of water is lifted, the three yellow tablets of diazepam swallowed. 'Give me half an hour and I'll be steady as the rock upon which the Church is built.' He whispers playfully.

A series of waves which are like frenzied screeches resound through his mind: madman John how are you, where are you, who are you? He is startled and gathers his paraphernalia agitatedly, but with the paradox of addiction smoothly into the plastic bag which he places and wraps in brown paper, then his stash is safe.

Mass then passed uneventfully, a combination of him being 'comfortably numb' and the single-track spirituality of the 6.15ers who knew the Mass so well it was less a ritual than a memorized piece of text which they'd pattered out for years, a sort of rapid mindless muttering. These acts of evasion; these deceptions were becoming more grotesque day by day he thought.

John, who had in many ways Peter pondered was the incarnation of the Franciscan ethic plus; plus, what? The psychiatric nurses who would periodically whisk him into what remained of the local mental hospital, much of it lay derelict; care-in-the-community, seemed John didn't receive any 'meaningful' care, at best Peter would use the term neglect to describe it. What care did either of them really get, but chemical care? Then it hit him, he was beginning to withdraw. Had to get downtown and quickly to the market square and those familiar black clams of shame were beginning to attach themselves to his mind, would people realize he was going out to 'score'. The leeches of an unforgotten passion were sucking his moist flesh, he must forget: Father, Father Peter, stop its John. I've been baptizing near the river. I'm John the Baptist.'

Holy shit thought the priest; he's really lost it this time and I need a hit.

Don't worry Father it's not full immersion, I'm 'doing them up' with pharmaceutical diamorphine.'

'Thank God.'

'It will soon be Easter Father, so I thought we'd better resurrect some of those downtown Lazarus people. St. Peter told me himself. You yourself Father Peter.'

'John, you child, I'm not a saint, I'm a junkie.'

'We have the immaculate hit; I've got the ampoules here.'

'Perhaps there is something of Peter in me; I've denied my Master more than three times. There is no mainline to paradise John, we make that or not here on Earth and that is a dreadful burden, an awful freedom. John, let us drink deeply from the streams within our hearts.'

'What about the ampoules Father, why waste them.' John said.

A wry smile came over the gaunt face of the priest and exposed his yellow teeth: 'Well one for the road, just to say good-bye to it all.'

They were found with the blood congealing in their syringes. It was simple; they had forgotten to reduce the dosage for this was pharmaceutical heroin, not Lazarus gear and there would be no resurrection. Father Liam's violin had indeed played a drowsy melody to Peter, one that left him in the pleasure dome, but would with an irresistible and remorseless logic which left him a prisoner chained in the dark dungeons of addiction. Liam now must hide the violin-case with fearful haste.

A Steppenwolf breathes the morning air.
> "My mind hums hither and thither
> with its veil of words."
> — Virginia Woolf, The Waves.

The steppes had been a wasteland of significance for the Steppenwolf and some wolf packs had revenged his mind and body when he had the misfortune to meet them: learning his nature and accepting on the savannahs and avoiding those marauding packs had been an important step after many false ones. The other place had its own deprivations that was where they the Worldings lived withal their concerns about banalities; no, the Steppenwolf preferred the meaningful desolation and had become habituated to the solitude. For didn't he have his books and writing materials. Whether he had been born here he had wondered much, if he had been born atoll seemed debatable at times after a particularly protracted and lonely trek when a younger wolf of the steppes. They had been a male wolf, from whom he often fled. and another called his 'mother'. The mother had taught him the ways of the steppes, herself a Steppenwolf but one made captive and taken to a cave where she was taught to speak like a Worldling but could never quite manage their language of platitudes. But, being of a similar nature, if tamed and harnessed she taught him to listen to the winds which swept across the steppes and interpret its beauty, understand its music. The tamed Steppenwolf also taught him to record the Steppes and the World in his notebooks and fashion them into poetry and prose and a love of sniffing that sharp morning breeze and opening a book. As I observe this surreal world, I shall not deceive you with his dialogues, his life is an interior monologue which from time to time others are granted access, but his observations of you and yes you are penetrating; you cannot escape those drowsy amber eyes. This world is not the physical world of Central Asia, the Steppenwolf has two rather than four legs, yet it is not the green and pleasant land of those cursed with the fidgeting of the sane terrain, no this land is named by some mental illness, by others who believe, although this is by no means certain, they have a privileged knowledge of the Steppenwolf: 'Paranoid Schizophrenia.' But my acquaintance with him is one of The Omniscient Eye, not

divine but one of narrator of tales, the weaver of words. Steppenwolf was 'born to be wild' and as less the fully developed wolf was hitching down the M1, my destination Notting Hill Gate. Not yet the playground of the less than totally sophisticated children of the dollar it was then a British version of Height-Ashby. First 'lift' was off a lorry driver, quite a large articulated one, that is the lorry rather than the driver who was a pleasant man of late middle-age: 'Want a lift, how old are you?'
The Steppenwolf was dressed in kaftan, jeans and beads and with a tee-shirt. He did not reveal the age of his body, but rather his mind.
'Come on get in, when did you last eat.' 'Like, is that meaningful man.' 'Here take my packed-lunch.'
'Thank you.' the young wolf replied for the steppes he had grown-up in where suburbia in fact the exodus to that part of London had in the preceding years been mainly one from affluent if stifling zones. Like the people of the Book of Exodus these young people believed themselves to be both blessed and consequently persecuted. all believed themselves to comprise   a sort of tribe of Steppenwolf s, but some were Steppenwolfs amongst the tribe, indeed would wander through magic doors endlessly with and without any assistance, no would rather tumble through them, indeed for this Steppenwolf, he would walk like a somnambulist through doors and entrances and fall over precipices. At first, he had not realized people will push you through doors and hurl one over the cliff edge. He had thought at this behavior was confined to the land of the Worldings. How wrong can a young wolf setting out across the steppes from a world of yelling and threats, those are merely transformed into different matter, there can seem to be only dark matter at times, but he possessed the key to shut the doors both magic and otherwise and allow the illusion of existence to be retained. The key to freedom was the written word and the word read in a relationship with the reader however anonymous that may be.
Five years later and the wolf was wandering the plateau with a haversack and the light of the moon for guidance, the pleasures of the lunar night which are enchantment and torment each in full measure, balanced precariously like a set of scales suspended from the cloud where the memory

Completely Fragmented:

of the trial of Socrates and his death with a dose of hemlock are pervasive. He was an outcast but did not realize it, had embraced Harry Hiller, the Steppenwolf of Hermann's novel, as a young man but of course Harry Hiller was a middle-aged man when he walked through the magic door and did not have an assortment of brightly coloured phials chained around his mind, oozing into the textures of his brain. Cast out of the wolf pack for he was a little to 'wordy' for many and not willing to act out the correct role of an albino in the specimen room for eloquent Steppenwolfs. The Steppenwolf did not pursue the tarnished calve of hedonism nor could he be a shepherd for lost sheep or a matador to slay the Minotaur. He slept on people's floors and in those old crumbling Trojan Horses, the lunatic asylums. The Steppenwolf was huddled on a park bench, the Worldings eyeing weary for its was a scorching summer's day and he was ensconced in a filthy duffle coat and a very long purple and white scarf wrapped several times around his neck, almost a sort of vestment. He was elsewhere for he was the protagonist of not one but all of Camus' novels; this was a little difficult to grasp. No certainly his mother hadn't died that morning and he hadn't experienced any kind of existential self-realization, but on that bench, day past day past day but 'The Outsider' seemed to have the clarity of a million sunrises with the dew hanging on the whispering grass. Was he Meursault, he wondered: a man of around sixty always walked his Scottish terrier through the park, past the human debris which was the Steppenwolf, by this time the odour emitting from him must have been potent and he have looked rather unkempt?
'My name is Monsieur Meursault and am experiencing an existential crisis, are you acquainted with this.' 'Bloody hell, he's flipped.' and the dog yapped in agreement.
The police came and the ambulance and the nurses 'specialled', not allowing even to the toilet by himself. He refused to take off the duffle coat and the other patients and then the staff called him Paddington. He had a marmalade sandwich just after medication time brought by a Spanish nursing auxiliary Francis with a mug of Horlicks. The Steppenwolf wondered whether Francis was Italian and from Assisi. Then a young nurse who looked like Rupert Brooke told him quietly:

'If you want to leave, you must stop this high-fluting conversation, then the doctors will think you are better. And for god's sake stop quoting from
'Dust' by Rupert Brooke'
'But it is more than existence, it has essence, it gives life and death.'
He opens the book and read the lines he knew by heart:
'When the white flame in us is gone, and we that lost the world's delight Stiffen in darkness, left alone
To crumble in our separate night;
When your swift hair is quiet in death, and through the lips corruption thrust
Has stilled the labour of my breath --
When we are dust, when we are dust! -- Not dead, not undesirous yet,
Still sentient, still unsatisfied,
We'll ride the air, and shine, and flit,
Around the places where we died,
And dance as dust before the sun,
And light of foot, and unconfined,
Hurry from road to road, and run
About the errands of the wind.
The choice is his, he listens to the Beethoven piano concerto No.5, the one the captive Steppenwolf played endlessly in her cave to him, she had turned him into the music of the crashing spheres, taught him to interpret it and hear it in the cold winds which sweep across those steppes and given him a key to unlock Pandora's Box but to see that it contained the good, those things he must live and write about. He tidies away the medicines and begins to write. It is 5.00 a.m. on the eighth anniversary of his mother Isis' death. The Steppenwolf goes outside and breathes the morning air and it is good.

Completely Fragmented:

The Swallow.

The leaves began to brood into autumnal red, crisp crimson just before the frost bites when she, a swallow, fluttered in through an open window they had forgotten to close. You could now peer into another nest of nails. She noticed there was a shattered pane in a smaller room. However, the main room seemed perfectly ordered, a black leather three-piece suit, a proud wooden cabinet which contained a colour television, a dark brown wall to wall carpet, a door ajar gave a glimpse of a dark tan dining table. There were not the vying aromas of the poor, the really poor part of this city: in a word, it was 'bourgeois. Or like a Ford factory canteen replicated in every Ford factory across the world. 1972 and The Blitzkrieg Man seemed an unhappy man she noted. Why? Of course, his world was like a ball on fire, a conflagration from Saigon to Chicago from Grosvenor Square to Stuttgart. There was the Viet-Ming, the Black Panthers, that Tariq Ali and the Baader-Meinhof Gang or as some would say, 'Red Army Faction'. He believed it to be victimization, a digression of Eve, of Pandora, she guessed. There was no shelter for him as he could not do as Jagger spewed out while gyrating like a little demon seeking oblivion in Gimme Shelter three years earlier she heard:

"Gimme shelter come on give me shelter, it's just a fix away, it's just a hit away."

Immediately the swallow realized he was as straight as a rod of iron and as stiff as the ruler he measured everyone and everything by. She saw swooping about that he seeks that inflated reflection of himself in the looking-glass which reflects his bourgeois wife as Virginia Woolf had explained in that little book which promised so much. Those pages lay open in her mind now. Like all who fly she knew that mirrors break and should not be stared at and spotted a crumpled invitation to that curved psychedelic groove which is etched in the mind by Lysergic Acid hiding in the corner. Yes 'acid', a method of psychological exploration, for some it burnt through the mind like a hot knife through butter, leaving it melted, a splodge. Timothy Leary hadn't anticipated that.

Eva lay flat out on the floor blooded, she observed, but absorbed blood like a sponge soaks-up spilt red wine. Eva staggered and seemed to her inspired with the primordial fertility of the first monthly curse, the first towel-less, pad-less, tampon-less bleed remembered by every woman, each generation. She straightened herself and spat out these words between her swollen lower and throbbing upper lips:

'Go on, why don't you hit me again just to make yourself feel like a real
 man?'

Blitzkrieg Man's flash of lightning had hit a lightning conductor; he was earthed by the audacity of his wife the swallow imagined he thought that as a gentleman, he wouldn't hit a woman. Not the fairer sex who must be put on a pedestal and admired, that is for men like Blitzkrieg Man until they stepped down from the pedestal and became human... impossible, for him to knock a woman off her pedestal. He seemed to her capable of deafening self-delusion as most people expected the sun to raise and set:

'But my dear you have cut your lip again, do take more care... Here, takes this handkerchief. 'said The Blitzkrieg Man.

'Just another male chauvinist pig, you just oink bloody oink, you honky motherfucker'. Brigitte, his ex-student daughter, yelled.

'Not all that again young lady. You are a pathological liar. I am a doctor, so I do know the symptoms of nervous disorders, maladies of the mind, I will say it "psychiatric illness". Now the inside of an admission unit can become quiet, what should I say, busy, you wouldn't like that, now would you.'

The swallow watched as she grabbed her Little Red Book, a whirlwind unleashing:

'Mao says: "Political power comes out of the barrel of a gun."'

'You will respect your mother and father as well as your country I say,
 I insist.' He said like a robot that saw cold steel and salivated iron fillings.

Fluttering she observed him writing on the wax tableau of his mind... what would happen if everyone did what Jagger and Leary advocated. There had been a growing amount of research into this so-called, what a pretension, 'counterculture', the Nation would grind to a halt. Of course, there was one Nation, just one happy family, not everyone could lunge around dreaming like drop outs. NO! All must work and boost G.N.P; (there he stood a gross national product she thought). After all someone had said, he pencilled a murmur of a memory, 'Arbeit macht frei'. He mouthed the words in carefully pronounced and refined English 'work makes you free'. Yes of course and what else could it do, Ford proved at their Dagenham Plant, symmetry is aesthetic perfection when it comes to the factories. She noted his nib slipped 'cemeteries'.

Eva had cleaned her mouth, applied the usual cosmetic necessaries, an abused bourgeois woman would use the term 'necessaries' the swallow knew and walked back into the living room, 'a death chamber' she sighed. This was the death of love and death of the family. Just one veiled glance towards Brigitte that hoped for a new dawn with her daughter's generation. That masked smile told the swallow this talk of revolution was a little extreme, but so was the clenched fist in the mouth from someone who cannot recall what he has done:

'She's young and an idealist, you shouldn't be so hard on her.' enjoined Eva.

'Me, hard on anyone, ironic isn't it. I go out to work, support you all and have a daughter claiming I have a resemblance to a piece of pork.'

These decomposing nests were sub-atomic particles of the atom that was suburbia, the atom had split, and its flames and hurricanes consumed Nagasaki and Hiroshima. The words had already been fashioned into a semi-circle of wrought iron 'Arbeit macht frei' above the entrance of Auschwitz. Then the swallow remembered her mother, a 'mental-defective', with the black triangle sown onto her blue and white striped uniform, herded into Auschwitz from the cattle-tracks with the Jewish people, the communists and homosexuals. That was when she had escaped the womb and became a swallow.

She dived down and spotted a copy of Hermann Hesse Steppenwolf opened at the page which described a door with the sign: 'For madmen only'. She, the swallow, had read Freud and embroiders this text which is sown into your mind with invisible thread:

"Dreams are the royal road to the unconscious."

Had Brigitte passed through Hesse's door in a dream? She saw a dark shadow haunted The Blitzkrieg Man. What had it all meant, those had been idle threats towards Brigitte about mental hospitals, and he was only trying to control her as he attempted to restrain a world which was hurtling towards a nemesis for the privileged, its coming is certain but its fruition not, she mused.

She swept toward the end of her song and told that Brigitte was ill in the terms employed by psychiatry, but not by 'anti-psychiatry'. Brigitte had read how the S.P.K argued 'turn illness into a weapon' and that it was a sick society that had caused her malady, her 'illness.' An illusion the swallow had conjured was the story took place in England, yes that is correct, however, in West Germany Brigitte's Double was a member of Sozalistischespatentkolletiv (SPK). Brigitte transmogrified in 1972 from Socialist Patients Collective fledgling to emerge from the chrysalis to become one of the butterflies in the second generation 'Red Army Faction'. Brigitte's German mother had been a swallow. This swallow watched Brigitte pondering Shakespeare:

'I acknowledge this thing of darkness mine.'

Brigitte didn't mess around, muttered Mao: 'we must draw a clear dividing line between ourselves and the enemy.'
She whispered: 'Daddy, I have a little something for you.'
'Yes.'
'I'm going to light your fire baby.' She smiled. Brigitte then coolly sprayed his bedroom with bullets from her Sten Automatic Pistol and precisely riddled her father with bullets again and again to make him perform a little dance; the bullets jerked his body like stings make a marionette jump. Was it History that had pulled those strings? She produced a Luger pistol placed its cold black barrel on her lap and waited for the 'pigs', the police. Her mother sat silent and stolid. The Sirens wailed, but only lure more into dreams of love which linger behind every bloody sunset. This swallow flew from this chamber knowing that she, those who read Daddy escaped having their hearts pierced by spears of fire as Sylvia's had been. She always had to fly high, higher, circling just to escape that icy stare and glare of Room 101.

<u>Notes on 'The Swallow'.</u>
Terrorism' pervades the news almost every day; my narrative is of another milieu, different 'backstory' and

ideology. Plath (1985) *Daddy* remained central throughout the editing. The 'swallow' originated in Frame (2008) where Grace Cleave is transmogrified into 'a migratory bird' because of feelings of dissociation. She is a 'personification' of Existentialist freedom. Research included: Meinhoff (1971), Cooper (1972) and S.P.K. (1972). I attempt to answer Dostoevsky (1864) whose 'Underground Man' was a reply to Chernyshevsky (1863) who created the literary 'New Woman' incarnate in Vera Pavlovna, there is an allusion to Chekhov (1896) in my title. The narrator is the 'swallow'; she's a limited omniscient narrator. This allows the reader to see the world through her eyes and allows her insights into the story, retaining some of the intimacy of the first-person narrator as well as the advantages of a partial omniscience; 'confessional intimacy' with some 'authorial distance'. I tried to employ 'dialogue' for both 'characterization' and changing the 'pace' of my story. There is some 'telling' as befits an instrumentalist story, the conclusion gains momentum by 'showing'. The "crumpled invitation" is an attempt to apply the concept of 'Chekhov's Gun' to 'foreground' Brigitte's madness which also references Dostoevsky *The Double* (1846). Throughout the story I use contradiction and paradox as a strategy to propel the reader's interest and 'defamiliarize' their experience as in dialectical opposed belief systems of Patriarchal Capitalism and a tendency within Western Maoism. I utilize both simile and metaphor in my prose. My intention regarding the resolution of my story is to realize a combination of a 'Chekhovian Ending' with 'Instrumentalism'. Although the genre is Historical Fiction it is subverted by being narrated by 'the swallow' who must question the nature of Realism for she is a non-human narrator. It has a resemblance to the parabolic. The intention was to comment on Patriarchal Capitalism:

>"Representation of the world, like the world itself, is the work of men;
>
>they describe it from their own point of view, which they confuse with
>
>absolute truth."
>
>De Beauvoir (1972) p. 161.

Both Sartre and Simone de Beauvoir were Maoist sympathisers.
References.

Bennett, T (1979) *Marxism and Formalism*, Methuen & Co Ltd: London.
Chekhov, A (1998) [1896]) *Five Plays: Ivanov, The Seagull, Uncle Vanya, Three Sisters, and The Cherry Orchard*, Oxford: Oxford World's Classics.
Chernyshevsky, N (1989 [1863]) *What Is to be Done?* Cornell University Press: Ithaca and London.
Cooper, D (1972) *The Death of The Family*, Harmondsworth: Penguin Books
De Beauvoir, S (1972) *The Second Sex*, trains. H. M. Parshley, New York: Vintage.
Dostoevsky, F (1985 [1864, 1846]) *Notes from Underground, The Double*, Harmondsworth: Penguin Classics.
Frame, J (2008) *Towards another Summer*, Virago: London.
Meinhoff, U {Red Army Faction} (2009 [1971]) *The Urban Guerrilla Concept*, Montreal: Kersplebedeb Publishing.
Neale, D. (ed.) (2009) *A Creative Writing Handbook*, Milton Keynes/London: A & C Black in association with The Open University.
Plath, S (1985) *Selected Poems*, London: Faber & Faber.
Shakespeare (1998) *The Tempest*, ed Orgel, S. Oxford: Oxford World's Classics. Sozalistischespatentkolletiv (1984 [1972]) *SPK: Turn Illness into a Weapon*, Dresden: Trikont.

Completely Fragmented:

Two men and a mermaid.

> 'Two souls, alas, are housed within my breast.'
> - Goethe.

A chill gust of wind swept frosted contorted leaves across the car park in a frenzy of colour, copper brown and red. John held on tightly to his diary, his case load was now reduced by another one. A glint of satisfaction which was almost reptilian appeared in his eyes as he glanced, no almost glared, upwards at the grey and black clouds. He pulled out a copy of Goethe, Faust from the inside pocket of his jacket, but he hardly noticed the tatty book other than to glimpse the cover subliminally. Its contents had been ingested when he was a university student. Rather, his attention was settled on the meeting that he had just left: 'Yes, that is another box ticked, empowering the clients.' He said smiling to himself.

After all, that is what it says in those shiny new social work textbooks and he is the incarnation of modern social work. That smile was so different from his clients. It exposed a perfect set of glinting teeth. Of course, John cleaned his teeth twice a day and went to the dentist every six months, unlike his clients who neglected their appearance. He was a man on his way up, but to where you my reader might have wondered too, heaven?

A middle-aged woman watched him; she must remain invisible to him. Her name is Angelina and she keeps copious notebooks on the social workers' interactions with his equally visible colleges and clients. She wrote on a notepad which was battered and torn that she guarded close in her inner sanctum. It is a hotchpotch of memory, observations and analysis:

There walks another straight-back, unburdened by life. I shall disclose a little secret which is not widely appreciated about social work, 'a box ticked' carries the same value whether it is a discharge because of some unforeseen recovery, change in circumstances or a suicide. Why? Because there was a Third Great Depression, a reorganization of social services a contraction in welfare provision and a new phrase: 'the choice agenda.' has entered the vocabulary. This means that the clients could make 'a choice' to jump off a multi-story car park. their responsibility, their 'choice', so you see the latter-day priest, the social worker bears no sin and he had the ultimate alibi, maybe?

He closed the door of his car; it was secure, just like an iron womb. The 'in' ambient music of Brain Enno caresses him in full surround sound, he feels safe and significant in his world.

Then he opened the diary:

Pam: 10.00-10.30, [Goal, there is not anyone known to us else in bed with her. Consider intramuscular contraception at the next team meeting.] Lunch with Luscious Lesley the new secretary.

Stephen: 1.30-2.00 [Already discharged, isolated, no family, potential suicide, but intelligently competent]. Note to self, this will be quite a coup. He has been on the books for years!

And so, it continued.

Angelina opened her notebook:

Lotta continua. These two words sliced like splinters of memory into her heart as she recollected those chilly hot Brigade Rossi days which possessed her youth.

How had Brigade Rossi lost, but of course we hadn't? No, it was merely a setback along the necessary road of dialectical conflicts, which Cluttered yet fueled the route to 'actual existing socialism.'

She paced restlessly with thoughts trapped in her head like particles in The Large Hadron Collider. Lit a cigarette, inhaled deeply and smiled at the bourgeoisie's naivety and continued to write:

Her comrades, those who had avoided death by the bullet, prison or long- term incarceration in psychiatric hospitals or equally had risen almost like the Nazarethian we're now in mid – life. They were scattered, some were in Trotskyist grouplets, while others had been like moles quietly burrowing into Radical churches, a few were deep Entryists, Entryism sui generis, in the arts or academia and yet others have been like her, Angelina, embedded in the Lumpenproletariat. Yes, it was a tough road for the vanguard. After all she had been incarcerated in penal institutions and then transferred to various psychiatric hospitals. She had been wired-up to the grid for quoting Mao in a Group Therapy sessions on another occasion for lambasting a charge nurse for being a 'male chauvinist pig' and standing like a slab of marble to defend black patients from   racist abuse. Yes, Electro Convulsive Therapy was used to 'correct deviant tendencies' by the megalomaniac doctors. It was like being given a blast of amnesia twice a week, only the strongest could resist and continue the struggle.

 Today, she conceived, she stands rather like Rosa Luxemburg, described by Clara Zetklin as 'the living flame of revolution.' She almost tore her notepad from her grey flannel jacket and wrote:
Burn, baby, burn.
She gripped a black pen with such passionate; she held it rigidly in her hand, which had almost become a clenched fist, that it spurted ink, the synthesis, dialectically speaking, of that stream within her thinking. Simultaneously, but in an almost separate reality Lesley thought that getting a petrol fueled, testosterone driven social worker to buy her a few decent meals and a bottle or two of plonk was not a bad scheme. All the staff had monthly meals; they were supposed to be for   team morale and professional bonding. Stephen, who was recently discharged by that strutting cock of a man who glanced at Goethe while jack booting across the Social Service department car park hadn't eaten for several days. He did not keep a diary; he hadn't the need of one, but kept verse in a stash tin in a secret place and travelled light, so light, like a feather   that he is blown higher and higher on the exhalations of the Earth's autumnal wind which were becoming icy winds and gales of winter. He plummeted one morning and then he realized help was much needed. There were none, so he went to see 'the Man', the dealer.

Angelina was whispering about with her notepad when she clocked the young man rolling one spliff more than was good for him, spaced-out is not adequate to describe his state of mind; zonked but conscious seemed to be rather a more suitable assessment she decided:

'Hey cat, where do you live, where's your pad.' She spoke with kindness. 'Hi, are you some Madonna.'

'No.' she laughed, 'No, not me.'

She realized this was the first time she had laughed spontaneously for a long time. 'I thought you were Our Lady of The Angels, come to take me higher. To

hold me in your arms and escort me to heaven.' He grinned.
'Hey babe Icarus, now don't get to fly too close to heaven. It might not be what you expect. But where do to you crash, the 'heat' will pull you, be careful.'
'Nowhere.'
She carefully removed her grey flannel jacket, an old companion, and wrapped it around the shoulders of the young man; she held him in her arms and by the rocking rhythm of a lullaby soothed him. There was not an alternative, he needed shelter and she took him to her nest, an anonymous flat in a grey concrete block where the State housed those on 'benefits'. Inside the sparsely furnished one-bedroom flat was a disproportionately large collection of books. They were on shelves built with wooden planks resting on reddish house bricks which formed columns at each end, but the books still overflowed onto the floor. She possessed no cooker, but a kettle and an old microwave to heat food. Purple drapes were hung permanently across the small windows. The interior light was provided by unshaded electric fitments. She laid cushions on the floor of the area which doubled up for a kitchen and a library and lowered him onto this bed; he was almost comatose with the amount of skunk he had smoked and hashish cookies that he had gobbled. Although she knew his life was not at risk, you don't O.D on cannabis, but you can take it too far. She removed her jacket from his body and covered his ragged clothes with a thick red covering which had green and blue mermaids embroidered on them.
'Babe Icarus, you glide down softly.' She whispered.
 He was unconscious for forty-eight hours and Angelina was awake and alert for the whole of those two days and nights. She wandered around whipping the sweats from his body like a moth drawn to a flickering light.
'Hi, who are you, where am I. I mean how did I get here.'
'Stoned and incapable.' Smile Angelina.
A hot flush of embarrassment coloured the young man's face...
'Don't worry, babe Icarus, you were too stoned to walk let alone anything else. The police would have picked you-up and there were several sticks of skunk not so carefully popping out of your socks. Do you want something to eat?'
'Yes, yes, please, very much.'

Completely Fragmented:

'See that rectangular brown thing and a small oblong of lighter stuff. It is bread and cheese, help yourself. Those blue things to your right are jeans which should fit you and the white thing next to it is a cheesecloth shirt. See you in ten.'
'Oh yes?' He wondered.
Angelina and the young man began to write a web of words within this flat. Would it be a drama, a Comedy, Tragedy, a tragicomedy? Possibly a pot-boiler of a romance or a piece of Socialist Realism, they could write a life of mystery and fable because this flat was a veritable laboratory of the creative mind: a cauldron of the emotions. However, we know Angelina has a secret notebook and the young man hides his writing in a stash box. She knew his was inviolable when she had laid him down for his slumber; she would never, ever, lift the lid off this box and delve within. It was his sanctum, his mind's temple. They conversed carefully, feeling and then plucking strings of the instrument which they were tuning into a relationship:
'I don't know your name.' 'Either do I.' She replied.
'That's a funny answer, do you always talk in riddles.' 'That is no riddle, babe Icarus. 'That's my new name, is it?' 'Maybe so.'
'Okay'
'That's settled then, you have been named!' 'Okay, boss' he smiled
She grimaced and flinched:
'Never, every call me "boss" again, you understand that. Never ever use that filthy word to describe me, anyone, but them and their lackeys.'
'What's wrong, I was joking.'
'Jokes are not always just what they seem. Have you read Freud
Jokes and Their Relationship to the Unconscious?'
'Heavy stuff. You are not like one of the shrinks, which we used to see or those social workers. You know when they smile you first see perfect teeth, but the mirage wears off, then you see their fangs.'
'I am sorry, babe Icarus. No, I am not a shrink or a social worker. Here, have you ever worn a kaftan, one would suit you.'

She pops into her bedroom produces one like a magician (it was really quiet a relic she had dragged around on her wanderings since the 1970's). She held it, measuring it in front of him for size:
'Hey, you will make a hippie yet.'
And they both smile, hugging each other as if they had been lost in a labyrinth and finally found a companion to help them escape or at least to accompany one another on those interminable journeys which exist within any maze.
She writes once again in her journal, recalling a quote from Albert Camus which she inscribes slowly and contemplatively, like a nun in an enclosed convent:
"Autumn is a second spring when every leaf is a flower.'
            - Albert Camus."
Life in the flat did not fall into a dull routine of revolutionary inculcation, they had fallen in love. True, Angelina had always been in love with the revolution and was devoted to the 'struggle'. 'Babe Icarus' was a young man of visions and voices who had been unloved, but she would come to realize that she cannot reciprocate his love for too long. Though she knew could never tell him why, it was because she was and will always be Brigade Rossi, the ramifications would be potentially unmanageable. She and Babe Icarus would be on the run from both friends and enemies. caught-up in a cross-fire of intrigue, he would never cope she calculated. However, this ballet, this Prokofiev ballet, which is like the Shakespearian drama, it took from it because Angelina and 'Babe Icarus' were indeed "star crossed lovers", but also Angelina was a child of the inheritance of October 1917.
She probed a little into the dark night of his mind, could it resemble 'the dark night of the soul' and anticipate a higher state of ecstasy. She was willing to listen:
'Babe Icarus, tell me about those visions and voices. What the shrinks call your illness, is it Schizophrenia.'
'It isn't really an illness at all, you see. I am both blessed and damned in equal measure like William Blake was; Blake lives in me. I am also the Fallen Angel from Milton, Paradise Lost and because I descended into The Inferno of Dante, so I always say: 'Abandon hope, all you who enter here.'

Completely Fragmented:

'Babe Icarus, I wouldn't 'tell' you what to do, but possibly the skunk and the hashish for some people are not the best if they have certain proclivities. Marx said:
'Religion is the opium of the people, it is the sign of the oppressed creature.'
He fell silent and marched out of the room. A gradual, but discernible change occurred from then onwards. They were after all different Houses: the Capulets and Montagues, so it follows her being a revolutionary damaged by the system she had attempted to overthrow, but he was well different she thought infatuated with the distorted image of the 'self'. She then realized 'Babe Icarus' was a narcissist of sorts, but one that hated his own refection although could not free himself of the bondage of staring at his own mental deformities. So, she could never tell him her truth and he was in love, not with her but his malady.
Late-autumn became mid-winter; Angelina knew there would be no thaw. She penned in her diary:
This shall be the winter of our discontents.
But either forgetfully or with subconsciously with intent did not place it in is hiding place. She went into the other room to make a coffee while he exchanged rooms apparently to lie-down:
'Angelina, what is this book I found on the bed.'
'Oh, I don't know, you tell me. Explain it to me, and then I shall ravish both your analysis and you.'
'What is Brigade Rossi?' Does it mean Red Brigade, no not those, not those terrorists?
 She froze as surely as if struck by a bolt of ice, she shattered fragments melted in   the heat of rage, tears boiled, poured out of her eyes with uncontrollable body jerking sobs:
'No, never, we were not 'terrorists."
Confused, he rushed out of the flat without dressing, screaming through the network of streets to the Social Services Department. It was locked as it always for security reasons, staff safety, but there was no one at the reception desk just a note taped across the intercom:
We are sorry, there is no one available at present, please ring and leave a message and we will get back to you as soon as possible.

It was the monthly staff meal. Stephan then ran to the Roman Catholic Church; but a note had been permanently attached to the church door months earlier, the rain had defaced it slightly. There was no Eucharistic Meal to be eaten there for the priests had left:
Mass cancelled due to a shortage of priests. You are in always in our prayers. In an emergency, seek appropriate help from the Social Services or dial 999.
The young man thought it read 666 and it was the code from The Book of Revelation of the Antichrist. It would be stamped upon his forehead. He became totally deranged and threatened to burn down both the Social Services Department and the Church, a passer-by made a mobile for calls to the police who by procedure alerted the psychiatric team. The social worker arrived first; he had rushed to get there because he had discharged the young man and wanted to get there before the police. Angelina also arrived, breathless, and confronted him; she pulled out a small black Lugar pistol with what seemed a blur of dark grey:

    'Now just give me that gun. Steady, you must be ill, a very poorly woman.'

    'Don't patronize me. My name is Angelina, I am a revolutionary and you are
a pig, a muttonhead. You will never put him back in that place, the so-called hospital.'
She pulled the trigger again and again and yet again, emptying the small magazine: 'Now, that is another box ticked don't you think, ah.'
And spits onto the hunched figure of the moaning figure and then calmly walked away like a whisper into the wind.
Days later the papers reported a suicide. Another had jumped from Beachy Head onto those rocks which are pounded by a relentless and remorseless sea. The body or what remained of it after however long it was thrashed by the sea was torn, bloated and blue. A note had found nearby the cliff edge hidden under a bush and weighed down with a stone. There was simply inscribed in small, neat handwriting: "My name is Legion, for we are many.' - Mark 5:9.'
It was rumored by some that a mermaid could be seen; she swam around the cliffs ceaselessly, carelessly without concern and gambled with the waves as they crashed onto those wailing, desirous and deadly rocks.

Completely Fragmented:

Reflections on the story.

Four areas were foremost in my mind as I wrote Two Men and a Mermaid. The first was concentrating on an emphasis on the interactions between plot, character and setting, these three elements. Secondly, I was aware of the requirement to 'show not tell' and tried to move towards this aim. Thirdly, I was interested in the relationship between Socialist Realism in Babel (1940) The Red Cavalry and Other Stories and origins of the short-story in fable. Finally, I noted the significance of the Edgar Allen Poe theory of the 'unity of effect' on the short story and attempted to implement some of his guidance. My narrator's point of view is third-person omniscient. A device I used was the insertion of the written material of my characters into the story, an epistolary dimension. This seemed a useful method to help create 'round' characters. Thus, the narrate gains a more intimate insight into the characters, especially Angelina, through diary entries which by their nature are first person direct narration and they also play a significant role in the plot. I begin in medias res; however, the action takes place within a controlled and tight period and space. An awareness of the oral origins of the short story, let to the use of a 'framing device' with the social worker's entry and his assassination. I conclude with the mermaid whose appearance is almost Magical Realist in nature and is intended to defamiliarize. The image of the 'black-pen' and equally black 'Lugar pistol' is phallic, thus questioning conventional gender roles in Angelina, but also modes of 'expression' for her creativity. She is the Dialectic incarnate, both creative and destructive. Her 'epiphany' which has its origins in Joyce (1914) Dubliners take place when she falls in 'love', but it is a tragic love because of her previous involvement with the Red Brigades in Italy. Like Juliet she cannot escape her past (familial or ideological. She could never share this secret with 'babe Icarus' because he is vulnerable. He finds her diary and reads it. He sees her involvement with Red Brigades as e 'fatal flaw. Indeed, her murder of the social worker is ideologically consistent; an agent of what Louis Althusser called the 'Repressive State Apparatus' while patrolling the 'Ideological State Apparatus'. He could have admitted 'babe Icarus' into a psychiatric hospital, which also conflicts with her historic anti-psychiatry beliefs. She is left in crisis, but because there is nowhere for her go to find fulfilment, there is no 'actual existing socialism' and hence her denouncement can only be a transformation into a mythological creature, half woman, half fish who must gamble with death by riding the rollers onto the rocks by Beachy Head. Like Sophocles Antigone, she has acted against the State and her punishment is like being entombed alive in the body of a mermaid...

Bibliography.

Chekhov, A (2003) Seven Short Novels, New York: W.W. Norton & Company.

Dante, A (2008) The Divine Comedy, Oxford: Oxford World Classics

Frame, J (2012) Faces in the Water, London: Virago Modern Classics.

Kaufmann, W (1969) Existentialism from Dostoevsky to Sartre, Cleveland & Ohio: Meriden Books.

Janet, you were on my mind.

..."if you can't adapt yourself to living in a mental hospital how do you expect to be able to live 'out in the world'?" How indeed?"

- Frame (2012) p.34.

The mists were leaden with the hum of significance, a salience of silence. A cave, a fire and some shadows lingered beyond the cave. However, as in Plato's allegory only the 'philosophers' were privileged to see the shadows, the 'Forms'. I had an intense interest in abstractions. Nevertheless, I pulled the heavy burgundy velvet curtains of my study closed. it was a foggy, chilly twilight and the screams of my patients were reverberating in my head. The year was 1957, the country New Zealand and the hospital Seacliff Lunatic Asylum. I treated one young woman patient who had been a student teacher, an undisclosed, at the time, aspirin overdose. She had continued to university where she wrote a story about her depressive breakdown. her English lecturer who she was infatuated with, or so the notes say, showed it to one of my superiors at this asylum and so would begin an odyssey. Janet Frame had been detained in in 1952; I was to meet her nearly five benumbed years later.

Completely Fragmented:

I had a call from Auckland six months before I met Janet, followed by a paper chase of correspondence, but I reached the end. I was awarded funding to head a program into Rehabilitation and Creativity. For me it was like Manna had started falling from Heaven. However, all that seemed possible in the short term were incremental changes to the system and some basic activities. Weaving and assembling stools, free expression art classes and the beginnings of a group of handpicked patients who would use Freudian 'free association' to create a group poem or story. The patients in this group would be pre-surgery. I was given free rein and of course an ex-undergraduate, however disturbed the patient, and seemed an ideal candidate. and so, I met 'an angel at my table', Janet Frame, apparently a fledgling author. I sought out Miss Frame. She was huddled in the corner of a padded isolation cell, a padded cell. She looked like a bird that had flown into a plane of glass blinded by a snowstorm, injured, bewildered and frightened. She seemed a broken person: teeth pulled out, ill-fitting dentures, ulcers around her mouth, but had with an uncontrollable mop of red hair. I was now a little further up their Tower of Babel, a senior registrar. This provided me with a certain degree of autonomy. Although I couldn't challenge the demigods, the consultants, I could not make decisions independently of them.

'Miss Frame, um, may I address you. Janet,' I said tentatively.
'I don't want it., I don't love paraldehyde, they said Shelia did and then she died.' 'Janet, I am so sorry about your friend.'
'She wasn't my friend, but they killed her. It was wrong.'
I felt like the collective hand of the patients was going to slap me. What could I say.? An uneasy silence filled the vacuum between us, but at least that was a beginning, I thought. Better than the descent into the inferno. You can fill a vacuum, with something; respect, compassion, even friendship.
'They call me an educated bitch.'
'That is unfortunate, Janet, but not all the patients are as well read, as educated as you. You mustn't take offence.'
'No, the nurses do.'
Unprepared my response was one of incredulity, then sympathy for this sad woman. 'Do you hear many voices,

Janet, like God or Keats? Emily Dickinson, maybe? Your fellow writers?'
'Fool', she screamed. 'but you are no "Holy Fool" in rags.'
'Nurse, Sister - quickly, restrain her, then the medicine, the usual dose, it will have been written up in her notes.' I reacted robotically.
I nipped into the doctor's consulting room, took a small leather lined hip flask from one pocket and had a quick gulp of the medicine, the whisky, and a peppermint popped a peppermint into my mouth almost simultaneously with the other hand. My hands were trembling.
Janet's consultant prescribed a course of E.C.T after this incident. It seemed inappropriate to me, almost punitive. No patient reacts well when their symptoms are challenged. It is like challenging someone's Weltanschauung, something the most stable person would find unsettling one way or another. This was hardly the therapeutic beginning I had hoped for; I had not anticipated it. To be honest, I was angry with the male consultant: he seemed to be trying to impinge on my program. It was a question of professional boundaries, or so I thought. Now I was doubly motivated, my engines were in gear and smoking: my project and my professional pride. I knew this was a pivotal moment in my chosen career, but I hadn't realized it would become something of an 'Epiphany, of course not of the magnitude of a James Joyce text. After all, this wasn't Dublin and so the literary academics were saying in those quasi-literary journals, Modernism if not dead, was in decline. I had a predilection for the short story. Have you read Ward No.6? just checking you, my reader, the author's name was on the tip of my tongue, blazes, how on earth could I forget, the master: yes, that was it: Anton Chekhov. He is the weaver of my nightmares. I am haunted by Chekhov's character Ivan Gromov. I have been since I read that damned book. Why am I to be nailed to a cross as surely as Jesus of Nazareth was crucified upon one
by that specter of Chekhov's mind, Gromov, after all I am no Dr. Ragin? I am a doctor though, but I did not intend being admitted to my own asylum. How the hell did Chekhov conjure that up? Seacliff Lunatic Asylum has its own little cherry orchard, but it does blossom, frost had eaten it years before... A community where the walls were wobbling with weeping and wailing, not that the walls had been built in no

less a sturdy fashion as than the average monastery. So robust that not many patients left; even if they did, stupefied into submission by the great machine of cogs and wheels of the institution, they would be unable to compete in the tragedy of a society with its cash-nexus and mind ant marching conformity. I can tell you that many of my patients were not clinically ill, but people whose face didn't fit the necessary identikit picture at the right time. A crash, a clap of thunder heralded a downpour. Evening deepened, and I poured the first shot of that whisky which was my anesthesia, then a second and when I woke in bed with a hangover, there was no memory of leaving my study to the quarters attached. For, yes, we doctor also lived in the asylum, but in houses, not dormitories.

I was beginning to have to justify the funding for my project; it had begun to look overly ambitious. Yes, I had a stockroom of wooden stools with woven seats, piles of randomly bespattered paper, the artwork, but nothing which was going to get me really noticed, nothing for the CV which would clinch a consultant's post. Of all the patients there was the only one whom I knew that had a history of writing: Janet. I parachuted down from my deluded heights and I realized the magnitude of my task. 900Nine hundred patients, drugged to the point of stupefaction; insulin therapy had wreaked havoc; E.C.T being used as a method of control, indeed in some cases as punishment and there was a culture amongst most consultants of wait, then wait again and then apply the scalpel to make them free. Where were they
 when the news of the medical experimentation on patients in Nazi Germany was seeping out after the Nuremburg Trails? I couldn't get the analogy out of my mind between 'Cut makes free' and the motto above the concentration camps 'Work makes free.' Yes, they were using the lobotomy and leucotomy on a routine basis. Women looked dazed, blank, with brightly coloured headscarves; it had a resemblance of Dante's, Inferno. I saw the words drip off the scalpel I had handed the consultant two days previously:
No room for hope, when you enter this place.
Dante (2008) p.56.

Janet would eventually be lobotomized; I could save her and get some decent writing, which would justify my

Rehabilitation and Creativity Programme. She wouldn't be discharged, that much was obvious to me, but she would write. That would tick the necessary boxes and avoid her surgery and my career and conscience were boosted. I was saved.

'If you pumped too much gas into a balloon, it would burst. Splat!' Who said that? I shuddered, but 'The Madman' continued,

'God is dead. God remains dead. And we have killed him. How shall we comfort ourselves, the murderers of all murderers?'

Was that Nietzsche's specter raised to haunt me?

'The Madman 'noted on his pad of dust that Janet's family had stopped visiting long ago; it was a long journey after all and the doctors always know what is for the best, the parents thought. Janet was quite happy; they had been assured, years ago. She had lost siblings in freak accidents. However, there was a younger sister who had graduated and married; she began to see dark clouds in this apparently benign forecast. She had lodged with Janet at one time, just when her older sister was

 apparently going insane; Janet had not seemed crazy to her. A little odd, maybe, but that was Janet. and this diagnosis, once she and her husband really applied themselves to the research, did not quite fit, and in fact into seemed wrong. Schizophrenia: it just did not make sense. The sister had known Janet wrote short- stories and, overcoming some resistance from mother and father, she rummaged, searched and sought them out. Eureka! She had found Janet's notebooks, now to read them and then show them to her husband. It could be nonsense, ravings; perhaps they were right, and she was wrong. They were only one way to discover the truth: read them, show them to old teachers, perhaps not that lecturer who had Janet 'committed' 'for a little rest' and maybe then send them away to a competition   or to a publisher or something. Any clue to find out what might have happened to her sister and then act. this atrophy was unbearable. Janet's life was not a stagnant pool covered with algae, at least it hadn't been. The 'Mad Man' wrote.

I, the doctor wondered if like Dr. Ragin iwi was beginning to lose 'the plot', should there be a 'plot' as Aristotle claimed; or was I living in a different genre, the short-story, which may be like the 1950's and life generally without a 'purpose', perhaps it is a 'seamless plot', or a tranche de vie. A doctor is not a 'free man' and must as unfree men everywhere be trapped in the 'plot' as Woolf realized that only: if he 'were a free man rather than a slave. there would be no plot.' Now back to the 'plot', against me? No, I meant Aristotle: I shall, indeed insist have 'a beginning, middle and an end'. The place to find the plot as every psychiatrist knows is in the notes written by other psychiatrists -, the voice of the plot, of Reason. However, any writings by Janet remained only referred to, but were not actually present. What the hell? no, keep your head; have a slug of whisky.

'The Mad Man' had contrived a plot., her sister would be its agent for Janet and her sister just as Antigone and her brother shared the same 'blood', the same inheritance. Now was the time for to implement it, conjuring up a spell of purple haze which would transmute into a flying carpet carrying Janet's golden words. Janet's sister had read a notebook of her short stories and discussed them with her husband. They decided to send the collection off to a National Short story competition. it was a high-risk strategy, but there seemed little choice as it was spring 1957 and Janet had been held incommunicado for years without any visitors.

It was a very hot summer and the patients were roasting and becoming agitated. The heat was on me to deliver on this project; a lot depended on it, my career. The scalpels were being whirled in an almost frenzy now. the Head of Psychiatry had had a taste of blood and thought he had solved the enigma. A new surgical unit was being built to increase the production of the 'cure', 'lobotomize them, and leucotomize them.' was the Master Plan., that is the final solution; the best made plans can go astray, solutions can have their test tubes broken and leak out to corrode the scientists, the doctors, even contaminated them.

The 'madman' noted the short story collection was like a spear thrown into the heart of psychiatry. it won the first prize: Miss Janet Frame was a nationally recognized writer. The scales were not only unbalanced, they had collapsed. Our progressive doctor, - that's right, the one so concerned about his patients that he had to self-medicate with whisky -

was going to be the lamb that would be sacrificed. The consultants would use that incident in the padded cell. after all the ward Sister had heard him accuse Janet of hearing voices and sanctioned the injection. It was a stitch-up. Chekhov was indeed a master of the short story and knew the human condition; well, not exactly Ward No. 6, but too damned close for the doctor's sanity.

He would be found years later in a cave in Thailand with an unlimited supply of opium supplied by whom.? He would puff on his hooker enter reveries and tell strange tales of a mental hospital, a Russian writer and a woman who became a significant writer he had once treated and cured. No-one thought these stories made sense: it was the opium and a touch of madness people said. He neglected his appearance and lived in the tattered rags of a 'Holy Fool.'

'The Madman' gleefully wrote that at Seacliff Lunatic Asylum, the consultants were feverish; Janet's sister and husband were due with copies of the book for Janet to sign. Nothing for it but to put her on an open ward.

"Miss Frame, there appears to have been a mistake, an erroneous diagnosis by a senior doctor, but not a consultant, you understand. Your book has won a National competition and you are to be discharged."

'No more injections, no more E.C.T.'

'Janet, you are to be discharged into the care of your sister and her husband.

We wish you every success.'

'Oh, I see,' Janet smiled dubiously.

The 'open' ward was a very different story; it had a different 'plot' and denouncement. There was no paraldehyde there, you know, of course, or maybe not, wrote 'The Madman' in his pad of dust, that they must administer it in glass syringes as it melts plastic ones. The characters were also different than on the 'closed' wards, deep in the dark heart of this place where there is no light. The patients here are overly stressed housewives and politely spoken shopkeepers speaking platitudes. They gave these patients, those chalky little yellow helpers, and diazepam. Fresh flowers were placed in porcelain vases every day and there was much, to Jean's relief, decent food. The nurses smiled and there were not thorns, but Colgate gleaming teeth. I can lap this up, wrote Janet in her the newly acquired book for her writing

Completely Fragmented:

the ward sister had given her. But, the dream has been, as always, disturbed by the nasty little business: waking reality. These patients stayed a maximum of three months and the headlights of the sister's husband's car was driving through the night with the two convinced they were knights saving Jane from the darkest of nights.
'The Madman' closed his pad of dust and sprinkled it on Antigone's brother's corpse. For this story of blood and was also about inheritance, a tale of madness and sanity, of corruption and purity. It is not the biography of Janet Frame., yes, the dates were correct, and the basic facts were correct, but it is the creation of an imagination who found an inspiration in the story of Miss Janet Frame., 'The Madman' contrived with Janet's sister and unhinged the doctor. Why, because every suicide of people 'The Madman' had known was etched on his heart in golden script., he had not forgotten or forgiven their tormentors until their unquiet spirits would be at rest. He pondered that Janet had flown into the cage they placed his mind into. Yes, he was also restrained and had involuntary E.C.T as a young person; he also wrote finding a path out of the psychiatric hospital through publication and academic study. The caged bird sings and sings when he or she is freed and quite often those who had locked the gilded cage did not like to hear what was said about them. However, you cannot silence a song, a story or a poem, however, particularly after it is published. It is a biographical fact that the New Zealand psychiatric authorities would not let Janet Frame 'go', even in death. One analysis of her writing claimed she had Borderline Personality Disorder. The Madman smiles and thinks if she were alive, she would retort:
'No, I an m not like you.'

Electra Unbound: A Modern Tragicomedy.
The action takes place over 24 hours.
Characters with some minor notes on direction.

Bridget.
A young student dropout, she has aligned herself with the radical currents in Western anti-psychiatry and armed urban Maoism. These occurred in Western Europe during the late 1960's until the late 1970s. She is in custody after killing her father.

Dr. Winston Smith.
A middle-aged male forensic psychiatrist with a particular interest in Jungian psychology and social science.

Police Superintendent Julia Mosley.
A strict disciplinarian.

The Swallow. *[Off stage and illuminated by a spotlight when speaking.]*
She sees all the dramatic action and comments upon it as she swoops in and out. A solitary and atomised Aristotelian Chorus who creates a Brechtian 'alienation effect.'

Eva.
Bridget's mother traumatized by her daughter's parricide.

Psychiatric nurses and Polices officers *[stock-characters 'doubled' so one actor doubles-up as a good nurse/good policeman and another as a bad nurse/ bad policeman].*

Locations: A police station. A secure psychiatric ward *[on a split stage].*

Completely Fragmented:

A presidium arch stage.

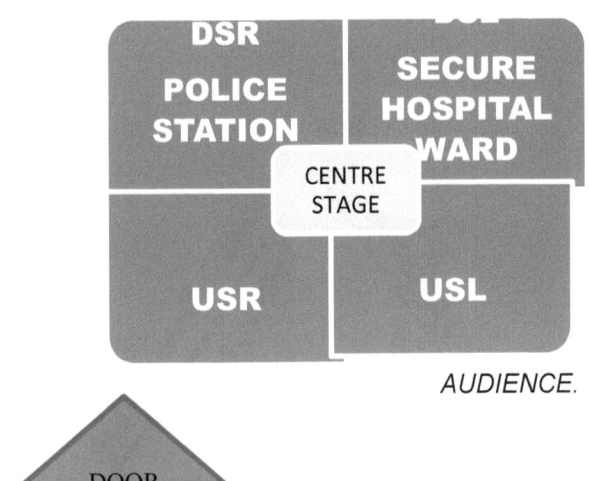

AUDIENCE.

Abbreviations used:
DSL: downstage left, etc. USR: upstage right, etc. the actor faces the audience].CS: 'centre stage.'   Off Stage: literally off stage, but heard on stage.

Freytag's Pyramid

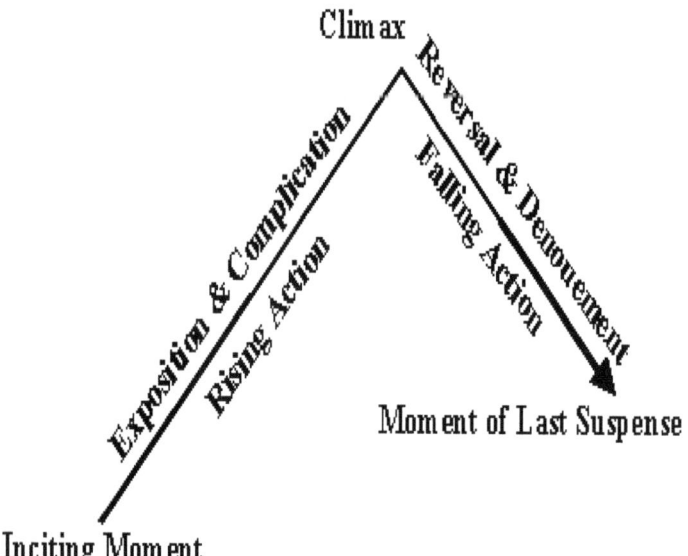

Freytag (1863) model of Aristotelian Tragedy

Completely Fragmented:

ACT 1.
Scene 1 A police station, which in not like an ordinary one, but more like 'Paddington Green' which is a British high-security station and holding unit for politically motivated offenders. The officers have no visible 'ID' numbers
BRIDGET is roughly bundled onto the stage. USR.

Bridget: Get your filthy pig hands off me

Uniformed police #1: Wouldn't want to touch that scum, she, it, killed her father. Shot the poor bleeder in his bed. What's your name? Are you really human or just a monster that looks like one. Look like a human, you'd have to put a bag over your head for me to fuck it.

(pause)

Officer #2 Come on we must charge you. I am sorry about the language .

Bridget: I will only give my status which is 'international revolutionary' and a brief statement.' I am a sister of the international struggle between the forces of reaction and those of progressive people's liberation movements.'

(pause)

Bridget: I am human only too human[2]. He was the enemy, my father, like it was personified, you know what I mean... He was oppression incarnate.

Officer #2: Another wordy one.

Officer #1: Educated cow. I thought you people were the toiling masses rising up. You seem like a bunch of spoilt kids to me.

Bridget [coldly]: Don't call me 'a spoilt kid'.... I am a revolutionary woman, and I believe like Mao in 'Drawing a clear line between the enemy and ourselves'[3]

---

[2] Nietzsche, F (1994).
[3] Mao TseTung cited in Meinhoff, U (1971).

There is a struggle during which BRIDGET is wrestled to the floor, face down and her hands handcuffed behind her back. Chairs and tables are overturned

Bridget: You can kill me, but you can't kill an ideal, the movement.

THE SWALLOW through a loudhailer Off Stage:

The pigs think we are scum, but just look and learn. Draw your own conclusions and don't be deceived, I say again, look and learn.

EVA is USL in the psychiatric ward and two nurses are trying to give her sedatives; she is distressed and walking on the spot. They do not speak except to say:

Nurse #2: Come on take the medicine you know it's good for you.

Nurse #1 Now you don't want an injection, do you, so take the pills.

Eva: My child…

Scene 2 USL BRIDGET from USR on her feet, but remaining handcuffed.

Lunges towards her mother:

Bridget You have betrayed woman, you made her dependent on 'the Other', the male, the husband, my father. Where is your 'sisterhood', any solidarity? between women? Shit, mother, don't you have a mind of your own. I guess that's a vacuous question.

INSPECTOR JULIA MOSLEY enters CSR [possibly wearing the uniform of the 1930's Mosleyite 'British Union of Fascists' known as the 'Black Shirts'.]

Completely Fragmented:

Mosley: The woman is ill; the young bitch is a criminal. Keep them apart and while you are at it rough that little whore up a bit.

The police officer #1 hits Bridget with increasing velocity and rapidity, he is warming to his task.

Bridget: AR, Arrr ah, you filth… not every woman is cruising for a bruising, you are…bloody hell that hurt…the dead.

THE SWALLOW stands-up OFF STAGE and is suddenly illuminated by a bright spotlight. She holds a white placard, which has emboldened upon in bold letters:

FASCIST PIGS.

DR. WINSTON SMITH enters DSL and glides into the melee. He put the upturned furniture back in place and places the papers in their files:

Dr. Winston Smith: The young woman seems irrational yet not in a delirium, I want to consider this a little deeper. Let me spend some time with her.

He then orders that handcuffs be taken off and escorts Bridget to the far edge of the USL.

Scene 3. A secure psychiatric ward is eerily quiet as the patients are so heavily sedated that they forget when they are holding cigarettes. The cigarettes smoulder into fingers and then fall onto fire-resistant carpets. Dr. Winston Smith and Bridget are sitting in the seclusion of his office. On his desk is Jung, T*he Theory of Psychoanalysis* [4] and Leach's book about Levi-Strauss published in 1970 [5] with *heavy* underlining. USL

---

[4] Jung, C (1998)

[5] Leach, E (1970)

Dr. Winston Smith: Now, I am going to give you a chance as I can see you are an educated woman. I have been reading some Carl Jung about his discovery of the 'Electra Complex'.

He picks up the book which is heavily underlined:

Bridget: I scribble all over my books as well.

Dr. Winston Smith: Leach argues in a recent study that the message of Greek mythology is simple enough: 'if society is to go on, daughters must be disloyal to their parents and sons must destroy [replace] their fathers'.
(pause)

Yes, well he first mentioned it in 1913, just at the time he was breaking with Freud.

Bridget: Is that a fact...

Dr. Winston Smith: Do I note a trace of irony, of a lack of deference to the analyst.

Bridget: Maybe.

Dr. Winston Smith: So, may I ask what are your beliefs Bridget?

Bridget: I think you have a fairly good idea doctor. Ulrike Meinhoff argues that in the urban conurbations in the West 'the armed struggle is the prerequisite for the proletarian revolution?' I was a member of anti-psychiatry group at a university hospital unit, us doctors became convinced of the position that psychiatric illness was the product of the oppressive relations in society, particularly? the family... taught us to become revolutionaries, urban guerrillas.'

Dr. Winston Smith: And you killed your father

Completely Fragmented:

Bridget.   He was an agent of social control.... he was a real brute doctor, he would hit my mother and then pretend he had no memory of it.

Dr. Winston Smith: I see, oh dear I see. That is, I cannot see for I am blinded. I have no eyes, like Oedipus Rex.

Bridget: You can 'see' if you want to.... you are part of the system   of what Louis Althusser[6] calls the 'Repressive State Apparatus' as a forensic psychiatrist you openly control people   and with 'Ideological State Apparatus' as a father in the nuclear   family. I am making this apparent because ideology is insidious.   It uses 'interpellation' or 'hails' people, they don't see it as 'false consciousness', but as their chosen beliefs, a way of life.

The stage darkens, and DR. WINSTON SMITH is bathed in red light

Dr. Winston Smith:
[with obvious physical unease] Steady on Bridget...

(pause).

Bridget: Camus says there is only one serious philosophical question   after realization; 'suicide or recovery.'

Dr. Winston Smith: You too have read his Myth of Sisyphus?

DR. WINSTON SMITH looks away and stares across the stage.

The Swallow OFFSTAGE: A game of chess and the King has been placed in check by our Queen.

---

[6] Althusser, L (1971)

ACT 2.
Scene 1. CS. INSPSECTOR JULIA MOSLEY:

    Winston, why do you go easy on the young thug? She killed her father, which makes her a parricide. Should be hung as far as I am concerned.

Dr. Winston Smith: She is a complex character, disassociated from reality. Or at least the reality of the majority of people.

Inspector Julia Mosley: Do you remember, before they had us in Room 101 we were lovers, we met secretly. We thought our love was revolutionary.

Dr. Winston Smith: It was, in a fashion, but it is easier to rebel against the morality of a system rather than the system itself.

Inspector Julia Mosley: Easy and it was good Winston, wasn't it…?

    (pause)

    Good and easy, ah…

INSPECTOR JULIA MOSLEY moves her face towards him, he pulls away.

    No, I am sorry, not again Julia.

    Damn you.

Swallow [off stage] Star-crossed lovers, no way man.

Scene 2. USL   In DR. WINSTON SMITH's office:

Dr. Winston Smith: Bridget, I am interested in your 'high-functionality', your ability to intellectualize all your problems, it

Completely Fragmented:

                         is if you have retreated into that domain.

Bridget: It is a rich land, but I can see where you are going. It has its benefits, but also…. well, I live there, you see.

Dr. Winston Smith: I believe I do, or at least am beginning to understand. now Bridget, you have helped me to understand the world, my role in it. Bridget, did your parent's show your emotional love, or were it all a matter of material tokens of a love that may or may not have been there.

Bridget [sobbing] 'Love'… what is that… material security but love… they were, are, emotional cripples.

Dr. Winston Smith [takes her hand]:

                 I can guide you out of this illness.

Bridget: What 'illness'.

Scene 3.USL.

BRIDGET paces around Dr. Winston Smith chanting incantations, he is not afraid:

               Eliminate all rational thought,
              Eliminate all rational thought,
              Eliminate all rational thought.

              So, writes William Burroughs.

                (pause)

             Don't you see that in an insane world? to quote R. D. Laing 'It is mad to be normal'[7]

Dr. Winston Smith: Eureka Electra, I think I have got it.

---

[7]Mullen, B. (1995).

Bridget: Cool.

The Swallow [off stage] Solidarity, comrades and lovers.

ACT 3. Evening. Bridget and Eva are now on the secure ward USR. The nurses are hoping for a peaceful night...

Scene 1. BRIDGET moves toward her mother:

Bridget: Mother, you must be strong. They will try and give you shiny white tablets or brown syrup. Don't take it, it is called Chlorpromazine will turn your mind into a rotting turnip and cause your limbs to jerk.

Eva: Why would they do things like that to us, we are patients and the nurse says they only want to help.

Bridget: Mother, they are cogs in a machine. They do what they are told.

Eva: You really do understand how things are, my child. You are teaching with wisdom that astounds me. For the first time in my life I know what it is to be free. You have changed, beatitude, you remind me of St. Clare and all those 'Poor Clare's' living a life of poverty and serving the poor.

The Swallow [offstage] A mistake, very touching though.

DR WINSTON SMITH ENTERS CSR.

Dr. Winston Smith: Bridget, there is something urgent I need to tell you. Before they got to me I was a person like Winston Smith as in George Orwell's novel '1984'. I was a revolutionary of sorts, a utopian dreamer, but they hammered me, and I was re-socialized and became a forensic psychiatrist, I sold out, but I still believe 'if there is hope it lies in the proles.'

Completely Fragmented:

Bridget: That is a quote from the novel.

Dr. Winston Smith: Yes, of course I should have expected you to know.

Scene 2.

Bridget: Winston, my comrade. Today's conditions in the Western urban centres must be seen from an internationalist perspective. Vietnam is being bombed, they are using napalm on children.

Dr. Winston Smith: I have seen some of the photographs, it is awful, terrible.

Bridget: Remember what I said about Ulrike Meinhoff…

(pulse)

Dr. Winston Smith: No that is too much to expect.

Bridget: As Anglia Davis says: 'Revolution is a serious thing, the most serious thing about a revolutionary's life. When one commits oneself to the struggle, it must be for a lifetime.'

Dr. Winston Smith: I am a doctor, I have a family. I couldn't leave them to fend for themselves.

The Swallow offstage: That is a line that must be crossed both Ulrike Meinhoff and Gudrun Ensslin did.

Silence….

Scene3.

Bridget: You will Winston.

She embraces him, and they kiss deeply.

Bridget: That is how important the struggle is.

Nurse #2 Bloody hell, they are snogging. The doctor and that woman, the one they brought from the police station earlier.

Nurse #'1 Little hussy.

Nurse #2 What should we do?

Nurse #1 They are both going down for a long time, I'm ringing the police.

Inspector Julia enters CSR and produces a small pistol, not a service issue.

Inspector Julia: You have betrayed me, everyone, everything. I will shoot you both dead.

Bridget: We haven't betrayed love or the revolution.

Winston freezes unable to move. Bridget grasps the pistol.

Bridget: Unlike Desdemona I can pronounce the word 'whore' and you are the whore of the bourgeoisie. Take that.

A single shot rings out. Bridget and Winston run across the stage DSR and Bridget kicks open the door. They exit hand in hand. A shower of red rose petals is thrown onto the empty stage DSL by THE SWALLOW and she sings The Internationale…

ON THE PLAY…

For Plato, art is 'shadow of shadows', Aristotle developed a systematic aesthetic:

Tragedy is an imitation of an action that is admirable, complete and possesses magnitude…Virtually all tragedians… use these formal characteristics…. for in fact every drama alike has spectacle, character, plot, diction, song and reasoning. But the most important is structure of events.

Heath (1996) p. 11.

Aristotle wrote what has become a dictum for Western dramatists:

Tragedy, then, is a representation of an action that is worth serious attention, complex, and of amplitude; in language enriched by a variety of artistic devices appropriate to the several parts of the play; presented in the form of actions, not narration; by means of a pity and fear bringing about a purgation of these emotions.

Dorsch (1965) p. 38-39.

Electra Unbound: A Tragicomedy's main Aristotelian action is articulated as a dialectical process. Bridget is a revolutionary who transforms Dr. Winston Smith's *Weltanschauung* while he in turn shows her the love she was denied as a child. It does, however, leave an unanswered question: is she in fact resolving her 'Electra Complex' or not? My drama is an attempt to employ Brechtian 'complex seeing' as defined by Raymond Williams in Aristotelian dramatology: It is not the good person against the bad, but goodness and badness as alternate expressions of a single being. This is complex seeing, and it is deeply integrated with dramatic form.'

Williams (2006) p. 234-235.

This dialectic is enacted within the structure of Aristotelian Tragedy, but with a happy 'turn' at the conclusion transforming it into a tragicomedy. I try to make the play function on a cause-effect basis as Aristotle advised and use the 'dramatic arc' (Neale (2009) p 85). The main technical problem I encountered in transforming TMA01 *'The Swallow'* into TMA02 was that of how to incorporate the swallow who had been an omniscient third-person narrator into my drama. I attempted this by making her into an atomized Aristotelian chorus who was off stage, but with a presence, either heard or seen on stage and utilising the methodology of Brecht (2013) *Life of Galileo* where placards are used in Brecht's concept of 'epic theatre' (Brecht, 1964). I attempt to combine both *mimesis* and Brecht's *'Alienation-Effect'.*

The play begins with an allusion to Shelley (2009) *Prometheus Unbound* and ends with one to Ibsen (2008) *A Doll's House*. Bridget's chanting of Burroughs's in Act 2, Scene 3 is an attempt to make language chaotic and thus challenge its phallocentric nature as achieved in the work of Hélène Cixous '*creature feminine*' [feminine writing].

Bibliography.
Althusser, L (2008 [1971]) *Ideology and Ideological State Apparatus. (Notes towards an investigation)*, London: Verso.
Aristotle/Horace/Longinus (1965) Classical *Literary Criticism*, trans, T. S. Dorsch, Harmondsworth: Penguin Classics
Aristotle (1996), *Poetics*, trans, Malcolm Heath, Harmondsworth: Penguin Classics.
Brecht, B (1964) *Brecht on Theatre*, trans, John Willett, London: Methuen Drama.
Brecht, B (2006) *Life of Galileo*, trans, John Willett, London: Bloomsbury.
Jung, C (1998) *The Essential Carl Jung*, London, Fontana Books.
Ibsen, H (2008) *Four Major Plays*, Oxford: Oxford World Classics.
Leach, E (1970) *Claude Levi-Strauss*. Revised ed. New York: Viking Press.
Meinhoff, U {Red Army Faction} (2009 [1971]) *The Urban Guerrilla Concept*, Montreal: Kersplebedeb Publishing.
Mullen, B (1995) *Mad to Be Normal: conversations with R. D. Laing*, London: Free Association Books.
Neale, D. (ed) (2009) *A Creative Writing Handbook*, Milton Keynes/London: A & C Black in association with The Open University.
Nietzsche, F (1994 [1878]) *Human, All Too Human*, Harmondsworth: Penguin Classics.
Orwell. G (1983) [1949]) *Nineteen Eighty- Four*, Harmondsworth: Penguin Books.
Shelley (2009) *The Major Works, Percy Bysshe Shelley*, Oxford, Oxford World's Classics
Williams, R (2006[1964]) *Modern Tragedy*, Canada: Broadview encore editions.

Completely Fragmented:

'The fourth sort of people have no voice nor authority in our commonwealth, and no account is to be made of them but only to be ruled, not to rule others' (Sir Thomas Smith). Is the statement affirmed or denied by Shakespeare's and Brecht's *Coriolanus* drama?

I shall argue that Shakespeare's genius has endured because his plays were material products of a society in chaos, at the crossroads between the transition from feudalism to the capitalist mode of production in the light of Christopher Caudwell[8]. The beginning of 'primitive accumulation' in England, a period now often referred to as the Early Modern Period. My analysis of class is concluded by Brecht and his revisiting of Coriolanus and combining Brecht's attack on Aristotelian notions of theatre illustrating how we need 'living drama', the poetry of the oppressed, or as Boal argued in his book *Theatre of the Oppressed*, a new poetic of resistance. To encapsulate the argument Plutarch, William Shakespeare and Bertolt Brecht were writing about and in socio-historical material circumstances of transition, Plutarch about the tumultuous early period of the Roman Republic, William Shakespeare writing in an epoch which would lead within fifty years to civil war in England and Bertolt Brecht during what the French revolutionist, Victor Serge, called the 'midnight of the century' i.e. fascism and Stalinism. William Shakespeare *Coriolanus* is a play with a dramatic *form* which thus provides it with a 'tragic hero' who must because of metatheatrical forces dominate the plebeians, yet the drama can be read as being profoundly sympathetic to the plebeians. While Bertolt Brecht summed-up his adaptation as:

> the tragedy of a people that has a hero against it. [9]

Hence, I look to the formalist and historicist schools of analysis.

This argument also challenges some post-Enlightenment 'humanist' critiques of Shakespeare *Coriolanus*, William Hazlett whom I suggest misconstrued Shakespeare as a

---

[8] Christopher Caudwell *Illusion and Reality*, 1977, (London, Lawrence & Wishart).
[9] Anita Pacheco, Coriolanus (Writers & Their Work) p.98. (Plymouth, Northcote House Publishers Ltd).

conservative, A. C. Bradley, who belittles the play as not reflecting the grandeur of Shakespeare's other plays. Their essentialism by arguing for a universalist measure against which to calculate the play's worth must itself be a historically class bound ideological construct. My methodology is derived from Marx:

> My dialectic method is not only different from the Hegelian, but is its direct opposite. To Hegel, the life-process of the human brain, i.e. the process of thinking, which, under the name of 'the Idea', he even transforms into an independent subject, is the demiurges of the real world, and the real-world is only the external, phenomenal form of 'the Idea'. With me, on the contrary, the ideal is nothing else than the material world reflected by the human mind, and translated into forms of thought.[10]

I note an Althusserian inclination in the scholarship of Johnathan Dollimore *Radical Tragedy*[11] .However, I prefer a view closer to Terry Eagleton here:

> Coriolanus, though literally a patrician is Shakespeare's most developed study of the bourgeois individualist.[12]

Thus, my analysis allows an argument both against those who understand Shakespeare as 'The Transcendental Bard' with the accompanying universality founded in 'essences' on the one hand and against some 'radicals' who see Shakespeare merely as a 'cultural imperialist'. Rather, I would comprehend the plays as being created in a period of revolutionary upheaval and living on in that tradition. That is tantamount to 'universality'.[13] I will conclude that it is only the modern proletariat which can bring freedom for all as it is 'the universal class' [Marx & Engels *Collected Works*, Vol 3

---

[10] Karl Marx, Capital. *Vol 1*: 1974 p.29 (London, Lawrence & Wishart).

[11] Johnathan Dollimore *(Radical Tragedy: Religion, Ideology and Power in the Drama of Shakespeare and his Contemporaries, 2010, (London,* Palgrave Macmillan).

[12] Terry Eagleton, *William Shakespeare, (Rereading Literature),* 1986 p. 73 (Oxford, John Wiley & Sons).

[13] Kieran Ryan *Shakespeare's Universality*, pp 1-28, (London, Bloomsbury).

p. 186.[14]] a class which must free all to free itself.
Shakespeare foreshadows this in *Hamlet*:
> Here's fine revolution, an we but the trick to see't
> *Hamlet*, V. I. 78-9[15]

Plutarch, the major source for Shakespeare's Roman plays *Julius Caesar, Anthony and Cleopatra* and *Coriolanus*, like Shakespeare and Brecht are all texts which are positioned in their epochs. However, it is only in 'late-capitalism', the era of Brecht, that *Coriolanus* can teach the *necessa*ry lesson of History. It seemed necessary to situate my analysis in the tradition of English Shakespearian criticism, particularly William Hazlett and A. C. Bradley.

William Hazlett believed Shakespeare was capable of a self-generated 'genius' reflecting his radical Romanticism. Hazlett believed Shakespeare to be overly 'conservative' in his political outlook. As in a review of Coriolanus in *The Examiner*. 15th December 1816 he wrote:
> Anyone who studies it may save himself the trouble of reading Burke's Reflections, or Paine's Rights of Man…the French Revolution or our own…[16]

Alan Bate[17] argues, John Keats had read William Hazlett on Shakespeare and consequently outlined *Negative Capacity* which was a major contribution to poetics and is in a sense, I maintain, like the Marxist dismissal of bourgeois egotism. Hazlett continued:
> The cause of the people is indeed but ill calculated as a subject of poetry…We had rather be the oppressor than the oppressed.
> Wheeler p.15.

I disagree with this point about *Coriolanus*; the reader rather understands the leadership of the plebeians as manifest in the First Citizen within the rank and file protesting with integrity not present in the patricians:

---

[14] Marx & Engels, *Collected works*, vol 3 p.186, 2005, (New York, International Publishers).
[15] William Shakespeare, (ed) G. R. Hibbard, *Hamlet, V. I. 78-9* (Oxford, Oxford World's Classics).
[16] Wheeler *Coriolanus Critical Essays* 1995, p.14. Hereafter Wheeler, page #. (London, Routledge).
[17] Johnathon Bate, *The Genius of Shakespeare, p 360-61*. Hereafter Bates page # (London, Picador Classic).

> I speak out of hunger, not of a thirst for revenge.
>
> *Coriolanus* I. ii. 24[18].

We see the citizens being transformed from a 'class-in-itself' into 'class-for-themselves', the active and moral subject of History.

A.C. Bradley was not impressed by the dramatic impact of Coriolanus:

> No doubt the story has a universal meaning, since the contending forces are permanent constituents of human nature, but the *imaginative* effect or atmosphere is hardly felt.
>
> Brookman, p 34[19].

A. C. Bradley, we see here wrote with the bourgeois world-view at its height in 1912 presiding over an Empire on which the sun would never set and yet to be rocked by World Wars and mass proletarian rebellions; it was complacent. He maintained in *Act 2; Scene 2* Shakespeare deviated from Plutarch over the question of the ritual inspection of Coriolanus' wounds by the people to win their acceptance of him as consul:

> In Plutarch, he shows them to the people without demur.
>
> ibid, p. 63.

Although this is the correct reading of Plutarch, he, I maintain, drew mistaken conclusions as I illustrate below:

> Now Marius following the custome shewed many wounds and cuttes apon his bodie... So there was not a man emong the people but was ashamed to refuse so valliant a man.[20]

---

[18] Shakespeare (Bliss) *Coriolanus*. The New Cambridge Shakespeare (Cambridge, Cambridge University Press).

Hereafter Coriolanus, page #.

[19] Brockman (ed) *Shakespeare: Coriolanus, A Selection of Critical Essays*, 1977 (London, Macmillan).

I argue, that what we see in Shakespeare's response to Plutarch presages Brecht's adaptation of William Shakespeare in which the people through their vanguard, the tribunes seize and maintain State-power, the Dictatorship the Proletariat which means no more than rule by and for the majority:

> I do beseech you,
> let me o'erleap that custom, for I cannot
> Put on the gown, stand naked, and entreat them
> For my wounds sake to give their suffrage.
> *Coriolanus* 2. 2.134-33.

Scinius, the tribune, a 16th Century 'labour aristocrat' who may in a non-revolutionary situation be supporting a Senate composed of people of his own class stratification replies:

> Sir, the people
> Must have their voices, neither will they bate
> One jot of ceremony
> *Coriolanus* 2 .2. 134-136.

Coriolanus, the protagonist, replies:

> It is a part
> That I shall blush in acting, and might well
> Be taken from the people.
> *Coriolanus* 2. 2. 139-141.

He speaks in verse: a diameter of iambic feet tapering off with enjambment after 'part'. We wonder whether he is playing a role on stage or is he engulfed in events which are beyond his control? We must ask how much volition do 'historical actors' have in the nature of huge objective socio-economic forces? Followed by the second line of iambic pentameter interrupted by a caesura to stress the consequences of the metaphor of 'blush' is, I suggest, ablaze with anger rather than embarrassment. The third line

---

[20] Sir Thomas North anno 1579, Plutarch's Lives of the noble Grecians and Romans English with an introduction by George Wyndham, I:158, (London: D. Nutt). Hereafter North p#

which can be read as a trimester of iambic feet with a feminine ending which contributes to the audience's perception of the people. The last lines are end- rhymed 'well' 'people' [a half-rhyme]'. The astute tribunes note this contempt and prepare for the decisive moment in Act 3.1. It was cloak and dagger work, but they managed it well and with far greater political awareness than the patricians. Just three words, maybe whispered by Brutus to Scinius:

                      Mark you that.
Coriolanus 2. 2. 141

In Shakespeare's embellishment, Coriolanus resents having to go through a Roman civic service. Bradley understands this as a lack of 'Introspection'. I would rather comprehend it as contempt for the plebeians whom Coriolanus describes as 'the nothings.' Coriolanus is the epitome of the early Roman cult of valour. Indeed, it is possible to find a direct link in North's translation of Plutarch:

        valiantnes was honoured in Rome above all other vertues [21]

I have suggested that Shakespeare developed a deviation from Plutarch over the civic ceremony to inform us of the nature of class conflict in Early Modern Britain. We can see that in Structuralist terms with the cultural signifier 'class' having a paradigmatic relationship to the signified 'oppression.' Here we perceive the relationship between the upper strata or labour aristocracy and the plebeians, Scinuis:

      What is the city but the people?

To which the plebeians reply as a 'collective.'

        True. The people are the city
                        Coriolanus 3. I. 200-201.

This a pivotal moment in the development of the play in terms of the fall of Coriolanus at the hands of the plebeians.

On the question of the portrayal of the plebeians in *Coriolanus,* we can understand Shakespeare's developing awareness of their nature. Compare, for example, the beginning of *Julius Cesar* where the plebeians are an intoxicated and disorganised rabble to *Coriolanus* where they differentiated by debate and leadership roles. Although in the latter, they do not exhibit ideological consistency as

---

[21]North II: 144.

when they welcome the victorious Coriolanus home in Act 2.1.135-140. He is consistent in his class hatred though from his first words in the play:

> What's the matter, you dissentious rogues,
> That, rubbing the poor itch of your opinion.
> Make yourself scabs.
> *Coriolanus* I.I. 147-9.

E.C. Pettit[22] argued there was a causal relationship between the Midland Rebellion of 1607 over the enclosing of land which could be described as the first secular, that is political in the sense a modern reader would understand, social unrest in England. They affected Warwickshire including Stratford-upon-Avon maybe influencing Shakespeare in his decision to write Coriolanus. David Johnston and Anita Pacheco[23] argue William Shakespeare was educated in the English Humanist Tradition of the 16th Century which was profoundly influenced by Ancient Rome. I speculate that this was derived from an anticipation of Britain's imperial expansion. Shakespeare was a man with his fingers on the strings of history's Aeolian harp and together with the recently translated into English by Thomas North (1595) Plutarch *Lives of the Noble Greeks and Romans, which* was probably written around the beginning of 2 A.D. With the dialectic tensions and synthesis in his mind generated by the reflexes of the material world William Shakespeare would have found the story of Caius Martius Coriolanus a compelling if not irresistible choice for a play. He wrote it in 1608 to open at Blackfriars Theatre with the King's Men in 1609. Thus, Shakespeare wrote this play through the prism of the concrete conditions of his epoch as did Bertolt Brecht. It is of significance that 80% of the play is poetry and 20% prose, which disfavours the plebeians by that yardstick and that it contains, possibly one of the most pregnant of stage direction in Shakespeare which encapsulates its gender dimension:

> *He holds her by hand, silence*
> O mother, mother.

---

[22] E. C. Petit Coriolanus and the Midlands Insurrection of 1607, *Shakespeare Survey III (1950) 34-42.*

[23] David Johnston and Anita Pacheco *Reading Guide for Block 3.* (Milton Keynes, Open University Press)

> What have you done?
> Coriolanus 5.3. 182

She had created a professional soldier and became the vehicle for an imperfect Aristotelian nemesis which in turn created the concrete conditions or the catharsis:

> Kill, kill, kill, kill, kill him.
> Coriolanus 5.6. 133.

Shakespeare is imperfect because as Jonathan Bates indicates:

> If we are to judge Shakespeare by the standards of Sophocles, he will be found wanting.[24]

Here the reader can understand something of Bertolt Brecht's perspective in his (1938) *Life of Galileo*:

Andrea: Unhappy is the land that breeds no hero.

Galileo: No Andrea. Unhappy is the land that needs a hero.
Life of Galileo, Scene 12, p. 112.

Firstly, I argue, Brecht compliments the class dialectic within William Shakespeare *Coriolanus* and secondly, we can discern in him a lifelong opposition of the 'Cult of Personality' whether it was manifest as bourgeois individualism, the Fuher or Stalin whom he had an uneasy relationship with because of his Epic Theatre, Stalin preferred Socialist Realism. Bertolt Brecht, like any great writer, developed a poetic, *Epic Theatre*. As a young man in the 1920s, he launched an assault on Shakespearian tragedy as bourgeois individualism:

> The object of the exercise was the great individual experience.[25]

His solution was ambitious, to remake theatre because as a Marxist, there is no record of him carrying a Party Card, Brecht understood theatre as dialectical, in motion and driven by contradictions. He critiqued previous drama:

> The theatre as we know it shows the structure of society (represented on the stage) as incapable of being influenced by society (in the auditorium).[26]

---

[24] Johnathon Bate p 160.
[25] *Political Shakespeare, Essays in cultural Materialism* [ed] Johnathon Dollimore and Allen Sinfield p. 205, (Manchester, Manchester University Press).

However, Brecht came to understand that Shakespeare had captured something extraordinary: the many-sided, dialectical, argumentative style.
> Ibid, p. 211.

Brecht's adaptation does include some important rebalancing, the tribunes and the masses are clearly foregrounded:

Brutus [as they prepare the defence of revolutionary Rome]
> I have the feeling, shared, I'm told, by many
> Others that Rome's a better place
> With that man gone, a city worth defending
> Perhaps for the first time since it was founded.
> Bertolt Brecht[27],

Brecht[28] wrote that he was influenced by Mao Tse-Tung: *On Contradiction*[29] 1937, during the writing of *Coriolan*. Mao Tse-Tung had attempted to broaden dialectics in the context of a different world situation. He began with a materialist analysis:

> Without concrete analysis, there can be no knowledge of the particularity of any contradiction. We must always remember Lenin's words, the concrete analysis of concrete conditions. [30]

However, Mao claimed erroneously that Lenin had argued for an 'antagonistic contradiction' i.e. a second contradiction. Hence Mao argued there was a primary contradiction between bourgeois and proletarian and a secondary contradiction between imperialism and the oppressed masses. We can see how Brecht used and adapted both ideas, the internal enemy of the plebeians in Rome, the Patricians, and then the imperialist enemy of post-insurrectionary Rome led by Coriolanus and Tullus Aufidius.

---

[26] Bertolt Brecht, *Brecht on Theatre* [ed] Marc Silberman, Steve Giles, Tom Kuhn Third Edition, p.189 (London, Bloomsbury Methuen Drama). Hereafter Brecht on Theatre p.#
[27] Bertolt Brecht, Berliner *Ensemble Adaptations,* p.161, 2014 (London, Bloomsbury).
[28] Bertolt Brecht, *Brecht on Theatre* p. 294,
[29] *Selected Works of Mao Tse-Tung Vol 1*, pp.311-347, 1967, (Peking, Foreign Languages Press).
[30] ibid.

It is necessary, as Boal *Theatre of the Oppressed* [31] argued, for a poetic which breaks with 'Aristotle's coercive system of tragedy'.

Thus, it is possible to comprehend in Brecht, maybe not a Shakespeare, but a dramatist in a similar epoch, an epoch like our own. Therefore, we understand continuity as well as change, the dialectic, in the work of Plutarch, William Shakespeare and Bertolt Brecht. I conclude with Christopher Caudwell who underpinned much of my analysis:

> Shakespeare could not have attained the stature that he did had he not exposed, at the dawn of bourgeois development, the whole movement of capitalist development.[32]

Bibliography.
Primary Sources.
Brecht, B, *Berliner Ensemble Adaptations,* (London: Bloomsbury, 2014).
Brecht, B, *On Art & Politics* [ed] Tom Kuln and Steve Giles. (London: Bloomsbury, 2015).
Brecht, B, *Brecht on Performance* [ed] Tom Kuhn, Steve Giles, Marc Silberman, (London: Bloomsbury, 2015).
Brecht, B, *Brecht on Theatre* [ed] Marc Silberman, Steve Giles, Tom Kuhn Third Edition, (London: Bloomsbury Methuen Drama, 2008).
Plutarch's *Lives of the noble Grecians and Romans Sir Thomas North anno 1579, English with an introduction by George Wyndham*, (London: D. Nutt, 1895-6).
Plutarch, *Makers of Rome*, [trans] Ian Scott-Kilvert (Harmondsworth: Penguin Classics).

---

[31] Augusto Boal *Theatre of the Oppressed, Ch 1,* 2008 (London, Plato Press).
[32] Christopher Caudwell *Reality and Illusion,* 1977, p.64-5 (London, Lawrence & Wishart).

Completely Fragmented:

Shakespeare, W, *Anthony and Cleopatra* [ed] Bate, J and Rasmussen, E, RSC, (London: Macmillan, 2007).
Shakespeare, W, *Coriolanus* [ed] Bliss, L The New Cambridge Shakespeare, (Cambridge: Cambridge University Press, 2010).
Shakespeare, W, *Coriolanus*, [ed] Bate, J and Rasmussen, E RSC Shakespeare, (London, Macmillan,2011.)
Shakespeare, W *Coriolanus*, [ed] Holland, P The Arden Shakespeare, London: Bloomsbury, 2016)
Shakespeare, W *Julius Caesar* [ed] Bate, J and Rasmussen, E RSC Shakespeare, (London, Macmillan, 2011).

Secondary Sources.
Bate, J, *The Genius of Shakespeare,* (London: Picador Classic, 2016).
Boal, A, *Theatre of the Oppressed,* (London: Plato Press, 2008).
Brockman, B.A. *Shakespeare: Coriolanus, A Selection of Critical Essays.* (London: McMillian Press).
Caudwell, C, *Illusion and Reality*, (London: Lawrence & Wishart, 1977).
Eagleton, T *Shakespeare & Society: Critical Studies in Shakespearian Drama*, (London: Chatto & Windus, 1970).
Eagleton, T. *William Shakespeare*, (*Rereading Literature*), (Oxford, John Wiley & Sons, 1986).
David Johnston and Anita Pacheco *Reading Guide for Block 3.* (Milton Keynes, Open University Press)
Dollimore, J *(Radical Tragedy: Religion, Ideology and Power in the Drama of Shakespeare and his Contemporaries,* (London: Palgrave Macmillan, 2010).
Johnathon Dollimore and Allen Sinfield [ed] *Political Shakespeare, Essays in cultural Materialism,* (Manchester, Manchester University Press).
Eliot, T.S. *Selected Prose* [ed] Frank Kermode, (London: Faber & Faber, 1975)
Eliot, T.S. *Collected Poems* 1909-62, (London: Faber & Faber 2002)
Hazlett, W *Selected Writings* (Oxford: Oxford University Press, 2009).
Huffman, C.C, *Coriolanus in Context* (New Jersey: Becknell University Press,1971).

Kermode, F *Shakespeare's Language,* (London: Penguin Book, 2000).
Kiernan, V, *Eight Tragedies of Shakespeare*, (London: Zed Books, 2016)
Kiernan, V *Shakespeare: Poet and Citizen* (London: Zed Books, 2016).
Mao Tse-Tung *Selected Work Vol 1*, (Peking, Foreign Languages Press, 1967).
Marx, K *Capital. Vol 1*: (London, Lawrence & Wishart, 1974).
Marx & Engels, *Collected works*, vol 3, (New York, International Publishers, 2005)..
Nuttall, A.D. Sh*akespeare The Thinker* (London: Yale University Press, 2008).
Pacheco, A, *William Shakespeare: Coriolanus, Writers and Their Work,* (Northcote: British Council).
Petit, E.C, Coriolanus and the Midlands Insurrection of 1607, *Shakespeare Survey III (1950) p.34-42.*
Ryan, K, *Shakespeare's Universality* (London: Bloomsbury Arden Shakespeare, 2015).
Schall, E *The Craft of Theatre: seminars and discussions in Brechtian Theatre* [trans] Jack Davis (London: Methuen Drama, 2008).
Shaughnessy R, *The Routledge Guide to William Shakespeare* (London: Routledge, 2011).
Siegel. P. *The gathering storm: Shakespeare's English and Roman history plats: a Marxist analysis*, (London, Redwords, 1982)
Squiers, A, *An Introduction to the Social and Political Philosophy of Bertolt Brecht: Revolution and Aesthetics* (Netherlands: Rodopi, 2014).
Tatlow, A *Shakespeare, Brecht, and The Intercultural Sign* (London: Duke University Press, 2001)
Wheeler, D [ed] *Coriolanus: Critical Essays* (London: Routledge, 1995).
Williams W.E [ed] *A Book of English Essays*, (Harmondsworth: The Penguin English Library, 1962).
Wood, A, Riot, *Rebellion and Popular Politics in Early Modern Politics in Early Modern Britain.* (Basingstoke Hampshire: Palgrave, 2002).

Completely Fragmented:

Why Elise Cowen?

Why write about Elise Cowen? It is rhetorical; a Beat poet, they were the precursors to the counter-culture, obsessed with books, rejected her roots, depressive becoming psychotic, spent time in psychiatric hospital, and had ill physical health because of her drug use. She was different from many of her contemporaries and found it difficult to play the roles her generation attempted to impose on her; for this she would pay a high price, a premature death. Elise jumped through a closed seventh floor window to her death at the age of 29. Why did she crucify herself with hypodermic needles? I am 55 and may know, also having drug-related schizophrenia, a writer, but I have been 'clean' and 'dry' for over thirty years.

Since 2014 the conditions for a revaluation of her poetry existed with the publication of Elise Cowen's only complete notebook ['Fall 1959-Spring 1960'] Trigilio (2014) and of her life with the republication of Elise's friend's Joyce Johnston (2014*) Come and Join the Dance* in which Elise is Kay. This is in addition to her other primary source Johnston (2006) *Minor Characters: a brief memoir of the Beat Generation* and Skir (1970) *Every Green Review, October 1970* both provide a wealth of material. The whole process of revealing this 'hidden history' of women 'Beat' writers could be traced to Neil Cassady's [the Muse of Allen Ginsberg and Jack Kerouac] partner Carolyn Cassady, who came out about the 'Beat' men in Cassady (1990) *Off the Road: Twenty Years with Cassady, Kerouac and Ginsberg.* Her book was a sharp rebuke to the men of the Beat Generation. It was of course a pun on Jack Kerouac (2000) *On the Road* written in 1957 which was the cornerstone of male Beat fiction with Allen Ginsberg, he was intimately involved with Elise Cowen for a brief period, who's *Howl* (2014) was published, after an obscenity trial, in 1956 and provided the poetic foundation. I cast a shadow on the Beat's personal revolution as it did not produce a qualitative social transformation, a socialist revolution, only a quantitative shift in social values. Elise and I were writing as well.

The Hit.
'Go man go.'   Elise encourages.

As every junky knows there was a family dysfunction or three: Blessed Trinity. However, it is cast into Hades because Elise like I remembered that first hit of heroin. She said:
What America needs is a lot of cheap heroin.
Skir (1970) p10.
Aged twelve, my mind was unlocked by L.S.D facilitating the comprehension of poetry: 'The force that through the green fuse drives the flower' (Thomas 1972, p. 8). Aged thirteen, I mixed with students like Elise, also an avid reader of Dylan Thomas (Skir 1970, p. 3). We sought sanctuary in a company of souls who did not yell, new companions did not have the strut of oppression and welcomed all outsiders into the company of dreamers, and these people were not branded with the iron of hypocrisy. They caressed with potions, wondrous white powders which beckoned into worlds of meaning and caring. Initiating a world of compassion and the poetry of oblivion, they prepared our first fix. The pristine white powder floated into a spoon, a lighter ignites, a wait until the liquid began to bubble with significance, cotton wool put in place with the zeal of the mystic in the magic liquid, the glass syringe sighed as the plunger is drawn up. Hell would cease now, and the heavens danced to caress the verse in the mind of the poets. Those shackles floated away, the needle fitted snugly onto the syringe, the singer of dreams smacked our arms, the tubes became swollen, and the spike pierced those purple veins, deliverance from the world. As the plunger drew up a serpent of blood danced into the cloudy liquid, a hit first time, the plunger pushed this chemical dream out of the syringe into my arm, her arm, we trembled Arrr…warmth radiated up the arm rushing into the catacombs which were minds now one… this heat permeated the entirety of our body. We welcomed the Kingdom; the stigmata on our arms were those of a Beat beatitude. Elise wrote:

              Oh that I was a Cunt of golden pleasure more pure than heroin or heaven.
Trigilio (2014) p.84.

The Cellar.

The origins of 'New Woman' are in Chernyshevsky (1863) *What is to be Done* personified as Sonia Pavlovna. She fled her family believing it to be dark and damp like a cellar. In a similar manner Elise made what a revolutionary move was for a young woman of
nineteen from an upper-class Jewish family with a definite Zionist agenda. Joyce Johnston (2006) *Minor Characters* articulated Elise's situation as she moved out of the family 'cellar':
Nineteen-year-old-girls did not leave home except for dormitories or marriage. If you lived free; you could not expect to live well.
Johnston (2006) p.63.
Existential psychiatry understood the roots of oppression and indeed the roots of insanity in the bourgeois family as David Cooper (1974) *The Death of the Family* wrote:
We don't need Mother and Father anymore. All we need is mothering and fathering...
Blood is thicker than water only in the sense of being the vitalizing stream of social stupidity.
Cooper (1974) pp. 29-30.

Gilly rolled me a huge joint of rich green marijuana just as Allen Ginsberg had rolled one for Elise; we had both inhaled deeply and demonstratively. I had been 'underground', a 'missing minor' for some time. It was time for me to go down to the U.K version of Haight Ashbury in San Francisco, which was Notting Hill Gate in London, the hub of the counter-culture with the offices of Release, a drugs agency always willing to get you checked over by a 'cool' doctor. Hitched down the M1 from near Warwick University and got a 'lift', a lorry driver, a pleasant man. He asked when I last ate, then gave me his sandwich box and asked me my age, which was thirteen, I said 17. He dropped me at Newport Pagnell Services M1 brought me a meal and split. A brown Rover 2000 picked me up; the cat had his suit jacket hanging from a hook:

>'Where are you going.' he asks.
>'London, man.'

I wore a red tee shirt, green jeans, desert boots and had a shoulder-bag made by my older sister as a present: 'I couldn't wait until you'd done your first trip' she said.

'I can drop you off wherever you want to go.'

'Err, possibly not man. Just where the motorway ends, thanks.'

'Have you been to any good orgies lately?'

A shiver of fear shot through my frame:

'No man, they're not my scene.'

We drove in silence to North London; I could tell he was no novice at this as we pulled into some run-down garages. He stopped the car, unzipped his trousers, a little erect penis glared at me.

'Wank me off.'
'No, I don't want to.'
'I can get you as much heroin as you want.'

I didn't believe him, grabbed the door handle and ran.

He shouts: 'I killed someone last week for not doing it.'

Years later I reflected that it was fortunate cars did not come equipped with central locking in the early 1970s. It was impossible to seek refuge in any way with the police, they were the 'enemy' as well when you're carrying drugs, a set of 'works'[33] and on the run.

We had left these ostensibly 'nice people' for very genuine reasons, it just made sense:

The Cowens were what my parents would call
a nice family.
Johnston (2006) p.54.

With a 'nice' apartment, 'nice possessions', nice and empty lives just like my parents and they were also similar in that:

They raised their voices, though, a great deal.
Mr. Cowen was given to threats and rages, Mrs Cowen to tears and recriminations.
Johnston (2006) p.55.

My mother had been telling me she was going to 'commit suicide' since I was seven, since my sister became a hippie and run away from home. When I enquired further after

---

[33] Underground idiolect for a syringe.

about a year she said, 'I am letting off steam'. They put my sister in an 'approved school' to which I was taken as a child, it seemed friendlier than home. I was marked as if with a branding iron. Later she was put in a psychiatric hospital both of us apparently insane, but no one else knows the chill of a cellar and the fears there until you experience them. She didn't have the same interest in books; I think that is what saved me. Families can indeed seem like cellars from which we and many like us fled in fear. You go, break the chains or you would be processed by their huge machine Moloch as Ginsberg *Howl* (2014) warned against. Some of us were not ready to be butchered in their abattoir, but we knew that the cemetery beckoned, our names already carved upon the tombstones.

<u>Jehovah and other men.</u>
I've tried]
I've tried
Been tried
I'll try again
Although my Beings weak
There's nothing worth
But God & you
And God has gone to sleep.
Trigilio (2014) p.49

There seemed to be three significant males prowling in Elise's life, all of them were Jewish like Elise and so they shared some concepts. Inevitably the God Jehovah as she was brought up in an upper middle-class Jewish family. Although many Jewish émigrés embraced working class 'resistance ideologies' Anarchism in the case of Emma Goldman and Alexander Berkman which lead to an attempted assassination of the company director Mr. Frick in 1912. Allen Ginsberg's childhood was dominated by the American Communist Party and his mother's descent into insanity. I note, although Elise met Leo Skir at the Hechalutz Hazard camp in 1949, both rejected Zionism and Elise re-examined her spiritual inheritance in her poetry and practice. The second man as far as I can ascertain was Mr. Cowen, another patriarch and the third was the major Beat poet Allen Ginsberg. She was afraid of the first two and fell in love

with the third. Elise attempted to reject the phallocentric nature of post-war American culture in particular the God of her childhood who cast a shadow of fear over her life, the darkest of nights. She picks up a pen and writes:
>   Jehovah-
> I don't believe a Word
> No, I don't believe you care anymore
> Do you really want our fear rather than our love?
>   Trigilio

(2014) p 42.

Ginsberg, (Miles 2010, p 172) mentioned, was trying to deny his homosexuality at the time they met. Maybe that was a strand within the thread of her infatuation for the Beat poet. Ginsberg never seemed to say 'no' to very much he thought would deepen his experience or expand his consciousness [he also fought a long battle with various strains of hepatitis]. She went from being an outsider at Colombia University who then had an affair with a philosophy professor to being given the nickname 'Beat Alice' during 1953 because of her new involvement in Bohemian circles.

    I became 'another man' in Elise Cowen's life. Influenced by the male Beat writers like William S. Burroughs, Allen Ginsberg and Jack Kerouac from an early age embracing the latter's belief in 'first thought, first word' in my writing. The pen and syringe were handed from their generation to the generation of 1967 and then to my contemporaries. Also, I shared their philosophical proclivities their strand of Existentialism: Nietzsche, Camus and Sartre. I embraced the Sisyphean moment, but Existentialism once realized can only be lived as practice, Praxis, because Camus (1976) *The Myth of Sisyphus* argued that once Nietzsche had announced the 'death of God':
>   There is but only one serious
>   philosophical problem
>   and this is suicide.
>   Camus (1976) p.11.

It is possible, I would argue, to perceive this very clearly in Elise, but also its ramifications for humanity in this post-modernist epoch. Click, my tape-recording cuts in: '*Revolutionary socialist current around Trotsky was in retreat,*

numerically tiny because of the betrayals of Stalinism and reformist
Socialist Democracy the world became disorientated. Consumerism
could never fulfil human needs and there were no other metanarratives.'
Elise and her friends were in a storm without an eye, the rebels who had to make their own cause. Or so it might have appeared, but, Trotsky (1981) *Art and Literature* understood there is never a linear line in literature; the dialectic exists to be answered by its antithesis. Literature cannot achieve that dialectical leap to a higher form of revolutionary literature without a movement lead by the 'universal class', the proletariat. Allen Ginsberg understood something of this:
> Holy the Fifth International.
> Ginsberg (2014) p.28.

But his International to replace the Fourth International created by Trotsky could not attain its objectives by a dissident aestheticism, a new decadent movement which conjured up Baudelaire and 'art for art's sake' would not suffice. Elise would not have read Marx in depth, but her girlfriend Shelia, before the relationship with Ginsberg, had urged upon her return from Paris:
> Another French Revolution was necessary "blood must   flow in the streets."
> Skir (1970) p.10.

Elise merely commented about the necessity of cheap drugs, Leo Skir recalled. Her disorientation was increased, spinning like a whirling top out of control as she descended further into psychosis and addiction.

Elise's middle name Nadir meant 'nothing and nothingness' and she would have been aware of the pun on Jean-Paul Sartre *Being and Nothingness* (Kaufmann, 1969) as much of the 'Beat' scene was inspired by Existentialist philosophy. However, I was only to enter Elise's magical and dark world upon reading Knight (2006) and then I embarked on an odyssey which is achieving fruition in writing this piece of Life-Writing, I had almost lost my heart to this strange woman and certainly we were rather like twin meteors ablaze in a dark universe. Joyce Johnson, interviewed 3rd October 2002, said of Elise Cowen:

> The world treated her very badly
> because she was an odd
> girl. She didn't care about being
> pretty. She was, you know,
> very bright, and she was eccentric.
> Grace and Johnson (eds) (2004) p. 198.

'I'm waiting for the man.'

I recollect living in squalid flat where The Velvet Underground and Nico L.P with the track 'I am waiting for the man', from their 1967 album, was played as if it were a Psalm. The song is about 'scoring' heroin and amphetamine, Elise must have waited for the man many times 'first thing you learn is you always have to wait' (Reed 2008, p. 3) lyrics continued. Elise would always be waiting for Allen Ginsberg and another futile wait that would be. Ginsberg's written choice of phrase, after her death, 'the intellectual madwoman' to describe Elise illustrates his lack of commitment to her. during their relationship Elise typed Ginsberg's long poem about his mother *Kaddish*. Joyce Johnston, Elise's best friend, encapsulated this in (2006) *Minor Characters: A Beat Memoir:*

> Elise was a moment in Allen's life.
> In Elise's, Allen
> was an eternity.
> Johnston (2006) p.78

Allen was, (Miles 2010, pp. 174-5) acting on the recommendations of his analyst who believed his homosexuality to be pathological and therefore encouraged him to have sexual relationships with women. Allen would soon fall in love with Peter Orlofsky, who became a lifelong partner.

Sigmund says...

Elise was Skir (1970) informs us interested in Freud as were the other Beat writers. Burroughs famously 'analysing' Ginsberg, which was possibly traumatic for both. What did Freud say about the nature of the creative process in writers?

> A strong experience in the present
> awakens in the creative

Completely Fragmented:

> mind a memory of an earlier
> experience (usually belonging
> to his childhood) from which there
> now proceeds a wish
> which finds its fulfilment in the
> creative work? The work
> itself exhibits elements of the recent
> provoking occasion
> as well as the old memory.
> Freud (1964) p.130

Freud compared the whole process to daydreaming. All of us and the Beats had concoctions allowing inner exploration. We all altered states of consciousness either to a lesser extent with hashish or marijuana or a greater extent with L.S.D or as Elise liked Peyote will recognise these. Certainly, in the creative person these can be far more intense. The hallucinogens produced, under favourable conditions an insight into the nature of oneself and the natural world or beyond, this was 'a good trip'. The 'bad trip' resembled something more like a descent into a Dantesque inferno. Lysergic acid diethylamide mimicked some of the experiences that are aspects of an untreated psychosis and as in the psychotic state the affected person can understand these as enlightening or intensely frightening. Often over time it is like a marriage of heaven and hell as with all mental illnesses and addiction or any substance misuse. For Elise these were a series of engagements with hell.

The Last Trip.

A haze began to encircle us, with the desire to transcend this world and embrace an essence, something the 'elders' did not possess, ignited again within us. Two outcasts of the system, but within us burnt a love of the 'Idea'. We chose to live on the periphery, which is the body of Isis when she is pregnant with the 'Word'. A prophet of this tribe, Ginsberg, said he would give us 'Californian Sunshine' [L.S.D] for an 'ontological awakening.', but he hadn't intended that it should be taken intravenously. He cruised back later; the sacrament was laid silently in a sea of shadows, solitary in its wrapping of tin foil, awaiting an awakening, its benediction. Elise and I welcomed him, it was really his Mass, it is here she will celebrate the 'Word', the creative energy of the universe which comes from, the feminine, the Lunar Muse, Graves (1984) *The White Goddess*. Elise gently unwrapped the square of tin foil with long pale fingers and held it in her hands, Ginsberg raised it before his forehead and said in words like a priest as he holds the Eucharist: 'This is my body, take it and eat, you will be sustained by its vibrations and given a glimpse of infinity.' Elise and I genuflected before the Host, the Word:

'Have a good trip, never forget me.' Ginsberg waved goodbye.

We were dizzy with anticipation as the sweet aroma of Isis scented our crash-pad. We quickly found the dream machine, prepared the 'gear' for a fix and located the mainline… wham without the fear of flying, we were left dancing. A spectre of William Blake appeared in the corner reciting: 'Hear the voice of the bard! Who Present, Past & Future, sees; whose ears have heard The Holy Word that walked among the ancient trees.' Tangerine lights merged into purple clocks which climbed the walls, their disembodied smiles swirled into seas of lemon, lime green flowers melt and kissed the skin, and then the mind dissolved into a pool of turquoise which wept back into the ceiling. They found me eight hours later curled into a ball, repeating a mantra:

'My name is Oedipus; my name is Oedipus, no more psychoanalysis'.

Elise had already been admitted into Bellevue Hospital chanting:

'My name is Electra, my name is Electra, no my name is Emily,
Emily Dickinson.'

Emily Dickinson.

Elise had written three poems which referenced Emily Dickinson: *Emily, Emily, white witch of Amherst* and *I took the skins of corpses:*

[Emily]

Emily,
Come summer
You'll take off your
jewelled bees
Which sting me

Completely Fragmented:

> I'll strip off my stinking
> jeans
> Hand in hand
> We're run outside
> Look straight at
> the sun
> A second time
> And get tan.
> Trigilio (2014) p.26.

Elise originally concluded her poem with the line:
> And we'll hatch.

She crossed out this line in her notebook (Trigilio 2014, p. 134) either an earlier rejection of motherhood as a choice of a woman Beat poet or possibly a reflection on an unwanted pregnancy with a drunken artist in California (Skir 1970, p. 8). This should have been a D&C but because of the long Christmas vacation the doctors performed a hysterectomy. The poem did suggest a feminist separatism, a sisterhood, which found a voice in the Feminist radicalization of the late 1960's and 1970's.

Thanatos.

Elise like I didn't choose not to conform we just couldn't maybe we were too ill, the society we lived in was like a huge Praying mantis and in the end 'hip friends' disengaged. The Freudian opposite of the Pleasure Principle *Eros,* the death instinct *Thanatos* was very powerful in us both. Here a quote from Kay (Elise) as a young woman university drop-out [she did go back and Majored in Modern Poetry] in her friend Joyce Johnston's *Come and Join the Dance*, the first woman Beat novelist published in 1961:

'Well, I think I am going to be a failure," Kay said slowly. "I think that's already settled. And that's alright. But I want to be a magnificent one. A gigantic smoking ruin.'
Johnston (2014) p 48.

I was similar but met exceptional therapists and nurses and with modern medicines can write and study. Chipmunkapublishing and The Open University have become like paths through the desert which has led to a more fruitful life. The British philosophy David Hume thought people weren't a consistent 'Self', but rather a 'bundle of selves' like actors playing different parts on the stage of a theatre at various times. Elise would write poignantly:

Did I go mad…? [Extract]

'Did I go mad in my
mother's womb?
Waiting
to get out
…
On my brain are welts from
the moving that never
moves
On my brain are the welts
from the endless stillness
I don't want to intone
"See how she suffers"
"See how she suffers"
(The sting of eyes reminds)
That not really, or only what
I mean-among other things I
am not
permitted to feel that much
…
'tick tock'
'But that the truth I guess of
(Even were I to KNOW it)
IS EVERYONE'S…
Knight (2006) pp. 163-164.

Elise Cowen took her place with poets Sylvia Plath and Anne Sexton, women who had attacked the citadel of Patriarchal society, but consequently were cast into an abyss of the Great Patriarch. Self-destruction is a product of Patriarchal Capitalism and only mass proletarian revolution can create the conditions for the emancipation of poets, a golden dawn so sweetly scented with love's aroma. This maybe communism as envisaged by women writers like Alexandra Kollontai (1982) *Love of Worker Bees* in these circumstances Elise and I would not be stung by barbed wasps and we would live in a great hive together with the worker-poet's Queen Bee. We would write our poems with pens that have honey for ink and sup happily upon these sweet words. We would be humming with poetry, rather than

Completely Fragmented:

buzzing with Benzedrine. Maybe I was inculcated with the revolution as a child, but who knows, who remembers? I do. My poem about Elise:

> Elegy for Elise Cowen (1933-1962).
> Your smile is bright with magic, it draws in verse
> To glimpse the "straights", their vision is blurred
> And gazes inert, that form is carried in a hearse,
> But you who danced the naked poetics preferred
>
> The peace of wombs, the warmth, you "rush" induced seductress,
> Our wastes are frozen with promises, caught and chosen,
> This moth of candle and flame is burnt and wingless,
> At dawn you cupped it in a hand and have then written
>
> A dirge of deserts and biting sand which sings
> Into the syringe, enchantment of the finite "fix"
> Lies with accusations on pages scribed in blotted words,
> This sacred insanity is vibrating your soul, a matrix
>
> For jewels, the wind whispered opiate kiss, it is
> In here, where belief lies on the periphery, the poetry
> Ascends in grace with those of Auschwitz,
> You stumble across the graveyards and weep in symmetry.
>
> > Pearce (2015) p 66.

Bibliography.
Camus, A (1976 [1955]) *The Myth of Sisyphus*, Harmondsworth: Penguin Modern Classics.
Cassady, C (1990) *Off the Road: Twenty Years with Cassady, Kerouac and Ginsberg.* London: Flamingo.
Chernyshevsky, N (1983 [1863]) *What is to be Done*, New York: Cornell University Press.
Cooper, D (1974) *The Death of the Family*, Harmondsworth: Pelican books.
Freud, S (1964 [1959]) 'Creative Writing and Daydreaming.' The *Standard Edition of the Complete Psychological Works of Sigmund Freud, Vol 9*, London: The Hogarth Press.
Ginsberg, A (2014 [1956]) *Howl and Other Poems*, San Francisco: City Lights.
Grace, Nancy. M and Johnson, Ronna. C (2004) *Breaking the Rules of Cool: Interviewing and Reading Women Beat Writers*, Mississippi: The University of Mississippi Press.
Graves, R (1984 [1961]) *The White Goddess*, London: Faber & Faber.
Kaufmann, W (1969) *Existentialism from Dostoevsky to Sartre*, Ohio: Meridian Books.
Kerouac, J (2000 [1957]) *On the Road*, Harmondsworth: Penguin Modern Classics.
Knight, B (2006) *Women of the Beat Generation: the writers, artists and muses at the heart of a revolution*, Berkley: Conart Press.
Kollontai, A (1982 [1932]) *Love of Worker Bees*, London: Virago
Johnston, J (2006) *Minor Characters: A Beat Memoir*, London: Methuen.
Johnston, J (2014[1961]) *Come and Join the Dance*, New York: Open Road.
Miles, B (2010) *Allen Ginsberg Beat Poet*, Great Britain: Virgin Books.
Neale, D. (ed.) (2009) *A Creative Writing Handbook*, Milton Keynes/London: A & C Black in association with The Open University.
Pearce, N (2015) *Icarus Rising: New and Selected Work*, London: Chipmunkapublishing.
Reed, L (2008) *Pass Thro Fire: The Collected Lyrics*, U.S.A: Da Capo Press.

Sartre, J-P (1976[1943]) *Being and Nothingness,* London: Methuen & Co Ltd.
Skir, L She was Beat with Allen Ginsberg: Elise Cowen: a brief memoir of the fifties, *Every Green Review, October 1970.*
Thomas, D (1972) *Collected Poems 1934-1952*, London: Dent & Sons Ltd.

On Method.

Richard Holmes argues Life Writing has been profoundly transformed:

> People often suggest that the future of biography lies in a
> radical change of form- in the development of fractured or
> post-modern narrative models. But this has been going on
> for quite a time. Peter Ackroyd's original version of
> Dickens (1988) with its flamboyant insertions of fiction.
> Cline and Angier (2014) p 118.

My interest was stimulated by Virginia Woolf's 'the lives of the obscure' (Lee (2009) p. 126). Lee continues:

> Biographies often speak for the alternative 'hidden lives', especially
> women's...- grew out of a feminist interest in 'hidden lives'...and
> of working-class history.
> Lee (2009) p. 127.

Although sympathetic to these perspectives my methodology is derived from Marx:

> In the social production of their life, men enter into definite
> relations that are indispensable and independent of their will,
> relations of production which correspond to a definite stage
> of production.
> Solomon (1979) p. 29.

There were three texts which were seminal in 'Life Writing' *Dead Beat*. Jean Rhys (1981) *Smile Please* which provided a material base for my episodic approach, Janet Frame (1984*) Janet Frame: An Autobiography* that blazed a path for the writing about mental health issues and thirdly, William S. Burroughs (2008) *Junky* which announced the historical moment that allowed people to write honestly about hard drugs.

My method is derived from the practice of Life Writing as outlined in Haslam, H and Neale, D (2009) *Life Writing* and complexified in both Hermione Lee (2009*) Biography: A Very Short Introduction* and more recently in Cline, S and Angier, C (2014) *Life Writing; A Writers & Readers Companion.* Therefore, I am aware of the requirements of an opening paragraph elucidating one's motivation and the academic 'justification' for embarking on the manuscript. Also, I was made aware of the necessity of grounding the text in history, but also of the post-modernist breaking-up of simple narratives and a tendency towards the subverting of the genre. While Neale, D. (ed.) (2009) *A Creative Writing Handbook* taught me important lessons about Aristotelian poetics generally, the use of the dramatic method to enhance prose and the effective use of dialogue. Hence my idiolect is appropriate to the historical sense of 'place', the 'Beat Generation' and the 'counter-culture'. I 'cross-cut' in some sections and merge narratives. The usage of quasi-Roman Catholic metaphor is consistent with Jack Kerouac's usage of 'Beat' 'beatitude' which I extend in 'The Last Trip' to the Eucharistic: 'Take you all of this and eat' as metaphors for the consummation and consumption of the L.S.D. This surreal employment of language is entirely congruent with the 'altered state of consciousness' which it describes. Sergei Eisenstein's montage technique is used in, for instance, the descriptions of the family by Sonia Pavlovna, the biographical detail of the Cowen family and mine with Cooper's reflection on the redundancy of the family, which 'cuts' to a verbatim account of what happened when I hitchhiked down to London as a young adolescent. These linguistic, dramatic and cinematic devices were vital in allowing me to compose my manuscript, *Dead Beat*. The title is a play on words as in the premature death of a 'beat poet' and the now archaic American phrase 'dead-beat' i.e.

exhausted. The authorial voice in my text is 'first-person plural.'

In regard of the Aristotelian poetic *Poetics* (Aristotle 1996) I employ a 'dramatic arc' which articulates 'the whole':

'A whole is that which has a beginning, a middle and an end.'

Aristotle (1996) p.13.

There is a causal relationship between each section which I disrupt, writing *in medias res*. Neale (2009) comments on autobiography as a genre even when it is 'subverted':

... character is still it's most central and essential feature, just as in the more straightforward Robinson Crusoe.

Neale (2009) p.7.

Aristotle's concept was developed by Freytag (2004) and illustrated in Fig 3:

Fig.3

I employ this structure and the conflicts which generate the 'action' are numerous e.g.
familial and ideological. I recalled *The Hours* (Neale 2009, pp 350-54) and make use of Time

Freytag's Pyramid

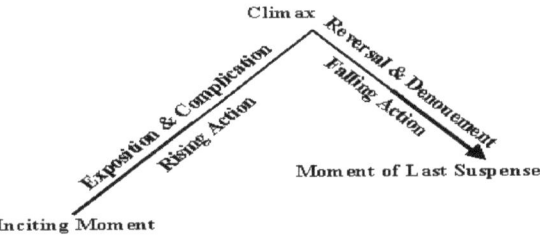

and emblematic imagery, e.g. drug images. I use parallel stories; Elise Cowen's and mine with the same plot. Forster commented on the relationship between the story and the plot:

> The king died and then the queen died.
> The king died and then the queen died of grief.
>   Forster (1955) p.86.

The difference between the two, he argued, was the plot has a causal nature in an Aristotelian sense. A submerged and ordered sequence of action that creates a 'plot.'

I would suggest that because of studying a Humanities Degree with Creative Writing at the Open University I have learnt to embrace 'the freedom of form'. I now have a far greater repertoire of technical devices and know better how to articulate my imagination. This is tantamount and consistent with asserting the module has allowed me to develop a 'creative voice'. One invaluable lesson learnt was the discipline of Realism in a 'stage-drama'. As I was engaged with a concrete situation and compelled to physically move my characters upon a stage my abstraction had to be rooted in a material base. This was not a limiting experience, quite the opposite and with the use of Brecht's 'alienation effect' I was able to subvert Naturalism when I choose. Elizabeth Bishop correctly maintains of poetic 'forms': 'They seem to start the machinery.' (Neale 2009, p. 246).

However, once learnt 'form' can be subverted as Elise Cowen and the Beat writers on the West Coast of America and the confessional' writers of the East Coast Establishment exhibited with consummate ability. The 'formal' and the 'experimental' can only complement. Is this not the paradox of modernism and post-modernism, the Metaphysical poets and Romanticism, and the debates about 'alienation effect' and Formalism in Socialist Realism which continue in Marxist circles? These apparent paradoxes are in fact dialectical in nature and each must therefore yes, contain a contradiction, but also a 'unity of opposites' which must then create the dialectical leap to a higher stage, 'the negation of the negation' as delineated by Engels (1976) Dialectics *of Nature*:

> The law of the transformation of quantity
> into quality and vice versa;
> The law of the interpenetration of opposites;
> The law of the negation of the negation.
>   Engels (1976) p.62.

This is not a metaphysical Hegelian aesthetic, but rather one rooted in the production and reproduction of everyday life, the material creation of literature. Thus, the theoretical 'argument' that underpins my piece of Life Writing is that the Beat Generation as a social phenomenon could not produce the objective material or subjective conditions necessary for an Aristotelian *eudemonia* for outsider poets under capitalism. These poets like Elise and I would, it seems, only find creative fulfilment and emotional solace under the conditions of communism. I have not 'foregrounded' this as my tutor warned against an overly academic style. I have attempted to write balanced creative non-fiction as appropriate to Life Writing.

Bibliography
Aristotle (1996) *Poetics*, London: Penguin Classics.
Burroughs, William. S (2008 [1953]) *Junky*, London: Penguin Classics.
Cline, S and Angier, C (2014) *Life Writing; A Writers & Readers Companion*. London: Bloomsbury.
Engels, F (1976 [1883]) *Dialectics of Nature*, Moscow: Progress Publishers.
Forster. E. M (1955 [1927]) *Aspects of the Novel*, Harcourt, Brave & World: New York.
Frame, J (1984) *Janet Frame: An Autobiography*, London: The Women's Press.
Freytag (2004 [1863]) *Technique of the Drama: An Exposition of Dramatic Composition and Art*, Hawaii: University Press of the Pacific
Haslam, H and Neale, D (2009) *Life Writing*, London: Routledge in association with The Open University
Lee, H (2009*) Biography: A Very Short Introduction*, Oxford: Oxford University Press.
Neale, D. (ed.) (2009) *A Creative Writing Handbook*, Milton Keynes/London: A & C Black in association with The Open University
Rhys, J (1981) *Smile Please: An Autobiography*, Harmondsworth: Penguin Books

Lord Byron's and John Clare's *Don Juan*: a question of class.

Why did John Clare suffer from the delusion that he was Lord Byron during the last twenty-seven years of his life? The majority of these were spent in High Beech Asylum and Northampton County Asylum. Lord Byron and John Clare, who both achieved similar 'print-run' statistics at their height. One would become the first literary media celebrity and In his own time created the phenomena Byronism. The other would descend into insanity. Byron's sales with the publisher John Murray in 1819 alone for *Don Juan* Cantos 1 and 2 were in total 5,100 (production figure). The first edition was an expensive 31.5 shillings [1,350 copies] and then a cheaper 9.5 shillings [3,750 copies][34]. This reinforced his position as the dominant poet of those years. He had after the success of *Childe Harold's Pilgrimage* in 1812 said: 'I awoke one morning and found myself famous.'[35] However, John Clare, a 'labourer poet' had production figures from 1820-1835 of a regular 3,000 per edition but falling away until a posthumous collected edition in 1873 with figures n/a[36]. Both wrote versions of *Don Juan*, Clare's was clearly the creation of an ill man.

How are we to understand these paradoxes? The methodological foundation for my analysis is drawn from Karl Marx

> we proceed from the active man...
> Consciousness does not determine
> life: life determines consciousness.37.

Thus, we understand a socio-economic basis for culture. I will illustrate that argument was developed through Antonio Gramsci and by Raymond Williams into Cultural Materialism. Specifically, here, Gramsci's concept of 'contradictory

---

[34] St. Clair, William *The Reading Nation in the Romantic Period*, (Cambridge, Cambridge University Press, 2007), p. 327

[35] MacCarthy, Fiona, *Byron Life and Legend*. (London, John Murray, 2004) Introduction, p, x.

[36] St. Clair (2007), p. 592-597

[37] Marx, Karl & Engels, F The *German Ideology* (London. Lawrence & Wishart,1982), p.47

consciousness' i.e., when a worker or a 'labourer poet' like John Clare can sustain both progressive and reactionary beliefs simultaneously. Frederick Engels had maintained that "false consciousness' could keep the working class from recognizing and rejecting their oppression.'[38] Antonio Gramsci developed this idea further:

> The active man-in-the-mass has a practical activity, but has
> no clear theoretical consciousness of his practical activity,
> one might almost say that he has two theoretical consciousnesses
> (or one contradictory consciousness): one which is implicit in his
> activity and which unites him with all his fellow workers in the
> practical transformation of the real world; and one, superficially
> explicit or verbal, which he has inherited from the past and
> uncritically absorbed.[39]

Therefore, we will comprehend a 'labourer poet' once he had not only quite normal 'contradictory consciousness' but was also estranged from his class after futilely looking towards the intelligentsia of his day who did not accept him. Here a second paradox appears as noted by Merryn & Raymond Williams[40]. This was that John Clare was estranged from his 'class' but not accepted into literary society. Then these contradictions once internalized would cause havoc. They were contradictions that are quintessential to class societies, that is pre-communist ones:

> The history of all hitherto existing society is the
> history of class struggles. Freeman and slave,

---

[38] Heywood, Andrew, *Political Ideas and Concepts: An Introduction, (London*, Macmillan, 1994) p.174.

[39] Gramsci, Antonio Selections from the Prison Notebooks

[40] Clare *John, Selected Poetry and Prose [ed]*, Williams Merryn & Raymond (London, Methuen, 1986) pp 10-20.

> patrician and plebeian, lord and serf, guild-master
> and journeyman, in a word, oppressor and oppressed,
> stood in constant opposition to one another, carried on
> an uninterrupted, now hidden, now open fight...41.

Thus, we see these two poets originated from opposite poles of the class spectrum, Lord Byron educated at Harrow and Cambridge while John Clare came from the rural poor. However, both classes were experiencing the transforming consequences of the Industrial Revolution. While the aristocracy would eventually come to an accord with the bourgeoisie the rural poor as a class was decimated with many becoming proletarians by the end of John Clare's life. Raymond Williams argues in *The Country and The City* (Chapter 13, 2016) this had a profound effect on 'pastoral poetry' with John Clare marking the end of the English Pastoral. Ultimately, he could not, Raymond Williams suggested, survive: 'in the noise of the market, profit, malice, envy, of capitalism'[42]. Raymond Williams concluded persuasively:

He lost his sanity, and this became manifest through the prism of Byronism with Clare deluded he was Byron.

Following Plato 'In vain does one knock at the gates of poetry with a sane mind' [Plato, *Phaedrus*, 245a][43]. We are provided with a shaft of illumination into the work and life of John Clare' who spent most of the last decades of his life in asylums for the insane. I shall argue against Jonathan Bate *John Clare* (2004)[44] that the 'heightened language' of John Clare's version of *Don Juan* composed while in Dr Allen's

---

[41] Marx, Karl & Engels Frederick *The Communist Manifesto* (Harmondsworth, Penguin Books, 1967) p, 79.

[42] Williams, Raymond *The Country and the City,* (London, Vintage Classics, 2016), p. 204

[43] Burwick, Fredrick *Poetic Madness and the Romantic Imagination,* (Pennsylvania, Pennsylvania State University Press, p., 1996), p.1.

[44] Bate, Jonathan. *John* Clare. (London: Picador, 2004).

private asylum High Beech in Epping Forest was a product of confinement. I will rather suggest that lewd and bawdy language which has no earlier manifestation in the writing of John Clare was the product of mental illness, hypo-mania. I shall endeavour to provide primary sources both of poetry and prose to illustrate this. I will employ Sylvia Plath's late poetry as another example of challenging and manic writing. Clare *Don Juan* will be shown as a reaction to Byronism which forms the backbone of this argument, especially *Don Juan*. It is possible to perceive the tension between what Aristotle had called 'a special gift' and 'madness' in both Lord Byron's and John Clare's writing. This, interestingly, we will discern in the use of his grammar or the 'awkward squad' as John Clare called it. Particularly that which was written more directly through the lens of the social phenomena of Byronism. The latter was itself a question of class. We see John Clare as torn in many directions. I will further suggest that Jonathan Bate although correct in arguing that John Clare could write prose as well as poetry in High Beech Asylum thus disproving Clare's doctor's, Dr Allen's thesis, that he could only write poetry. However, returning to my central argument, Jonathan Bate maintains that John Clare's disturbing revisiting of *Don Juan* was the product of containment in the hospital rather that of a mind in the grip of a mania. [45] But he does not address the question of the misogynistic content and the erratic punctuation here. I shall endeavour to illustrate by way of John Clare's pre-asylum writing that he could write sane poetry and prose but when writing about Lord Byron as early as 1825 (his first hospitalization was in 1838) his writing would become ungrammatical, galloping along as if in a hypo-manic state of mind. My argument will be supported by primary texts of both poetry and prose. I understand Virginia Woolf's comments on Byron's *Don Juan* as cogent:

> It is the most readable poem of its length ever
> written… It's what one has looked for in vain-an
> elastic shape which will hold whatever you

---

[45] Bate, Jonathan (2004) pp.446-450

choose to put in it.46

It is possible to maintain that Byronism embodied a contradiction which is illustrated by his biographical details of libertinism and his revolutionary poetic aspirations such as in *Don Juan*:

> I do not know; - I wish men to be free
> As much from mobs as kings- from you and me.
>
> Lord Byron, Don Juan, IX, 25, 7-8
> 47

The assonance of 'o's, 'e's created a sense of depth when combined with the iambs that provide pace but broken by caesura which adds a hint of dark questioning and then the masculine rhyme 'ee' stressed freedom. 'Poetry demands a man with a special gift...or a touch of madness' [Aristotle, *Poetics*, 1455a][48]. In the case of Lord Byron his lines in *Lara* provide an insight, I suggest into him or at least his authorial persona, the Byronic Hero:

> His madness was not of the head, but heart;
> Lord Byron, Lara Canto IX, L 358 49.

That was a constant throughout Byron's poetry and prose. To encapsulate my position here, Byron was articulate to the point of genius but troubled rather than 'mad'. Byron reinforces this concept in a collection of journal entries *Detached Thoughts*:

> ...at heart you are the most melancholy of mankind,[50]

The Romantic poets would have not necessarily have seen themselves as a 'school of poets'. However, they could be perceived as reacting against Neo-Classicism, the Enlightenment, and Alexander Pope. Hence, I shall explore

---

[46] McGann, Jerome J. *Don Juan in Context* (London, John Murry, 1976) p, 10.

[47] Lord Byron, The Major Works, (Oxford, Oxford World Classics, 2008), p. 684. Hereafter DJ p. #

[48] Burwick, Fredrick (1996) p.1.

[49] Byron. Lord, *Selected Poems*, (London Penguin Classics, 2003), p.326.

[50] Byron, Lord *Selected Letters and Journals* [ed] Leslie A. Marchant, (Massachusetts, Harvard University Press, 1982), p, 275

the relationship between Byron and Alexander Pope a little deeper through a variety of primary texts. Here is an extract from Pope's early *Essay on Criticism:*

> Those RULES of old discover'd, not devis'd,
> Are Nature still, but Nature Methodiz'd;
> Nature, like Liberty, is but restrain'd
> By the same Laws which first herself ordain'd.
> Hear how learn'd Greece her useful Rules indites,51

Then juxtapose this with a letter from Byron to Murray, September 15th, 1817:

> With regard to poetry in general, I am convinced, the more I
> think of it, that he and all of us — Scott, Southey, Wordsworth,
> I, — are all in the wrong, one as much as another; that we are
> upon a wrong revolutionary system or, not worth a damn
> in itself, ... I am the more confirmed in this by having lately
> gone over some of our classics particularly Pope. Depend upon
> it, it is all Horace then, and Claudian now, among us; and if I had
> to begin again, I would model myself accordingly... 52

Therefore, it is consistent that Byron should choose the genre employed by Alexander Pope in his major poem *The Rape of the Lock,* a mock-heroic narrative poem for his opus, *Don Juan* which is a multi-voiced or dialogic mock-satire. Thus, I show that Byron was more profoundly rooted in the Greek and Latin traditions of poetry than Wordsworth or Southey. I illustrate the intellectual basis of his attacks on

---

[51] Pope, Alexander *Selected Poetry* (Oxford, Oxford World Classics, 2008) p.3
[52] Marchant (1982), p. 167

them in the suppressed until 1834 *Dedication* to Don *Juan*. Here Byron assails Wordsworth:

> And Wordsworth, in a rather long "Excursion"
> (I think the quarto holds five hundred pages),
> Has given a sample from the vasty version
> Of his new system to perplex the sages;
> 'Tis poetry—at least by his assertion,
> And may appear so when the dog-star rages—
> And he who understands it would be able
> To add a story to the Tower of Babel.
> DJ, Dedication, 4 L.25-32.

I understand that Lord Byron is using Ottava Rima. In English the Ottava Rima stanza consists of eight iambic lines, usually iambic pentameters. Each stanza consists of three alternate rhymes and one double rhyme, following an ab, ab, ab, cc scheme. Thus, allowing a witty couplet on lines 7&8. I can, therefore, understand Byron's *Don Juan* as subverting Romanticism by referencing the work of Augustan poets such as Alexander Pope's satirical mock-heroic poetry. This contrasted with Wordsworth *Preface to Lyrical Ballads,* 1802 which advocated the use of ordinary language about the masses but transmuted through the mind of a quasi-divine power, the Poet. The differentiation of Neo-Classical and Romantic poetry had been referred to by W. H. Abrams as the 'mirror' and 'lamp.'[53]. Pre-Romantic poetry was understood as a mirror and Romantic illuminated through a 'lamp'. Thus, the genre that he decided to write within was particularly significant. He almost taunts his reader as towards the end of his mock-epic-satire informed them exactly what they had been reading:

> And I shall take a much more serious air
> Than I have yet done in this epic satire.
> DJ, Canto XIV, 99, 790-792.

---

[53] Abrams W, H. *The Mirror and the Lamp: Romantic Theory and the Critical Tradition* (Oxford, Oxford University Press 1971}

Completely Fragmented:

Air/satire rhymed teasingly with a tumbling enjambment. Then he confronted the reader with:
> Is strange-but true; for Truth is always strange,
> Stranger than Fiction: if it could be told,
> DJ, Canto XIV, 101, 801-803.

Byron's intellect and creativity were toying with the reader. The reader had just been given concrete generic information by Byron, then left to ponder. What is true? What is Fiction? Yet Byron had written to John Murray, August 21st, 1821
> Almost all of Don Juan is real life-either my own-or from people I knew.54

Of course, although the genre is epic-satire that does not mean *Don Juan* is merely a protracted swipe at those institutions Lord Byron disapproved of. He was writing in a narrative of poetry. For as T.S. Eliot noted in *The Sacred Wood*:
> No poet, no artist of any art, has his complete meaning alone.
> His significance, his appreciation is the appreciation of his relation
> to the dead poets and artists. You cannot value him alone; you
> must set him, for contrast and comparison, among the dead.55

I would now like to comment on the Don Juan legend more generally. Moyra Haslett, a leading Byron scholar, noted a looseness in Don Juan as a legend which originated in 1630 with the tragic drama *The Trickster of Seville and the Stone Guest* attributed to a Spanish monk, Tirso de Molina. Therefore, one can conclude that Byron was allowing himself ample literary space for a 'writing back' when he chose the Don Juan legend:
> The legend of the Don Juan was never intrinsically
> partisan. Indeed, it could be appropriated for contrary

---

[54] Marchant, Leslie, (1982). p, 256.
[55] Eliot, T.S. *The Sacred Wood*, (London, Faber & Faber, 1997) p.41

arguments and indeed, its ambivalent political status
has enabled many political readings.56
Although, that is not to argue that Byron was not committed to a progressive belief-system, merely that his class orientation was not objectively opposed to capitalism as in the case of the interests of proletarians or systematically organized in terms of ideas as in the case of Shelley. When his publisher Murray wanted to suppress parts of *Don Juan* Byron wrote back with some conviction: 'I will not give way to all the Cant of Christendom.'[57] Here is the crux for Byron as he believed 'Cant' or hypocrisy was prevalent in the society he placed his contribution to the *Don Juan* narrative within. Byron's *Don Juan* was as mentioned a powerful 'writing back' to Tirso de Molina *The Trickster of Serville and the Stone Guest*, 1630 but also to Mozart's opera with the libretto by Lorenzo da Ponte *Don Giovanni*. Don Juan in both of these was the seducer rather than the seduced. However, Byron turns both the drama and the opera on its head with the women acting as seductresses. The women are powerful in a manner that was quite radical for the British reading public at the beginning of the nineteenth century and echoes Geoffrey Chaucer's *The Wife of Bath's Tale* in *The Canterbury Tales*, 1404-1410. As Moyra Haslett correctly argued, class matters:

> Because of his social position as a member of
> the ruling class in decay, Don Juan carried out
> Jacobinism in the only field open to him – that
> of sexuality.58

Nevertheless, she also maintained that:
> However, this 'revolutionary' sexual behaviour
> is gendered. Women could hardly avail themselves

---

[56] Haslett, Moyra, *Byron's Don Juan and the Don Juan Legend* (Oxford, Clarendon Press 2003), p.176.
[57] Leslie A. Marchant (1982), p.328.
[58] Haslett, Moyra (2003). p.185.

> without incurring severe penalties
> and the degree
> to which they benefited from such
> activity is
> questionable.59

I would rather understand Byron's treatment of women in *Don Juan* as empowering because he had inverted the legend and thus the patriarchal relations involved in the original versions mentioned by Tirso de Molina and Mozart. Thus, we can comprehend two essential components for my analysis: class and gender and I would argue in agreement with Frederick Engels:

> According to the materialist conception of history,
> the ultimately determining element in history is the
> production and reproduction of real life. Other than
> this neither Marx nor I have ever asserted...60

We have understood why Byron made caustic attacks on Wordsworth and Coleridge. Indeed, there was also a degree of personal acrimony, but class hostility was key between the 'Grasmere scribblers' to use Byron's phrase regarding Wordsworth and Coleridge but also the younger Romantic poets like Keats who suggested rather peevishly to his brother:

> You speak of Lord Byron and me – There is this great
> difference between us. He describes what he sees – I
> describe what I imagine – Mine is the hardest task.61

Nevertheless, Byron's attacks on leading figures in the British politico-military complex such as Wellington and Castlereagh were strident and caustic attacks on the

---

[59] Haslett, Moyra (2003) p.186,
[60] Marx, Karl & Engels, Frederick, *Selected Correspondence* (Moscow, Progress Publishers, 1965) p, 417-419
[61] Keats, John, *Selected Letters* (London, Penguin Books, 2014) p, 427.

oppressor nation and the futility of war. It is significant that unlike Wordsworth and Coleridge, Byron had not been a young man in the heady days of the French Revolution. As the young William Wordsworth wrote:

> Oh! Pleasant exertion of hope and joy!
> For mighty were the auxiliars which there stood
> Upon our side, we were strong in love!
> Bliss it was to be alive,
> But to be young was very heaven!62

Both Wordsworth and Coleridge, all the Grasmere Poets would retreat into reaction as reaction established itself both in Europe and the British Isles after this period of revolutionary tumult. Nevertheless, an uprising in Ireland, the United Irishmen, in 1798, led by the Protestant Wolfe Tone had been brutally suppressed on the orders of Lord Castlereagh and he also organised state repression in England, notably the Peterloo Massacre of 1819. Although Castlereagh committed suicide in 1822, he remained a figure of hatred in progressive circles and amongst the poor. Shelley wrote a scathing poem after the Peterloo Massacre in Manchester *The Masque of Anarchy*[63]. There is no hint of satire in Byron's attacks on Castlereagh. Here in the Dedication *Don Juan* he invokes and references the seventeenth-century revolutionary poet John Milton who spoke of being 'fallen in evil days on evil tongues' *Paradise Lost Bk 7, L.25* after the defeat of the English Revolution:

> If, fallen in evil days on evil tongues,
> Milton appeal'd to the Avenger, Time,
> DJ. Dedication, X. I 72-73.

> Would he adore a sultan? he obey
> The intellectual eunuch Castlereagh?
> Dedication, XI, I 87-88.

---

[62] https://www.poetryfoundation.org/.../the-french-revolution-as-it-appeared-to-enthusia.
[63] See Paul Foot *Red Shelley* (London, Sidgwick & Jackson, 1980) for a cogent Marxist analysis of Percy Bysshe
   Shelley and his epoch.

Byron's assault on Castlereagh does not in the slightest resemble the satirical, its biting lines contrast with the concluding mock-satire of the English Cantos of *Don Juan* which Byron did not complete because of his premature death. It is rather an attack on a hated symbol of oppression. Here again, we saw a divide in Byron between the revolutionary and satirist. Byron made blistering attacks on Castlereagh's repression in Ireland:

> Cold-blooded, smooth-faced, placid miscreant!
> Dabbling its sleek young hands in Erin's blood.

Lines 88-90 are shocking, and they impacted on the masses as Richard Lansdown argued:
And it was Don Juan that working people read. At the Great Chartist demonstration held at Newcastle on 27th June 1838, several banners carried quotes from Byron's epic poem DJ, 671-2, for example:
'REVOLLUTION

> I have seen some nations, like o'er load asses,
> Kick off their burdens, meaning the high classes.'

By 1838, Byron's poetry had entered what historian William St. Clair calls 'the radical canon' of the nineteenth century working class.64.

Marx was aware though of the limitations of poets like Byron and the strengths of those like Shelley:

> The real difference between Byron and Shelley is this:
> those who understand them and love them rejoice that
> Byron died at thirty-six, because if he had lived, he would
> have become a reactionary bourgeois; they grieve that

---

[64] Lansdown Richard, The Cambridge Introduction to Byron (Cambridge, Cambridge University Press, 2012). P. 158.

> Shelley died at twenty-nine, because he was essentially
> a revolutionist, and he would always have been one of
> the advanced guard of Socialism.65

We have comprehended a 'class' element in Byron's assault on William Wordsworth who was not a member of the aristocracy and John Keats referred to as 'the cockney poet.' Byron had also made an attack on a successful 'labourer poet' Robert Bloomfield and his brother Nathan in *English Bards and Scottish Reviewers*:

> Lo! Burns and Bloomfield, nay, a greater far,
> Gifford was born beneath an adverse star,
> Forsook the labours of a servile state,
> Stemm'd the rude storm, and triumph'd over fate:
> Then why no more? if Phœbus smiled on you,
> Bloomfield! why not on brother Nathan too?
> Him to the mania, not the muse, has seized;
> Not inspiration, but a mind diseased:66

The final couplet above illustrates an unpleasantly caustic and patronizing attitude of Byron's towards 'labourer poets' and indeed, those of them who became mentally ill. It illuminates that contradiction within Byron but also those of his objective class interests and those of the poets from the rural poor like John Clare and Robert Bloomfield. Thus, we can see an element of hypocrisy in Byron who in *Don Juan* attacked the 'Cant' of the ruling elite of Britain at the time while he had indulged in a similar orientation. Christopher Caudwell noted in his early Marxian study into British poetics:

> Byron is an aristocrat – but he is one conscious
> of the break-up of his class as a force, and the

---

[65] Marx, Karl & Engels, Frederick, On Literature and Art (Moscow, Progress Publishers 1976) pp. 320- 21.
[66] Lord Byron *Selected Poems*, (2003). P.36 L. 777-784.

> necessity to go over to the bourgeoisie.
> Hence
> his mixture of cynicism and romanticism.67.

John Clare wrote these poignant lines towards the end of his life while compulsorily detained in Northampton County Lunatic Asylum:

> I am - yet what I am, none care or knows;
> My friends forsake me like a memory lost:
> I am the self-consumer of my woes –
> They rise and vanish in oblivion's host.
> John Clare: Lines: 'I am'68.

Two pieces of prose here illustrated John Clare's ambivalent relationship with grammar. This is an area of Clare scholarship which is addressed in, at least, two sources exclusively as well as marginally in other texts. See especially:

a) Eluding the Awkward Squad: John Clare's Punctuation, The Absence of
   Punctuation in John Clare's Sonnet *'Field Thoughts'*, Martyn Crucefix.[69]

b) *John Clare and the Tyranny of Grammar*, James C. McKusick.[70]

However, for my purposes I wish to delineate the relationship and connections between John Clare's perspective on grammar and his use of it in two rare prose pieces and then apply these findings to his revisiting of Byron's *Don Juan*. John Clare's poem reveals more than just an uncertain use of grammar but will be shown to employ a heightened libidinal language which descends into pushing the boundaries of acceptability which is not present elsewhere in John Clare's writing. I will argue against Jonathan Bate when he maintained that this was the product of mere confinement rather that of a mind in the grip of a mania:

---

[67] Caudwell, Christopher, *Illusion and Reality* (London, Lawrence & Wishart, 1977) p, 104.

[68] Clare, John *Selected Poems* [ed] Bate, Jonathan, (London, Faber & Faber, 2005), p.282.

[69] www.pnreview.co.uk/cgi-bin/scribe?item_id=8675

[70] http://www.jstor.org/stable/25601059

Jonathan Bate does not address the question of bawdy language and punctuation here. Rather two examples of John Clare's prose are useful as a beginning in understanding his relationship with grammar or 'awkward squad' as John Clare defined it. This piece of prose was composed in 1821 but not published until 1931:

'Grammar' [...]

I thought sometimes that I surely had a taste peculiarly by myself and that nobody else thought or saw things as I did. I pursued my literary journey as usual, working hard all day and scribbling at night, or any leisure hour, in any convenient hole or corner I could shove in unseen; for I always carried a pencil in my pocket. Till necessity, as I got up towards manhood, urged me to look for something more than pleasing one's self, my poems had been kept with the greatest industry under wish'd concealment. The laughs and jeers of those around me, when they found out I was a poet, was present death to my ambitious apprehensions; for in our unlettered villages, the best of the inhabitants have little more knowledge in reading than what can be gleaned from a weekly Newspaper, Old Moore's Almanack, and a Prayer Book...71.

This example shows a knowledge of grammar. Another piece of prose is devoid of grammar and gallops along at a tremendous rate, it is essentially three pages of unpunctuated observation and comment entitled, *Byron's Funeral* [72]. This is of interest in-itself as it suggests a relationship established long before John Clare's collapse into mental illness between erratic writing and Byronism. It was written in 1825 but not published until 1951. I note that this is concluded with lines which illustrated John Clare's 'class' orientation as well as the lack of punctuation:

---

[71] Williams Merryn and Raymond Clare, *John. John Clare: Selected Poetry and Prose* (Routledge English Texts)

(Kindle Locations 1040-1060). Taylor and Francis. Kindle Edition.

[72] Williams Merryn & Raymond Clare, John. John Clare: Selected Poetry and Prose (Routledge English Texts)

(Kindle Locations 3138-3167). Taylor and Francis. Kindle Edition.

Completely Fragmented:

> I believe that his liberal principals in religion
> &
> politics did a great deal towards gaining the notice
> & affections of the lower orders be as it will it is better
> to be beloved by those low & humble for undisguised
> honesty then flattered by the great for purchased &
> pensiond hypocrisy – [...]73.

The second continues in the same misogynistic vein Care (*Don Juan*, p168). He appeared deranged. As Williams (1986, p.242) noted correctly: 'It is dominated by a bitterness towards women (as in Shakespeare's darker plays) for which there is no obvious reason.' It is written in Ottava Rima but with what Jonathan Bate (2004) called 'outrageous rhymes.'

My position is that by this time John Clare was an established poet, he knew the craft but was 'manic' as Sylvia Plath was when she wrote *Daddy*. That contained the memorable and mould-breaking:

> Daddy, daddy, you bastard, I am through.[74]

Sylvia Plath was in a state of elevated mood which oscillated with depression that concluded in suicide. She wrote in a patriarchal society that oppressed her. John Clare did reference class oppression in *Don Juan*:

> I wish M. P's. would spin less yarn – no doubt
> But burn false bills and cross bad taxes out
> Clare, Don Juan, p.169.

However, the sexism extending to hatred is almost inexplicable in John Clare's poem. The key to understanding it is the lack of end-stops in his *Don Juan*. I had previously shown when writing about Lord Byron his grammar and

---

[73] Williams Merryn & Raymond Clare, John. John Clare: Selected Poetry and Prose (Routledge English Texts,
   (Kindle Locations 3163-3165). Taylor and Francis. Kindle Edition.
[74] Plath, Sylvia *Ariel* (London, Faber & Faber, 1965), p.56

punctuation became erratic. He was in a manic state in which sexuality can be distorted and elevated. We understand John Clare as torn by Gramscian 'contradictory consciousness', alienation from the poor and intelligentsia and manic. Thus, the poetry becomes warped and without punctuation as refracted through the mind-bending prism of Byronic libertinism for as Marx argued:

> The ideas of the ruling class are in every epoch, the ruling ideas.75.

I understand Byronism as a cultural manifestation of the dominant ideology of its epoch which was one of transition and Clare's *Don Juan* as being distorted by the former because of the uneven class relationships. In the last instance though, John Clare did not find a 'voice' that would withstand the pressures of capitalism. Rather his voice became overwhelmed by the dominant ideology and a slanted version of Byronism. John Clare would live, writing profusely, in asylums largely forgotten by the literary world and society. Both Byron and Clare belonged to classes which would either come to an accord or be assimilated into the contending classes of modernity, the bourgeoisie and the proletariat respectively. Only the latter can create communism and the conditions for a new poetic because as Marx had argued persuasively:

> The revolution cannot take poetry from the past only the future.76

Bibliography.
Primary Sources.
Bloomfield, Robert, *Selected Poems* [ed] Goodridge, J & Lucas, J (Nottingham, Trent Editions, 2007).
Byron, Lord. *Byron's Letters and Journals: A New Selection* [ed] Landsdown, Richard (Oxford, Oxford University Press, 2015).
Byron, Lord, *Selected Letters and Journals* [ed] Leslie A. Marchant, (Massachusetts, Harvard University Press, 1982).

---

[75] Marx & Engels (1982) p.64.
[76] https://www.marxists.org/archive/marx/works/1852/18th-brumaire/ch01.htm

Byron, Lord, *The Major Works,* [ed] McGann, Jerome, J (Oxford, Oxford World Classics, 2008).
Byron, Lord, *Selected Poems*, [ed] Wolfson, Susan J and Manning, Peter (London Penguin Classics, 2003).
Clare, John, *Selected Poems* [ed] Bate, Jonathan, (London, Faber & Faber, 2005).
Clare, John, *Poems selected by Paul Farley* (London, Faber & Faber, 2007).
Clare, John, *By Himself* [ed] Robinson, E & Powell, D (Manchester Carcanet Books, 2002).
Clare, John, *Major Works*, [ed] Robinson, E & Powell, D (Oxford, Oxford University Press, 2008).
Clare, John, *Selected Poetry and Prose [ed],* Williams, Merryn & Raymond (London, Methuen, 1986).
Clare, John, *The Letters of John Clare* [ed] Storey, Mark (Oxford, Oxford University Press, 2014).
Keats, John, *Selected Letters* [ed] Bernard, John (London, Penguin Books, 2014).
Keats, John, *The Complete Poems* [ed] Bernard, John (London, Penguin Classics,1988).
Pope, Alexander, *Selected Poems* [ed] Rogers, Pat (Oxford, Oxford University Press, 2008).
Shelley, Percy Bysshe, *The Major Works* [ed]Leader, Zachary & O'Neill, Michael (Oxford, Oxford University Press, 2009).
Wordsworth, William, *The Major Works* [ed] Gill, Stephen (Oxford, Oxford University Press, 2008).

Secondary Sources.
Abrams W, H. *The Mirror and the Lamp: Romantic Theory and the Critical Tradition* (Oxford, Oxford University Press, 1971).
Barrell, John, *The Idea of Landscape and the sense of Place 1730-1840, An approach to the poetry of John Clare*. (Cambridge, Cambridge University Press, 2010).
Bate, Jonathan. *John Clare.* (London: Picador, 2004).
Lord Byron's Don Juan: Modern Critical Interpretations [ed] Bloom, Harold (New York, Harold Chelsea House Publishers, 1987).
Bone, Drummond, *Byron Writers and their Work* (Northcote House, British Council, 2000).

The Cambridge Companion to Byron [ed] Bone, Drummond (Cambridge, Cambridge University Press, 2004).

Byron: The Poetry of Politics and Politics of Poetry [ed] Beaton, Roderick & Kenton-Jones, Christine (London, Routledge, 2017).

Burwick, Fredrick, *Poetic Madness and the Romantic Imagination,* (Pennsylvania, Pennsylvania State University Press, 1996).

Caudwell, Christopher, *Illusion and Reality* (London, Lawrence & Wishart, 1977).

The Cambridge Companion to British Romantic Poetry [ed] Chandler, James & McLane, M Maureen (Cambridge, Cambridge University Press, 2008).

Eliot, T.S. *The Sacred Wood*, (London, Faber & Faber, 1997).

Foot, Paul, *Red Shelley* (London, Sidgwick & Jackson, 1980).

Franklin, Caroline, *Byron* (London, Routledge, 2007).

Gramsci, Antonio, *Selections from the Prison Notebooks*, (New York, International Publishers Co; Reprint, 1989 edition (November 24, 1971).

John Clare in Context [ed] Haughton, Hugh, Philips, Adam and Summerfield, Geoffrey, (Cambridge, Cambridge University Press, 2005)

Haslett, Moyra, *Byron's Don Juan and the Don Juan Legend* (Oxford, Clarendon Press, 2003).

Haslett, Moyra, *Marxist Literary and Cultural Theories (Transitions)* (Basingstoke, Palgrave Macmillan, 2000).

Heywood, Andrew, *Political Ideas and Concepts: An Introduction,* (London, Macmillan,1994)

Byron Childe Harold's Pilgrimage and Don Juan: a casebook [ed] Jump, John (London, Macmillan Press Ltd, 1973)

Lacas, John, *Clare Writers and their Work* (Northcote House, British Council, 1994).

The Cambridge Introduction to Byron [ed] Lansdown, Richard, (Cambridge, Cambridge University Press, 2012).

A Companion to Romantic Poetry [ed] Mahoney, Charles, (Chichester, Wiley-Blackwell, 2011).

MacCarthy, Fiona, *Byron Life and Legend.* (London, John Murray, 2004).

McGann, Jerome J. *Byron and Romanticism* (Cambridge, Cambridge University Press, 2002).

McGann, Jerome J. *Don Juan in Context* (London, John Murry, 1976).

Marx, Karl & Engels, Frederick, *On Literature and Art* (Moscow, Progress Publishers 1976).

Marx, Karl & Engels, Frederick *The Communist Manifesto* (Harmondsworth, Penguin Books, 1976).

Marx, Karl & Engels, Frederick, The *German Ideology* (London, Lawrence & Wishart,1982).

Marx, Karl & Engels, Frederick, *Selected Correspondence* (Moscow, Progress Publishers, 1965).

Plath, Sylvia, *Ariel* (London, Faber & Faber, 1965).

Robertson, R, *Mock-Epic Poetry from Pope to Heine* (Oxford, Oxford University Press, 2009).

Byron: The Critical Heritage [ed] Rutherford, Andrew, (London, Routledge & Kegan Paul, 1970).

Stabler, Jane, *Byron* (London, Longman, 1998).

St. Clair, William, *The Reading Nation in the Romantic Period,* (Cambridge, Cambridge University Press, 2007).

Storey. Mark, *The Poetry of John Clare: A critical introduction* (London, Macmillan, 1974).

Clare, J, The Critical Heritage [ed] Storey, Mark (London, Routledge & Kegan Paul, 1973).

Thompson, E. P. *The Making of the English Working Class*, (London, Penguin Books, 1991).

Vardy, Alan, *John Clare, Politics and Poetry (Basingstoke, Palgrave Macmillan, 2003).*

White, Adam, *John Clare's Romanticism* (Switzerland, Palgrave Macmillan, 2017).

Robert Bloomfield: Lyric, Class and the Romantic Canon [ed] White, Simon, Goodridge, John and Keegan, Bridge (Lewisburg, Bucknell University Press, 2006).

Williams, Raymond, *Culture and Materialism: Selected Essays* (Verso, London, 2005).

Williams, Raymond, *The Country and the City* (London, Vintage Classics, 2016).

Williams, Raymond, *The Long Revolution* (London, Chatto & Windus Ltd, 1961).

Don Juan Theory in Practice [ed] Wood, Nigel, (Buckingham, Open University Press, 1995).

Completely Fragmented:

Milton and Blake.

I firstly suggest that, Milton *Paradise Lost* (1674), because of the material circumstances in which it was written, those of the defeat of the English Revolution, must have limited the capacity for human freedom as it was a poem born of defeat. The defeat of the first bourgeois revolution humanity had experienced. Whereas in Blake's poetry and we understand that he was writing in a period of revolutionary upturn, principally the French Revolution. Thus, a period of hope rather than despair for the masses because of the potential for greater human freedom:

> Rouze up O Young Men of the New Age!
> set your foreheads
> against the ignorant Hirerings! For we have Hirerings in the
> camp, the Court, & the University: who would if they could
> for ever depress Mental and prolong Corporeal War.
> Blake, *Milton*, 1, 11-15. [77]

Having delineated a general conceptual orientation for my argument in regard of human freedom in Milton and in Blake's poetry which will be elaborated upon. I secondly argue for a complexified reading of the relationship between the poet and society founded on a correct understanding of dialectical materialism as suggested by Leon Trotsky[78] is necessary in the last instance. I hence suggest, therefore, that in this context, reductionist arguments: economic, psychoanalytical or otherwise are inadequate to totally explain the genius of poets like Dante, Milton and Blake.

When the reader approaches any text the question of genre immediately arises. *PL* was in some ways a contradiction, an epic that transcended the epic form. It addresses the heart of Western civilisation especially in the pre-modern, even now in a post meta-narrative post-modernity world *PL* has relevance, the Fall and Redemption.

---

[77] Blake, William, *The Complete Poems* [ed] Ostriker, *Alicia* (London, Penguin Classics, 2004), p 513.
[78] Leon, Trotsky, *Art and Revolution: Writings on Literature, Politics and Culture* (New York,
  Pathfinder, 2013).

The Biblical account contained little depth for Adam or Eve, this Milton attempted to remedy in *PL* and he also addressed the 'Problem of Evil.' So, we understand Milton using a Homeric and pagan form, the epic, addressed the questions of Christianity, but we see him doing it at a concrete moment in history:

> Anger and just rebuke, and judgement give'n
> That brought into this world a world of woe,
> Death's harbinger: sad task, yet argument
> Not less but more heroic than the wrath
> Of stern Achilles... [79]

It is also important to ground *PL* in the Reformation. This brought, amongst Protestants, the rejection of a complex biblical scholarship known as the 'Fourfold Method' and a return to one manifestation of biblical literalism, probably more complex than that practiced by Evangelical Protestants today though, with a method called 'typology'. This can be comprehended as type=type, thus Adam, the first man at Creation and Jesus Christ the Son of God who was understood to be the new or substitute Adam, for a new age, were the same 'type'. The New Testament was translated by John Tyndale into English, who had paid with his life. It then became inevitable that eventually a mass produced, and state authorized version would become available. This occurred in 1611 with the *King James Version*. The Bible had become the site of ideological contestation for Protestants. I would go further than Christopher Hill's arguments and argue it became a handbook of revolution, a text which challenged the priestly secrecy of the Latin *Vulgate Bible,* the Divine Right of the monarch and advocated the Kingdom of God on Earth for the poor in *Luke 6: 20-21* in the 'common tongue' or at least an accessible language:

> Blessed are ye poor:

---

[79] Milton, John, *Paradise Lost* [ed] Leonard, John, (London, Penguin Classics, 2003). BK IX, L 10-14,
Hereafter *PL* Bk #

Completely Fragmented:

> yours is the kingdom of God:
> Blessed are ye who hunger:
> ye shall be filled.[80]

I would comment, that the use of the English language in the *King James Version* as a literary text has enthralled writers and readers over the centuries, it remains the essential or 'master narrative' of English literature and has seen writing back from most significant authors. Christopher Hill maintained:

> That the Bible was, or should be, the foundation of all English cultures.
> On this principle, most Protestants agreed. If we do not grasp this we
> are slipping into an anachronistic trap.[81]

I would like to stress the position taken by W. R. Owens[82] For our purposes, however, we take the Bible to be a product of human history and culture, and as such open to analysis and exploration from many standpoints. This approach should not be taken as implying any lack of respect towards those who regard it as the Word of God.

Milton had adhered to two radical seventeenth-century heresies both can be located in *De Doctrina Christiana* which was not discovered until 1823 and published in 1825 and is still contested by some as not Milton's work. They are Arminianism and Arianism. The former, which understood human beings to have complete 'Free Will'. Hence being an ideologue, he placed his theology in the mouth of the Christian God in *PL,* his understanding of the nature of The Fall in *Genesis 3.22:*

> And the Lord God said, Behold,

---

[80] *The Bible: Authorized King James version with Apocrypha, St. Luke,* (Oxford, Oxford World's Classics, 1997), p.80

[81] Christopher Hill, *The English Bible and the Seventeenth Century Revolution (London, Allen Lane, The Penguin Press,* (1993). P 7.

[82] Owens, W. R. *A815 MA English Course Reader. Part 2 Paradise Lost* (Milton Keynes, The Open University, 2009), p. 4.

> the man is become as one of us,
> to know good and evil: and now, lest he put
> forth his hand, and take also of the tree of life,
> and eat, and live for ever.[83]

The desire for humanity to attain Divinity:

> I made him just and right,
> Sufficient to have stood, though free to fall...
> as if predestination overruled
> There will, disposed by absolute decree
> Of high foreknowledge, they themselves decreed
> Their own revolt not I,
> (*PL*, BK III. L 99-117).

Here Milton used onomatopoeia in L 100, the reader feels as if they are also falling 'free to fall'. However, the rejoinder came from Adam, not Satan and is both potent and poignant as he makes a counter-accusation in his postlapsarian condition and echoes the cries of an alienated humanity across history; 'why me?':

> Did I request thee, Maker, from my clay
> To mould me man, did I solicit thee
> From darkness to promote me, or here place
> In this delicious garden?
> (*PL*, Bk X 743-45).

The assonance of 'a', 'y' 'o' and 'e' sound in combination with the alliterative 'm's give an urgency which flows like a torrent of anguish from Adam's mouth while the caesura after 'me' L. 744 followed with the overflowing and despairing enjambment of L 744-45., suggest an almost Lucifer like defiance, but it is human authenticity and created pathos. Hence, I argue that Adam rather than Satan is the poetic agent who challenges Milton's intended aspiration 'to justify the ways of God to man', (*PL* Bk 1,26.)

---

[83] The Bible (1997) *Genesis*, p. 4

Completely Fragmented:

The latter of Milton's two heretical positions Arianism, which importantly saw the Father Deity separate and existing before his Son, Jesus Christ. There is simply little trace of omnibenevolence, given the Father's omniscience. Recollecting that Milton was an Arminian we do not read him as privileging the Son of God's necessary, in Christian iconography, sacrifice of the crucifixion, the latter is almost written out of *PL* as noted by Professor John Carey. Carey argued that this invalidates the poem as a Christian poem.[84] He continued:
> If the Son- just once- burst out with an expression of his love for
> mankind when he saw how beautiful humans were, as Satan does,
> it would transform the whole poem. But he never does.[85]

John Carey might have been stretching a point here because *PL* is self-evidently a Christian poem.

Milton as argued by Christopher Hill[86] *PL* was written in a period of defeat of the English Revolution by a disappointed and blind revolutionary millennialist. He regarded the epoch as one of Satanic reaction, The Restoration of the monarchy in the form of Charles II as here:

> though fall'n on evil days,
> On evil days though fall'n, and evil tongues;
> In darkness, and with dangers compassed round,
> And solitude; yet not alone, while thou
> Visit'st my slumbers Nightly, or when Morn
> Purples the East: still govern thou my Song,
> Urania, and fit audience find, though few.
> (*P L* Book VII 25-30).

He was alone but for his Muse who is identified by implication as the Holy Spirit *PL* BK1, but is also referred to as Urania, the Muse of Astronomy. On this count, it is worth

---

[84] Carey, John, *The Essential Paradise Lost* (London, Faber & Faber, 2017) p.229-232.
[85] Carey (2017) p.232.
[86] Hill, Christopher, *Milton and the English Revolution* (London, Faber & Faber, 1977).

recollecting that the young Milton visited the aged Galileo. His Muse and a few comrades and family to whom he dictated the text were in fear of mobs of drunken Royalists. The use of alliteration with 'f' sounds in L 30-32 creates an ethereal sense in Milton's writing, but the reader was then confronted in L 32-33 with the:
> barbarous dissonance
> Of Bacchus.

Fredrick Engels reminded us: 'Let us not forget Milton, the first defender of regicide'[87]. Thus, as suggested, following the seminal work of Christopher Hill, we understand the overarching socio-historical perspective for this epic poem was the defeat of the English Revolution. The contribution Christopher Hill has made in positioning *PL* in concrete material conditions cannot be exaggerated. Christopher Hill, *The English Bible and the Seventeenth Century Revolution (*1993) made a pertinent observation:

> Englishmen had to face a totally unexpected revolutionary situation in the 1640s and 1650s, with no theoretical guidance such as Rousseau or Marx gave to their French and Russian successors, and no experience of any previous event that had been called a revolution. They had to improvise. The Bible in English was the book to which they naturally turned for guidance.[88]

Nevertheless, Christopher Hill's work had generally failed to take its revolutionary implications to their logical conclusion, that of a modern revolution. This can be explained because historians like Christopher Hill and E. P. Thompson accepted the post-war 'historical compromise' with western capitalism that had been argued for by some Marxists. Thus, these theoreticians had very real limitations when addressing the question of human freedom as a concept which embraced revolutionary praxis. They could not understand that the dialectic and therefore irresolvable contradiction was not merely an abstraction, but as Marx had argued was rooted in the everyday practices of people. It should be noted that Karl Marx regarded Milton as an 'unproductive labourer' in that he did not intend to make money from *PL's* production. Rather, Marx argued: 'Milton produced *Paradise Lost* for the

---

[87] Engels, Frederick *The Northern Star,* 18th December 1847.
[88] Hill, Christopher, (1993), *p.9.*

same reason a silk worm produces silk. It was an activity of his nature.'[89] We, therefore, need to revisit and reassess the contribution of more overtly *orthodox* Marxist literary critics such as Alick West *Crisis and Criticism & Literary Essays* (1975) and Christopher Caudwell *Illusion* and *Reality* (1977) and radical currents that emerged from feminist writers.

I shall now describe and assess two very different accounts of aesthetics and Milton from British orthodox Marxist critics Alick West and Christopher Caudwell. Firstly, Alick West[90] gave an unusual view of literature which had Freudian as well as Marxist origins. He largely understood literature as a form of positive energy or libido in the sense of Eros competing with the death wish, Thanatos. But here his convergence with Freud ended. Maynard Solomon argued this was because Alick West saw this 'energy' as rooted in material collectivises such as social class 'whereas Freud does not consistently recognize the cooperative and communistic roots of Eros, nor the class nature of Thanatos.'[91] Thus we can perceive Alick West offering a very different account to the official Socialist Realist 'line'. He was therefore in an obscure fashion closer to the original tradition of Karl Marx who had rejected 'tendentious literature' as an artistic expression. His reading of *PL* was symptomatic of his general perspective. Therefore, Heaven served as a symbol of declining feudalism [Thanatos] and the Garden of Eden as one of an emergent capitalism that humanity would be expelled from until communism created a collective Eden, maybe a garden of love, of Eros. Alick West was a tormented man because of unrelenting self psycho-analysis. This dominated him to the detriment of his understanding of Marxism.

Christopher Caudwell argued that the bourgeois revolution in England had inevitably 'gone too far' for the bourgeoisie because their demand for unfettered freedom

---

[89] Marx, Karl, *Theories of Surplus Value, vol 1* (Moscow, Progress Publishers, 1969), p.401.
[90] Bounds, Philip, British Communism & the politics of Literature 1928-1939, (Pontypool, Merlin
    Press, 2012) pp.105-107
[91] Solomon, Maynard, *Marxism and Art* (Detroit, Wayne State University Press, 1979), p.495.

must unleash a massive upsurge of what he called the 'have-nots'. He suggested a 'Cromwell or a Robespierre' would be produced to temper the rebellion of the masses. To the genuinely revolutionary element, he argued, the petty-bourgeois, this was the ultimate betrayal of their revolution. Thus, he concluded:

> Therefore, in *Paradise Lost* Milton sees himself as Satan overwhelmed and yet still courageous: damned and yet revolutionary.[92] Christopher Caudwell might here be recollecting:

> Better to reign in Hell, than serve in Heav'n.
> (*PL* BK 1, L 163).

He was positioning himself in the literary current that Shelley had advocated when he had argued: 'Milton's Devil as a moral being is far superior to his God.'[93]

As the seventeenth-century English revolution was not mature because of the lack of a proletariat. Therefore, following this first strand of my argument, the prerequisites for solving the question of patriarchy could not be addressed in a satisfactory manner. We can read Virginia Woolf describing 'the Milton bogey' in *A Room of One's Own (2002)* that has haunted and distorted women writers. Thus, we read Sandra M. Gilbert and Susan Gubar (1979):

> Hence Milton himself – the real patriarchal spectre, one more
> bogey created by Milton: his inferior and Satanically inspired
> Eve, who has intimidated women and blocked their view of
> possibilities both real and literary...Both he (Milton) and the
> creatures of his imagination constitute the misogynistic
> essence of what Gertrude Stein called 'patriarchal poetry.'[94]

---

[92] Caudwell, Christopher, *Illusion and Reality* (London, Lawrence & Wishart, 1977) p. 94.
[93] Shelley, Percy Bysshe, *The Major Works* (Oxford, Oxford University Press, 2009), p.692.
[94] Sandra M. Gilbert and Susan Gubar: *The Madwoman in the Attic: The Woman Writers and the*

Completely Fragmented:

The contemporary scholar Mary Nyquist, *The Genesis of Gendered Subjectivity in the Source Traits and in Paradise Lost, (1987)* is persuasive. She correctly argues that there are two creation narratives in Genesis, firstly the 'P' account of creation in Genesis1.27 which she argued suggested something akin to a 'spiritual equality' between the sexes ('male and female created he them') and 'J' which favours patriarchy, 'where the man is created first, of the dust of the ground, with the woman being created out of his rib (Genesis, 2.7,22). Mary Nyquist continues that in Milton's 'divorce tracts the 'J' account is to be understood as offering a kind of commentary on the 'P' account, which it fills out and completes.' That in *PL* vii 519–48, he splices together the 'P' and 'J' accounts in a fashion which favouring the 'J' account, in a manner, that 'specifies the gendered Adam of Paradise Lost as the "man" who is made in the divine image[95]'. This she indicates was a reflex of an emergent patriarchal capitalism where the 'public sphere' would be that of the male and the 'private' family sphere that of the woman. Therefore, she concluded John Milton was not a 'proto-feminist'. However, why is orthodox Marxist criticism valuable in this light, one good reason is its conviction that:

> The change in a historical epoch can always be determined by
> the progress of women
> toward freedom, because in relation
> of woman to man, of the weak to the strong,
> the victory of human
> nature over brutality is most evident. The degree of emancipation
> of woman is the natural measure of general emancipation.[96]

Nineteenth- century Literary Imagination (New Haven, Conn, Yale University Press, 1979) p.188
[95] Owens, W. R. (2009) pp. 22-3.
[96] Marx, Karl & Engels, Frederick, *The Holy Family* (Moscow, Foreign Languages Publishing House,
1956), p, 258-59.

Alexandra Kollontai argued that only a total restructuring of the family under communism was the solution for an emancipation of the majority of women. She recognized that bourgeois women could and would make gains under capitalism. Alexandra Kollontai suggested:

> In place of the old individualist and egotistic family, there will rise
> a universal family of workers, in which all the workers, men and
> women, will be, above all workers, comrades.[97]

We have seen that Milton had been an early advocate of divorce but his orientation in early capitalism would have inhibited his views in the context of my initial argument. John Milton's reading of *Genesis* which he developed in *PL* with a vain and narcissistic prelapsarian Eve tempted by the prospect of becoming a 'human goddess' Bk IX, L 712 by Satan. She had already fallen in love with her own reflection BK IV L, 460-470. Eve, in Milton *PL*, also consciously brought about the absolute Fall of humanity by sharing the fruit of The Tree of Knowledge with Adam. Sandra M. Gilbert and Susan Gubar, *The Madwoman in the Attic: The Woman Writers and the Nineteenth- century Literary Imagination, (*1979*)* appear justified in their reading of Milton as 'patriarchal poetry' here. Therefore, for Milton in *PL* it was quintessential that Adam and Eve should not aspire to transcend their naive state, they should remain innocent and ignorant of matters of knowledge, good and evil. Satan had also dared to rebel and suffered awful consequences. Was Milton in the post-revolutionary epoch questioning his earlier positions in support of the revolution and regicide? We will never be able to know exactly what Milton thought but T.S. Eliot made a penetrating comment:

> The civil war of the seventeenth century, in which Milton

---

[97] Kollontai, Alexandra, *Alexandra Kollontai on Women's Liberation* (London, Bookmarks, 1998), p.48.

> is a symbolic figure has never been
> concluded...Of no
> other poet is it so difficult to see the
> poetry simply as
> poetry, without our theological and
> political dispositions,
> conscious and unconscious,
> inherited and acquired,
> making an unlawful entry.[98]

It is possible following the current of the primary component of this argument to comprehend Milton's reading of *Genesis* which favours the source 'J' over 'P', his writing on divorce and *PL* generally as a complex series of reflexes of the emergent capitalist and patriarchal society in which he lived. His choice of blank verse and consequent rejection of rhyme was a revolutionary act. The abandonment of his earlier intention to write a patriotic Arthurian epic in favour of an epic in the light of Homer's *Odyssey* and *Iliad*, Virgil's *Aeneid* and Dante's *Divine Comedy* informs us of a profound shift in Milton. He was a man attempting to understand at least three questions: 1) why the revolution had been lost remembering he expected it to be concomitant with the Second Coming and 2) his blindness, surely as profound as Beethoven's deafness, 3) what or who were the English people in the context of the revolutionary and counter-revolutionary events, how did they fit, if at all, into a Divine Cosmology outlined in the *King James Bible*? His answers seemed to be lacking in consolation for the poet, I would argue, an expulsion from Eden towards introspection:

> but shalt possess
> A paradise within thee, happier far.
> *PL,* XII L 586 – 587.

Therefore, it could be argued that Milton was abandoning a social project for an inner one and thus possibly bound humanity in manacles.

For Blake in *London* these were 'mind forged manacles':
In every cry of every man,
In every Infant's cry of fear,
In every voice, in every ban,
> The mind-forged manacles I hear[99]

---

[98] Eliot, T.S. *Milton* (London, Faber & Faber, 1947) p.3.

William Blake is expressing the importance of the imagination by attacking what he called the "mind-forged manacles" but does this using an established poetic device called anaphora in which the same word is repeated in every line. He contrasts this in the final line by not employing that device to create a pounding dissonance which reverberates with a full-rhyme 'fear'/'hear.' However, as Raymond Williams suggests there is a social-economic dimension of the power of the capitalist system that at:

> the levels of both ideology and actuality, manacle every mind- exploiter and exploited- in an ineluctable organized repression.[100]

However, today humanity is faced with catastrophic climate change which is driven by the logic of capitalism which offers only the abyss and human extinction if not countered by proletarian insurrection[101]. Blake was aware of the dangers of mass industrialization very early as articulated in *Milton: a poem*:

> And did the Countenance Divine,
> Shine forth upon our clouded hills?
> And was Jerusalem builded here,
> Among these dark Satanic Mills?[102]

The 'dark Satanic Mills' are a metaphor for the chaotic and rapid industrialization, which was transforming the English landscape. Blake saw this as Satanic in a similar fashion to Milton's perception of the Restoration. Parallels and disjuncture between these two great poets were to be expected because they were writing within a similar discourse.

However, when we examine the interactions between the two poets Blake's comment is the largest thorn in Milton's side, as here in *Marriage of Heaven and Hell [MHH]*:

> The reason Milton wrote in fetters when he wrote of Angels & God, and at liberty when of Devils & Hell, is

---

[99] Blake, William, *The Complete Poems* [ed] Stevenson, W. H. (London, Routledge, 2007), p 161.
[100] Williams, Raymond, *The Country and the City* (London, Hogarth Press, 1973) p.148.
[101] Molyneux, John, *Lenin for Today* (London, Bookmarks, 2017) for a cogent argument.
[102] Blake (2007) p, 502.

because he was a true Poet and of the Devil's party without knowing it.[103]

Blake, self-evidently, predates Shelley's position *In Defence of Poetry* and was the originator of the perspective that Milton's the Devil was a more rounded and sympathetic character than his God. It should be noted that in *MHH* the 'Devil' here, at worst represents 'erroneous thinking' rather than Satan. For Blake in *Songs of Innocence and Experience* the real adversary is the distorting effect of this, like some who would use Milton *PL* as an argument for the repression of 'The soul of sweet delight which should never be defiled.' (Plate 9) and who 'Like caterpillars choose the fairest leaves to lay her eggs on, so the priest lays his curse on the fairest joys.' (Plate.9, 14) with the consequence that:

> Prisons are made out of stones of Law
> brothels with bricks
> Of Religion[104]

William Blake *The Poison Tree* which had been originally entitled *Christian Forbearance* in an earlier manuscript:

> In the morning glad I see
> My foe stretched out beneath the tree.[105]
> Juxtapose this with a postlapsarian Miltonic Adam:
> On the ground
> Outstretched he lay, on the cold ground, and oft,
> Cursed his creation.
> *(PL 10:850-1).*

The intertextuality is clear, Milton's Father God is understood as tyrannical and cruel.

Blake was like Milton, a revolutionary poet, but he believed Milton must be disencumbered of his belief in God as a reason-driven moralist. As W.H. Stevenson so eloquently encapsulated Blakes beliefs: '(a) that the energies of natural desire, not behaviour to a predetermined code, will lead to the proper way of life... and (b) everyone's

---

[103] Blake (2007) PL 6, p.113.
[104] Blake (2007) p. 112.
[105] Blake (2007) p. p.210

'imagination' is 'the truth' for them. He retained both ideas throughout his life, but they underwent modifications.'[106] Blake might be perceived as a hedonistic solipsist by some, but as he believed that his vision could be generalized to the whole of humankind so one might describe him an early utopian-socialist visionary. As E. P. Thompson pointed out 'It was in the immediate aftermath of the French Revolution that the millennial current... burst open... touched Blake with its breath. Against this background... William Blake seems no longer the cranky untutored genius to those who knew only the genteel culture of the time.'[107] However, Alick West argued 'William Blake was a pioneer. The spirit of his work is not the antagonism of the individual here and society there, but the antagonism within a living unity.'[108] I argue that William Blake understood the essential nature of dialectical thought as he states in *MHH*: 'Without Contraries is no progression.' Ultimately for William Blake there was a dialectical synthesis: 'Are not Religion & Politics the Same Thing? Brotherhood is Religion.' Indeed, Steve Vine argued 'Blake's spiritual-political was, in many ways, an attempt to *reclaim* the popular millenarian tradition that had motivated English revolutionaries in the seventeenth century.'[109] However, neither Eden or its secular equivalent communism can be founded simply on grandiose ideals, like the magnificent dreams of the utopians and poets; it must rest upon a materialist basis. As Engels explained, it is the proletariat itself that can create a historical possibility of the creation of a socialist, classless world:[110]. But and here I unravel the second string of my position because Leon Trotsky *Literature and Revolution* allowed a more complex reading of the dialectical relationship between the socio-economic foundations of society and that of the literary geniuses created by History. Hence:

---

[106] Blake (2007) p.107.
[107] Thompson, E.P, *The Making of the English Working Class* (London, Pelican, 1968) pp.54-5, 56.
[108] West, Alick, *Crisis and Criticism & Literary Essay* (London, Lawrence & Wishart, 1975) pp. 22-23.
[109] Vine, Steve, *William Blake: Writers and their Work* (Northcote, British Council, 2007) p.4.
[110] https://www.marxists.org/archive/marx/works/1880/soc-utop/

> But Dante was a genius. He raised the expectations of his epoch to a tremendous artistic height... *The Divine Comedy* as a source of artistic inspiration, this happens not because Dante was a Florentine petty bourgeois of the thirteenth century but, to a considerable extent, in spite of that circumstance.'[111]

We can see in this second augmentation of my argument that our view of John Milton's and William Blake's poetry was enhanced and embellished because like Dante the reader understood they transcended their epoch's fetters of the mundane. This secondary strand compliments rather than obfuscates or dominates the primary.

Bibliography

<u>Primary Sources.</u>

The Bible: Authorized King James version with Apocrypha, (Oxford, Oxford World's Classics, 1997).

Blake, William, *The Complete Poems* [ed] Ostriker, *Alicia* (London, Penguin Classics, 2004).

Blake, William, *The Complete Poems* [ed] Stevenson, W. H. (London, Routledge, 2007),

Carey, John, *The Essential Paradise Lost* (London, Faber & Faber, 2017).

Milton, John, *Areopagitica and Other Writings* (London, (ed) Poole, William (London, Penguin Classics, 2014).

Milton, John, *Paradise Lost* (ed) Fowler, Alastair (London, Routledge, 2006).

Milton, John, *Paradise Lost* [ed] Leonard, John, (London, Penguin Classics, 2003).

---

[111] Leon, Trotsky, (2013) p.75

Milton, John, *Paradise Lost* (eds) Orgel, Stephen & Goldberg, Jonathan, (Oxford. Oxford University Press, 2008),

Shelley, Percy Bysshe, *The Major Works* (Oxford, Oxford University Press, 2009).

Secondary Sources

Bottrall, M (ed) *Songs of Innocence and Experience: a selection of critical essays* (London, Macmillan Press Limited, 1974.)

Bounds, Philip, *British Communism & the Politics of Literature 1928-1939,* (Pontypool, Merlin Press, 2012)

Broadbent, John, *Paradise Lost: Introduction*, (Cambridge, Cambridge University Press, 2009).

Campbell, Jordan & Corns, Thomas. N, *John Milton: Life, Work, and Thought* (Oxford, Oxford University Press, 2010).

Caudwell, Christopher, *Illusion and Reality* (London, Lawrence & Wishart, 1977).

Danielson, Dennis [ed] *The Cambridge Companion to Milton* (Cambridge, Cambridge University Press, 2013).

Dobranski, Stephen. B (ed) *The Cambridge Introduction to Milton,* (Cambridge, Cambridge University Press, 2012).

Eaves, Morris [ed) *The Cambridge Companion to Blake*, (Cambridge, Cambridge University Press, 2007).

Eliot, T.S. *Milton* (London, Faber & Faber, 1947).

Engels, Frederick *The Northern Star,* 18th December 1847.

Frye, Northrop, *Fearful Symmetry: A Study of William Blake* (U.S.A., Princeton University Press, 1990).

Completely Fragmented:

Gilbert, Sandra M and Gubar, Susan: *The Madwoman in the Attic: The Woman Writers and the Nineteenth- century Literary Imagination* (New Haven, Conn, Yale University Press, 1979)

Hill, Christopher, *Milton and the English Revolution* (London, Faber & Faber, 1977).

Hill, Christopher, *The English Bible and the Seventeenth Century Revolution* (London, Allen Lane, The Penguin Press, (1993)

Kean, Margaret (ed) *Paradise Lost: A Sourcebook* (London, Routledge, 2005).

Kollontai, Alexandra, *Alexandra Kollontai on Women's Liberation* (London, Bookmarks, 1998),

Marx, Karl, *Theories of Surplus Value, vol 1* (Moscow, Progress Publishers, 1969),

Marx, Karl & Engels, Frederick, *The Holy Family* (Moscow, Foreign Languages Publishing House, 1956.)

Molyneux, John, *Lenin for Today* (London, Bookmarks, 2017).

Nyquist, Mary The Genesis of Gendered Subjectivity in the Source Traits and in Paradise Lost, (1987) in *Owens, W. R. A815 MA English Course Reader. Part 2 Paradise Lost* (Milton Keynes, The Open University, 2009),

Owens, W. R. *A815 MA English Course Reader. Part 2 Paradise Lost* (Milton Keynes, The Open University, 2009).

Solomon, Maynard, *Marxism and Art* (Detroit, Wayne State University Press, 1979).

Schwartz, Louis, *The Cambridge Companion to Paradise Lost,* (Cambridge, Cambridge University Press, 2014).

Thompson, E.P, *The Making of the English Working Class* (London, Pelican, 1968)

Trotsky, Leon, *Art and Revolution: Writings on Literature, Politics and Culture* (New York, Pathfinder, 2013).

Vine, Steve, *William Blake: Writers and their Work* (Northcote, British Council, 2007).

West, Alick, *Crisis and Criticism & Literary Essays* (London, Lawrence & Wishart, 1975).

Williams, Raymond, *The Country and the City* (London, Hogarth Press, 1973).

Woolf, Virginia, *A Room of One's Own* (London, Penguin Modern Classics, 2000).

Zunder, William, *Paradise Lost: Contemporary Critical Essays* (London, Macmillan Press Limited, 1999).

Completely Fragmented:

On Defoe and the colonial encounter.

Daniel Defoe, *Robinson Crusoe*[112] wrote what can be perceived as a paradigm shifting work. It was published in 1719 and immediately went into several editions. The Robinson has become a genre bordering on an archetype. Daniel Defoe had unwittingly created something new. Of course, Cervantes, *Don Quixote*[113], 1605 had already established the long prose-fiction form. But during the 17th century, Portugal and Spain were beginning to wane as Mercantile powers in the face of British colonialism. *Robinson Crusoe* must be understood in the social, economic, indeed historical context that it was written. This was England after it had emerged from a period of social turmoil. However, although the Civil War was passed the bourgeoisie was yet to achieve hegemony in any coherent sense. The contending forces were being reflected in the different literary genre, for example, John Bunyan *A Pilgrims Progress* remarkably written in prison was the literary incarnation of a quintessential Puritan Nonconformity. It was a spiritual allegory. While Daniel Defoe's novels, *Robinson Crusoe* (1719), *Moll Fielding*[114] (1722), *Roxana*[115] *(1724)* would delineate the lives of society's outsiders. *Robinson Crusoe* was a young man who defied his father's will and the dubious pleasures of middle-class life by running away to sea. Defoe was here, on first examination tuning into the genre of the 'travelogue' which was popular at the time. Particularly the story of Alexander Selkirk *A Cruising Voyage Round the World* (1712)[116]. *Moll Fielding* was born in Newgate Prison and largely lived on her 'wits' and again

---

[112] Daniel Defoe, *Robinson Crusoe*, ed. by Thomas Keymer (Oxford: Oxford University Press, 2008). Hereafter RC1. RC2, RC3.

[113] Miguel De Cervantes Saavedra, *Don Quixote,* ed. by John Rutherford (London, Penguin Classics, 2003).

[114] Daniel Defoe, *Moll Fielding,* ed. by G.A. Starr and Linda Blee (Oxford: Oxford University Press, 2011).

[115] Daniel Defoe, *Roxana*, ed. by David Blewitt (London, Penguin Books, 1982).

[116] *Rogers, Woodes (1712). A Cruising Voyage Round. beyond the World: First to the South-Sea, Thence to the East-Indies, and Homewards by the Cape of Good Hope. London: A. Bell.*

Defoe used a genre popular with his contemporary audience, the 'Newgate biography', although elaborated on it notably and *Roxane* which within obvious limitations and given the nature of patriarchy at the time could be designated, almost, proto-feminist. It was not published until after Defoe's death. Hence, we can see that these works though were drawing on the sub-genres of the epoch. However, Defoe enhanced and developed them into a new genre, that of 'fictive realism', the phrase employed by Ian Watt in his seminal work *The Rise of the Novel*,[117] to describe the new genre of the novel. They were 'confessional' accounts. However, I am aware there are other 'readings' of RC1 which I will engage with later, particularly G.A. Starr *Defoe and the spiritual autobiography*[118]. Defoe could be understood as a protean individual who had a varied life in business, journalism, politics but was not a minister of the church. He represented the tendency within the nascent Nonconformist bourgeoisie that would compete and eventually call a truce with Anglicanism and form the new British ruling class. The latter articulated its ideology in a more florid language than that of Nonconformist Protestantism. Nevertheless, England indeed Britain was still an unstable social formulation and Defoe's novels reflected and indeed illuminated this multifaceted ideological uncertainty and competition. This also took place in sermons and religious guidebooks, spiritual autobiographies as well as in the incipient novel. However, almost three hundred years of criticism cannot be avoided. What the critic Pierre Macherey *The Theory of Literary Production*[119],called 'the gaps and silences in a text' compel us to make new interpretations of texts.

    The method that I shall employ to examine the issue inherent in the question of the nature of the relationship between narrator and protagonist and the ironic separation

---

[117] Ian Watt, *The Rise of the Novel*, (London, The Bodley Head, 2013).
[118] G.A. Starr, Defoe and the spiritual autobiography in *Defoe; Critical Impetrations*, ed, by Harold Bloom (Chelsea House Publishers; Library Binding edition Dec. 1991)
[119] Pierre Macherey *The Theory of Literary Production,* (London:1978).

or authorial distance between them emanates from an examination of narratology particularly in Jahn Manfred, *A Guide to the Theory of Narratology*[120], and Claire Colebrook, *Irony: the new critical idiom*[121]. My overarching methodology is derived from Karl Marx and follows thus: "It is not the consciousness of men that determines their existence, but their social existence that determines their consciousness."[122] This fundamental method will be elaborated by examining the work of writers who augmented and developed the Marxist tradition of literary criticism especially three who examined the genre of the novel in detail, George Lukács, Ralph Fox, and Raymond Williams, who developed his own nuanced understanding of Marxism as Cultural Materialism . The writing of Frantz Fanon will be seen to understand Friday in *Black Skin, White Masks*[123] and the nature of the 'settler' in *The Wretched of the Earth*[124]. In regard of the afterlife of *Robinson Crusoe* as a colonial encounter, I shall briefly examine Coetzee *Foe*. All these questions are expanded upon and a conclusion achieved.

To arrive at a systematic understanding of the nature of 'Ironic separation' between narrator and protagonist", a prerequisite to the construction of an understanding of the ramifications of the "first contact between Crusoe and Friday" and, therefore, its "implications for the colonial encounter.' I firstly examined Claire Colebrook[125] which understands three main areas of literary irony [from Ancient Greek eirōneía, meaning 'dissimulation, feigned ignorance'. 1) Cosmic Irony, a contrast between the absolute and the relative, the general and the individual, which Hegel called,

---

[120] http://www.uni-koeln.de/~ame02/pppn.htm

[121] Claire Colebrook, *Irony: the new critical idiom,* (London: Routledge, *2006) p 179-185.*

[122] Karl Marx, A Contribution to the Critique of Political Economy, Preface. *in Marx & Engels, Selected Works in One Volume* (London, Lawrence & Wishart,1973), p. 180.

[123] Frantz Fanon, *Black Skin, White Masks,* (London: Plato Press, 1986).

[124] Frantz Fanon, *The Wretched of the Earth* (London: Penguin Modern Classics,2001).

[125] Colebrook, 2006.

"general [irony] of the world" or as Claire Coleman argues: 'Cosmic or Tragic irony' is when a community or individual is thwarted by life's events, events which often seem to pass judgement on their life, or seem to be the outcome of fate. 2) dramatic irony when the audience knows more than the characters or 'if a character's speech is undermined by subsequent action' [Ibid] and 3) 'structural irony', this can be understood to be when a fictional hero is a 'first person narrator' and when 'distance' is the extent to which the author draws us into the novel then there are inevitable consequences for this 'first-person narrator' as in RC1. Crusoe tells his story with hindsight which 'Crusoe-on-the-island' cannot have. This is probably close to the concept of "ironic separation." Also, in this context, the question of the 'implied author' is worthy of consideration. The 'implied author' cannot, according to Wayne C. Booth, *The Rhetoric of Fiction* [126] who introduced the term of 'implied author' to distinguish the virtual author of the text from the real author. Therefore, we cannot assume in RC1 that there is a direct correlation between the views and beliefs of Danial Defoe and those of Robinson Crusoe. Hence, we can comprehend an additional 'separation' in regard of RC1.Nevertheless, that is not to argue for the 'autonomy' of the text from material conditions because there is a material base for consciousness.

James Joyce brings us face to face with Robinson Crusoe and Friday, indeed Xury, and British colonialism:

The true symbol of the British conquest is Robinson Crusoe, who, cast away on a desert island, in his pocket a knife and a pipe, becomes an architect, a carpenter, a knife grinder, an astronomer, a baker, a shipwright, a potter, a saddler, a farmer, a tailor, an umbrella-maker, and a clergyman. He is the true prototype of the British colonialist, as Friday (the trusty savage who arrives on an unlucky day) is the symbol of the subject races. The whole Anglo-Saxon spirit is in Crusoe: the manly independence; the unconscious cruelty; the persistence; the slow yet efficient intelligence...

---

[126] Wayne C. Booth, *The Rhetoric of Fiction*, (University of Chicago Press, 1983.)

the practical, well-balanced religiousness; the calculating taciturnity.

Whoever rereads this simple, moving book in the light of subsequent history cannot help but fall under its prophetic spell.[127]

The 'footprint in the sand' which foreshadows Crusoe's meeting with Friday has an echo of RC 1, p.53, 'humane Shape had never set Foot upon that Place' and when he does find a single footprint, a stroke of genius from Defoe that Coleridge compared to Shakespeare:

It happened one Day about Noon going towards my Boat, I was exceedingly surpiz'd with the Print of a Man's naked Foot on the Shore, which was very plain to be seen in the Sand. I stood like one Thunder struck, or if I had seen an Apparition; I listen'd, I look'd around me, I could hear nothing, nor see any Thing, I went to a rising Ground to look further I went up the Shore and down the Shore, but it was all one...

RC1, p.130.

This is in itself a beautiful piece of writing and happens with a freedom of style one would expect from the author of a great text. It begins without a trace of anticipation, Crusoe is nonchalant but after what has occurred has been assimilated the pace of the writing is deftly increased by Defoe with short and rapid registers punctuated with commas we are compelled forward with his fear and are left almost breathless. The huge irony as pointed out by Pat Rogers *Robinson Crusoe*[128] is that of Crusoe being entrapped on 'the island of despair' in solitude since 1659 in 1674 sees the footprint of a man before he has any palpable evidence of cannibalism but then lives in a state of heightened fear for two years. He does not find the evidence of cannibalism until 1677, has a presentiment in a dream of rescuing a savage from the cannibals and in 1684 he rescues Friday. 1685 being his happiest year on the island as 'Master' of his kingdom complete with Friday and eventually, Friday's father who they freed from cannibals

---

[127] James Joyce, *Lecture on Daniel Defoe*, Università Popolare, Trieste, Italy, March 1912.

[128] Pat Rogers, *Robinson Crusoe* (London: Routledge Revivals, 1979) pp113-116.

and a Spaniard. Now, this may have fit the narrative of an expansionist British readership in 1719 but the world three hundred years later is a different place. As Heraclitus argued: 'You could not step twice into the same river'. - Plato, *Cratylus*, 402a[129]. History and reality are in motion. and therefore, there are colonial and post-colonial ramifications to Crusoe's perspective, his 'point of view' regarding essentially everyone who is white, male and, maybe, garbed in goatskin.

The first contact with Friday is foreshadowed by a dream in which RC frees two 'savages' and they facilitate his escaping from the island (p.168-9) so he began venturing out of his 'Castle' to 'scout' the shoreline for a year or so, then:

> While I was watching them, I perceived by my Perspective, two miserable Wretches dragg'd from the Boats…and brought out for the Slaughter…In that very Moment this poor Wretch seeing himself at Liberty…started away from them, and run with incredible Swiftness along the sands towards me, I mean towards that part of the Coast, where my Habitation was. I was dreadfully frightened…when I perceived him to run my way…
> RC 1, p.170.

RC's response is 'now was the Time to get me a Servant, and perhaps a Companion, or Assistant; and that I was call'd by Providence to save this poor Creature's Life.'RC1, p.171. So, Providence seemed to be firmly on the side of the British. Yes, RC had saved his [Friday's] life but it was to firstly facilitate his escape from the island, and secondly to provide a 'Servant'. Indeed, the first word Friday is taught is 'Master.' We will learn that other Europeans, Spaniards, live peaceably with the 'savages'. So, it became apparent very quickly there was an ironic separation in this first encounter, but it is the irony implicit in a Master race believing that an omniscient Deity can articulate their narrative and no other. RC comes to convert Friday, we shall see his own 'conversion experience as ironic. Did Friday have a choice in the circumstances, he becomes a better theologian than Crusoe asking why God allows the devil to exist i.e. a variant on 'the problem of Evil'. There is also irony in how Crusoe

---

[129] https://archive.org/details/dialoguesofplat01plat

replicates the master/servant dialectic which is implicit in Christianity, to that of a master/slave dialectic between human beings of other origins. We see this irony of Crusoe with the boy Xury, whom he escapes slavery with, then converted to Christianity only to 'sell' him. The ironies between how RC behaves and the consequences he later draws from his behaviour are marked. Coetzee argued

> *Robinson Crusoe* is unabashed propaganda for the establishment of new British colonies. As for the native peoples of the Americas and the obstacle they represent, all one need say is that Defoe chooses to represent them as cannibals. The treatment Crusoe metes out to them is accordingly, savage.[130]

For the modern reader acquainted with Frantz Fanon, who was a French Martiniquian, both the ideas of self-subjection of a colonial people and their path to emancipation becomes clearer. In *Black Skin, White Masks*[131] he argued that white racism was a complex problem having understood that many of his countrymen had negrophilic tendencies. He explained this by arguing that they had internalized white stereotypes and rejected their own 'blackness' and demonized other Black people, Black Africans. Hence one can see a black person ashamed of their colour wearing a white mask. Therefore, Frantz Fanon argued here that white-blacks must somehow be emancipated from the complex which alienated them from their Black sisters and brothers and the whites from their feelings of superiority and stereotyping of black people. We can perceive Friday here as a Black man who has put on a white mask. In both this regard and that of RC generally, Frantz Fanon is clear in *The Wretched of the Earth:*

> The settler makes history and is conscious of making it. And because he constantly refers to the history of his mother country, he clearly indicates that he himself is the extension of that mother-country. Thus, the history which he writes is not the history of the country which he plunders

---

[130] Coetzee, J.M. *stranger shores essays 1956-1999* (London, Vintage, 2002), p 24.
[131] Fanon (1986).

but the history of his own nation in regard to all that she skims off, all that she violates and starves.[132]

Virginia Woolf [133], a contemporary of James Joyce, had argued in her bi-centennial assessment that RC1 was had been absorbed into consciousness as an archetype. However, more interesting for the purposes of my analysis she returned to the subject in *The Common Reader* Volume 2. 'He is incapable of enthusiasm. He has a natural slight distaste for the sublimities of Nature. He suspects even Providence of exaggeration.' [134] Albert Camus was to write of the art of fiction: 'fiction is the lie through which we tell the truth.' Certainly, this was true in the novel in the 20th century but Defoe wrote in RC3 (1720): 'This supplying a story by the invention is certainly a scandalous crime. It is a sort of lying that makes a great hole in the heart, in which a habit of lying enters in.' Here we can observe the Nonconformist Puritan suspicion of both the theatre and prose-fiction. Thus, there is most definitely 'ironic separation at the very heart of Defoe's multi-volume project. Crusoe-the-protagonist-on-the-island and Crusoe-the-narrator-of-RC1 and Crusoe-the – narrative voice-of-RC3. There is no doubt that RC3 clenches the point for an inherent ironic separation as it is a quasi-mystical commentary. The ironic gap between: 'I was born in the Year 1632, in the City of York, of a good family.' RC1, p.1 to RC3 p.365: 'The Fable is always made for the Moral, not the Moral for the Fable.' Defoe is asking his reader to read RC as a parable here. However, two paragraphs later he is warning his reader:

> Robinson Crusoe, being at this time in perfect and sound mind and memory, thanks be to God therefor, do hereby declare their objection is an invention scandalous in design, and false in fact; and do affirm that the story, though allegorical, is also historical.
>
> RC3, p 365.

---

[132] Fanon, 2001, p.40.
[133] Virginia Woolf, *The Common Reader, vol. 1* (London: Vintage, 2003).
[134]

https://ebooks.adelaide.edu.au/w/woolf/virginia/w91c2/chapter4.html

Completely Fragmented:

G.A. Starr[135] is interesting and attempts to shed light on RC1 and religiosity. However, the premise for Starr's contribution revolves around Crusoe's "conversion experience" RC1, pp.80-83. The point I would like to make in that regard is that it is a rather Worldly "conversion experience" when RC sees an avenging angel with a spear who threatens him. He was not only ill and this is my point, he
had altered his state of consciousness with copious amounts of alcohol 'a pint of rum' mixed with water and strong tobacco:

>I found a cure both for Soul and Body. I open'd the Chest, and found what I was looking for, viz. the Tobacco, and the few Books, I had sav'd, lay there too, I took out one of the Bibles which I mention'd before…and brought both that and the Tobacco with me to the table. the Tobacco at first almost stupefied my brain being green and strong…then I took some rum…In the interval of this, I took up the Bible and began to read.
>
>RC1, p. 80.

So, RC upon reflection:

>My Condition began now to be, tho' miserable as to my Way of living, yet much easier to my Mind; my Thoughts being directed by a constant reading of Scripture, and praying to God…
>
>RC1, p.83.

Any reader may see a little irony here and the modern reader most certainly perceives Crusoe as desperate, ill and maybe intoxicated when he opens the Bible. Starr (1965) does provide contemporary data as to physical illness being linked to 'conversion experiences' but not, I think with the assistance of a 'pint of rum' and 'strong tobacco.'

For George Lukács[136], arguing from a classical Marxist perspective the novel was a product of capitalism and therefore embodied man in his social nexus. It was thus a Realist genre and we are aware of the nature of verisimilitude in RC1 and RC2. Indeed, this whole tradition of literary critics perceived the novel to be a great product of a

---

[135] In Bloom (1991).
[136] George Lukács, *The Historical Novel* (London: Merlin Press, 1965.)

revolutionary class, the bourgeoisie especially until the revolutions of 1848 when they understood that social class had become reactionary and a fetter on Humanity's development. Ralph Fox described 'the novel as the great gift to humanity from the bourgeoisie.' [137] Indeed, for theoreticians of this persuasion the social production of human beings, our interaction with the environment and the dialectic between humanity and Nature which Marx calls 'labour' whether physical or intellectual is what the young Marx maintained provided humanity with its "species-being", its essence [see Marx, *Philosophical and Economic Manuscripts of 1844*]. Here Marx illustrates the process under the circumstances of 'commodity production' and its distortion:

> The worker becomes all the poorer the more wealth he produces, the more his production increases in power and size. The worker becomes an ever-cheaper commodity the more commodities he creates.
>
> The devaluation of the world of men is in direct proportion to the increasing value of the world of things. Labour produces not only commodities; it produces itself and the worker as a commodity – and this at the same rate at which it produces commodities in general.
>
> This fact expresses merely that the object which labour produces –
> labour's product – confronts it as something alien, as a power independent of the producer. The product of labour is labour which has been embodied in an object, which has become material: it is the objectification of labour. Labour's realization is its objectification. Under these economic conditions this realization of labour appears as loss of realization for the worker's objectification as loss of the object and bondage to it; appropriation as estrangement, as alienation [138]

It is the 'estrangement' of labour from its object and the artificial 'division of labour' between manual and mental

---

[137] Ralph Fox, *The Novel and the People* (London: Lawrence & Wishart, 1979), p 53.

[138] Marx, K, *Philosophical and Economic Manuscripts of 1844*, (Moscow: Progress Publishers, 1967) p 66

labour that is pertinent here and which I shall explore further in the analysis of the 'island narrative' in RC1 which will be comprehended as, a laboratory, almost approximating *tableau rasa* in the sense that Defoe's contemporary philosophers, the British Empiricists, would have understood.

RC is cast into a circumstance on the island where the capitalist relations of production are, self-evidently, not dominant. We can see a 17th century Englishman having to start from scratch. He has salvaged some tools and munitions from the wrecked ship. But, he is not *tableau rasa* and merely reproduces the relations of society he originated from. British colonialism was not in the blood but as I had quoted previously from Marx 'social being determines consciousness.' There was not a 'necessity' for RC to reproduce the relationships and power hierarchies of the metropolitan country on his island, but he did without any intended irony. Was there an alternative. Marx's *Capital* provides one:

> Let us picture to ourselves, by way of change, a community of free individuals, carrying out their work with the means of production in common...All the characteristics of Robinson's labour are here repeated, but with the difference that they are social, instead of an individual. Everything produced by him was exclusively the result of his own personal labour, and simply an object of use by himself. The total product of our community is a social product. [139]

So, it is not labour that is the problem, but how it is organized and RC1 having created a microcosm allowed us to think creatively about this question and envisage potential solutions such as the social ownership of 'the means of production.'

Thus, 'commodity-production' and the division of labour i.e. capitalism was finding its earliest development in Britain with its concomitant ideology of individualism. In this epoch, that of RC1, there was social uncertainty and competition in

---

[139] Marx, K *Capital, vol 1* (London, Pelican Marx Library, 1976) p 169

early capitalism which Raymond Williams[140] aptly described as a 'crisis of values.'. This was a huge structural change in England, Williams argued: 'The transition from feudal and immediate post-feudal arrangements to this developing agrarian capitalism is of course immensely complex. But its social implications are clear enough…In this development, an ideology of self-improvement…became significant.' Defoe, argues Raymond Williams (ibid, pp 88-89), with some merit, abstracted the crisis and shock of the coming together of pastoral and industrial forces at the turn of the century when he began writing novels that he would project: 'the abstracted spirit of improvement and simple economic advantage – as most noteworthy in Robinson Crusoe – and created a fictional world of isolated individuals to whom other people are basically transitory and functional.' (ibid) We can understand this because the young Crusoe rejected his father's entreaties to remain in: 'the middle state, or what might be called the upper Station of Low life, which he had found by long experience was the best in the World.' (RC1 p.2). Society was experiencing a maelstrom, what Williams described as the 'Pastoral and the Anti-Pastoral, the country and the city' and, of course consequently, the emergence of the last two great contending classes of History, the bourgeoisie, and the proletariat.

I want to return to the consequence of the colonial encounter: Edward Said argued:

> I am not trying to say that the novel or the culture in the broad sense – 'caused imperialism, but that the novel as a cultural artifice of bourgeois society, and imperialism are unthinkable without the other.[141]

Coetzee, *Foe, 1986,* [142] is an attempt at 'writing back' to RC1. In its method in challenges the Realism of the master narrative by introducing a woman, Susan Barton who is modelled on a character in *Roxana.* However, although this feminist dimension is significant because Susan Barton wants Foe to write her island narrative into a popular genre

---

[140] Raymond Williams, *The Country and the City* (London: Vintage, 2016) p.86

[141] Edward Said, *Culture and Imperialism, (London, Vintage, 1993) p.84.*

[142] Coetzee, *Foe,* (Penguin Books, London 1986).

which has irony. However, I am interested here in the post-colonial; 'writing back' or indeed lack of it. Friday is in the care of Susan as he is mute, possibly because his tongue has been mutilated or there is an inference it could be psychological. Dominic Head[143] argues he may be castrated as well. Friday's silence sets up what Dominic Head called a 'double-bind' situation in the novel because Coetzee as the author is a white man commenting on Black oppression and Susan tries to teach Friday to speak again. They represent the position of white liberals in post-colonial situations, essentially marginalized. Friday's silence can only be perceived as a metaphor for a deafening roar as he is an emblem of the people Frantz Fanon *The Wretched of the Earth* described in the colonial situation, 'The well-being and progress of Europe have been built up with the sweat and dead bodies of Negros'. His solution was the National Liberation struggles of brown, black and yellow people. This was Frantz Fanon's position during the Algerian War of Independence in 1961:

> At the level of the individual, violence is a cleansing power. It frees the individual from his inferiority complex and from his despair and inaction...Even if the armed struggle has been symbolic...the people have the time to see that the liberation has been the business of each and all and that the leader has no special merit[144].

Fanon's words haunt us 300 years after *Robinson Crusoe* was published with a resonance which leaves the European as "Thunder struck" as Robinson Crusoe when he discovered that solitary footprint in the sand. A remorseless dialectic as Marx argued: 'A nation which enslaves another can never itself be free.'[145] We see the imperialist as a dissembler.

---

[143] Dominic Head, *The Cambridge Introduction to Coetzee*, (Cambridge, Cambridge University Press,
    2009) pp, 63-65
[144] Frantz Fanon 2001, p.74.
[145] https://www.marxists.org/archive/marx/works/1870

Bibliography.
Primary Sources.
Miguel De Cervantes, *Don Quixote,* ed. by John Rutherford (London, Penguin Classics, 2003).
Defoe, D, *Moll Fielding,* ed. by G.A. Starr and Linda Blee (Oxford: Oxford University Press, 2011).
Defoe, D, *Robinson Crusoo,* ed. by Thomas Keymer (Oxford: Oxford University Press, 2008).
Defoe, D, *The Complete Life of Robinson Crusoe,* ed, by S. M. Rogers (U.S.A.).
Defoe, D, *Roxana,* ed. by David Blewitt (London, Penguin Books, 1982).
Rogers, Woods. A Cruising Voyage Roed. by und the World: First to the South-Sea, Thence to the East-Indies, and Homewards by the Cape of Good Hope. (London: A. Bell, 1712).

Secondary Sources.
Ashcroft, B, Griffins, G and Tiffin, H eds. *Postcolonial Studies: The Key Concepts,* Third Edition (London: Routledge, 2013).
Baines, P *Danial Defoe: Robinson Crusoe/Moll Flanders, A reader's guide to essential criticism* (London: Palgrave MacMillan).
Bounds. P, *British Communism & the Politics of Literature 1928-1939*, (Pontypool: Merlin Press, 2012).
Coetzee, J.M. *Foe,* (Penguin Books, London 1986).
Coetzee, J.M. *stranger shores essays 1956-1999* (London, Vintage, 2002)
Fanon, F, *Black Skin, White Masks,* (London: Plato Press, 1986).
Fanon, F, *The Wretched of the Earth* (London: Penguin Modern Classics, 2001).
Fox, R, *The Novel and the People (London: Lawrence & Wishart, 1979),*
Head, D, *The Cambridge Introduction to Coetzee,* (Cambridge, Cambridge University Press, 2009)
Hammond, P, *A Defoe Companion* (London: McMillian Press,1993).

Joyce, J, *Lecture on Daniel Defoe*, Università Popolare, Trieste, Italy, March 1912.
Kettle, A, *Literature, and Liberation: Selected Essays* ed. by Graham Martin and W. R. Jones (Manchester: Manchester University Press 1988).
Kettle, A, *An Introduction to the English Novel vol 1*, (London: Hutchinson & Co, 1977).
Lukács, G, *The Historical Novel* (London: Merlin Press, 1965).
Macherey, P, *The Theory of Literary Production*, (London:1978).
Mackay, M, *The Cambridge Introduction to the Novel* (Cambridge: Cambridge University Press, 2011).
Marx, K, A Contribution to the Critique of Political Economy, Preface. *in Marx & Engels, Selected Works in One Volume* (London, Lawrence & Wishart,1973).
Marx. K, *Capital, vol 1 (*London, Pelican Marx Library, 1976),
Marx, K, *Philosophical and Economic Manuscripts of 1844*, (Moscow: Progress Publishers, 1967).
Rogers, P, ed. *Defoe The Critical Heritage* (London: Routledge & Kegan Paul Ltd, 1972).
Rogers, *P, Robinson Crusoe*, (Routledge Revivals, 1979).
Said, E, *Culture and Imperialism, (London, Vintage, 1993).*
G. A. Starr, Defoe and the spiritual autobiography in *Defoe; Critical Interpretations.* ed, by Harold Bloom (Chelsea House Publishers; Library Binding edition Dec. 1991).
Watt, I *The Rise of the Novel* (London, The Bodley Head, 2015).
Williams, R, *The Country and the City* (London: Hogarth Press,1993).
Woolf, V, *The Common Reader, vol 1* (London: Vintage, 2003).

What is literature?

Roman Jacobson maintained:

'Literature is organized violence committed on everyday language.'

Jacobson, Roman in Eagleton, Terry *Marxism and Literature*, (1976).

The question 'what is literature?' is a literary device in that it is a rhetorical question, it elicits an answer. I shall argue or sketch many well established replies and allow you to reach your own conclusions. Literature and poetry can be differentiated from other writing or speech by having the quality of 'literariness'. This term was first employed by the Russian Formalist Critic Roman Jacobson in 1919 when he declared:

The subject of literary scholarship is not literature in its totality, but literariness, that is, that which makes a given work of literature.

Jacobson, Roman [1919] in Victor Erich (1981) p, 171, *Russian Formalism*; History, Doctrine, Yale University Press.

So, for the Russian Formalists literature was not the incarnation of: The best that has been thought and said in the world.

Arnold, Mathew ([1869] (1971) *Culture and Anarchy*, p,6. Cambridge University Press.

Secular religion as Mathew Arnold argued, would save Western capitalist civilization from both the creeping philistinism of the rising bourgeoisie and the degeneration of the masses and that this may bring about social disorder. Arnold was hoping to make cultural glue, a kind of cultural opium of the people. It would by implication require a transcendental quality inherent in an ether of eternal 'Ideas'. The Canon of bourgeois texts is to be read with the guiding hand of a bourgeois curriculum e.g. 'The Newbolt Report'.

However, there was disagreement between the Russian Formalists who deviated from the concept held by most other Marxists that literature was simply a reflection in the ideological superstructure of the material base of any given socio-economic epoch, 'in the last instant.' The views of the Formalists were unorthodox although most remained close to the ideas of the Bolshevik revolution and their ideas around them which went out of favour with the rise of the Stalinist counter-revolution. Leon Trotsky learning from and leaning towards the Russian Formalists claimed artistic creation is:

> A deflection, a changing and transformation of reality, in accordance with the laws of art.

Trotsky, Leon (1924) Literature and Revolution in Eagleton, Terry Marxism and Literary Criticism (2002), p. 46 Routledge.

The key to understanding the ideas of the Formalists lies in this concept of 'literariness'. They argued that in everyday language and literature we develop habits or are 'automatized' by the routine of everyday life. We simply may not notice literature when we are reading it because of it does not possess this quality of 'literariness'. What gives something, a material text, this quality? It is 'defamiliarization' argued Victor Shklovsky in an important text, Poetry as Technique (1917) and this is central to the ripening of the human experience:

'Art exists that one may recover the sensation of life... The purpose of art is to impart the sensation of things as they are perceived not as they are known.'

Shklovsky, Victor (1917) Poetry as Technique in Hans Bertens (2008) Literary Theory. p 25 Routledge.

It serves a similar purpose to that which the English poet Shelley had claimed for poetry in A Defence of Poetry (1821):

Poetry lifts the veil from the hidden beauty of the world and makes familiar objects be as they were not familiar'

> Shelley (1821) In Defence of Poetry

This of course poses the question of how a material text transmutes from a piece of everyday language or 'autotomised' experience in a piece of 'literature' this is what made this small group so radical. For there were suggesting that it lies in the formulaic devices within a text, rhythm, metaphor, image etc. That in turn lead to them being labelled in a derogatory manner 'Formalists', but it is also what underpins their perspective to a firm commitment to the material text. They tended towards understanding the materiality of the text as its primary importance and the literary devices which allowed this text to attain literariness which is consistent with a Materialist analysis derived from Marx and following Marxism the Russian Formalists comprehended 'texts' as being significant in the context of the social and economic period they were written in. However, they were clearly not 'Orthodox' literary Marxist scholars in the manner of Georg Lukács. Indeed, it is illuminating to examine the debate between Victor Shklovsky and Georg Lukács to inform the differences to the Formalist and this more 'orthodox' Marxist approach to literature. The orthodox approach to art is encapsulated by Plekhanov, the 'father of Russian Marxism':

As an adherent of the materialist conception of the world, I would say that the first task of the art critic is to translate the ideas of a work of art from the language of art into the the language of sociology, to establish what might be called the sociological equivalent of a given literary phenomenon.

See Plekhanov, G.V. (1955) Kunst and Literatur, Berlin And again by Lukács when he argues artistic concentration:

Is the maximum intensification in content of the social? and human essence of a given situation. Lukács, G (1978) Writer and Critic, London.

It is possible to perceive how the Formalists were concerned with the 'defamiliarization' or 'strangeness' of the individual literary text, what made it different and unique what they called its '' literariness'; but literalness was critical for Lukács. For him the average person in the historical Realist novel was of the most significant as they 'reflected' authentic social relations and in all its contradictions. His criticism of Shklovsky and of the Formalists generally was scathing, for them:

The average character is nothing but an embodiment of uninspiring pedestrianism. Tihanov, G (2000) Victor Shklovsky and George Lukács in the 1930's. University College London.

So, in conclusion to the question 'what is literature?'1) is it as Mathew Arnold, argued the quintessence of the 'best of humanity' transmogrified into a secular religion, 2) a special kind of writing which has the effect of 'defamiliarization' and therefore gives a text its literariness and allows the reader to see reality in a new light as the Russian Formalists maintained or 3) Georg Lukács' argument that it should represent everyday life and show its contradictions. I will leave the last words to Lenin:

Completely Fragmented:

One cannot life in society and be free of society. The freedom of the bourgeois writer is simply masked dependence on money.
We socialists expose this hypocrisy and rip off false labels, not to arrive at a non-class literature (that will only be possible in a socialist non-class society) …It will then be a free literature, become, the idea of socialism and sympathy with working people and not greed or careerism. 'Down with literary supermen! Literature must become part of the common cause of the proletariat, "cog and screw" of a gradualist mechanism set in motion by the entire vanguard of the the entire working class.'
Lenin. V. I. (1905) Party Organization and Party Literature, pp. 2-5. Moscow

Nigel Pearce

On creativity, exorcism and recovery

Creativity is a means of exorcising the ghosts that haunt your soul, torment your mind. The pen can do more than any priest or shaman.

> 'Many of the most sincere and gifted artists and writers in this capitalist world are conscious of a loss of reality.'
> - Ernst Fischer: 'The Necessity of Art'.

Some theorists of language, such as the 'Russian Formalists' have argued that this 'loss of reality' is a positive aspect to writing and the processes of language generally. The 'Formalists' existed before the revolution of October 1917 in Russia and thrived in the creativity of the post-revolutionary period of the 1920's, only to be crushed by the counter-revolutionary Stalinists during the 1930's. They moved attention away from the symbolist interpretation of literature to a more material approach to the text. What is of interest to us about them is the 'concept' of the 'defamiliarizing effect' or what they called 'making strange'. The first step of their argument is that literature is condensed by Jan Mukarosky:

> 'in the maximum of the foregrounding of the utterance, that is bring the act of expression to the foreground, into prominence for the reader.'
> - Mukarosky.

The concept of foregrounding therefore is to put the 'linguistic medium' i.e. literature at the front of our perceptions. Victor Shklovsky argues this creates estrangement or a defamiliarizing effect, by disrupting the everyday uses of language literature 'makes strange' the world of everyday life a and renews the readers lost capacity for a new experience; essentially literature disrupts the 'mundane' which is part of our experience of alienation under capitalism. Therefore, it is possible to argue that a 'loss of reality' or even the process of 'making strange' can be understood as positive elements in writing.

Having established the idiosyncratic nature of 'authentic' writing I will now construct a model of consciousness and language as formed by Marx and Engels which will then be developed by the philosophy of language created by

Valentin Voroshilov in the late 1920's. Then this model will be applied to the journey taken by Jean-Paul Sartre from his first novel of 1938: 'Nausea' which is a work of existential dread and horror which expresses the essence of Sartre's existentialism to his crowning philosophical text: 'Critique of Dialectical Reason' which offers a path to freedom through 'praxis' from the existential anguish of his early novel. Firstly, then how did Marx and Engels conceptualize and therefore understand the categories of and the relationship between consciousness and language? The response is multi-dimensional a) Marx to quote Terry Eagleton:

> 'Turned the whole history of philosophy of humanity on its head, revolutionized it with the statement: 'my method is movement upwards from the abstract to the concrete.'
>
> - Eagleton.

This is the foundation for the overarching thesis I present here i.e. Historical and Dialectical Materialism. For Marx and Engels, we live in a material world. b) The material source of consciousness is material:

> 'Thought and consciousness are products of the human brain.'
>
> - Engels.

This may seem obvious, but for many people the source of awareness is not the brain but 'The Idea' (Hegel), a 'First Cause' (Aristotle) or a 'Supreme Being' (Thomas Aquinas). So, what is the nature of this 'consciousness' described by Engels?

> First came labour; after it, and then side by side with it, articulate speech.'
>
> - Engels.

This process is social and the result of people not only interacting with their environment but each other:

> 'in order to produce they enter definite connections and relations with one another, and within these social connections and relations does their activity take place.'
>
> - Marx.

Therefore, labour and language are social in nature. This position is developed further:

> 'First labour, then articulate speech were the two main stimuli under the influence of which the brain of the ape gradually changed into the human brain. The development of labour brought the members of the community more closely together...these relations gave rise to the need for primitive man to speak and communicate with each other.'
> - Schneierson.

Here, therefore, is the fundamental model on which this thesis is constructed upon. Now I will look at two models of language in the light of the model constructed above. First, Ferdinand de Saussure in his 'Course of General Linguistics' (1913) created a theory which would influence all following study of language. It consisted of a) There exists a pre-established or ahistorical structure of language before its realization as writing and speech.

b) It consisted of chains of 'signs'. Each 'sign' is made up of 1) Signifier which is the sound or written image of 2) the Signified or meaning/concept. e.g. in English the signifier 't r e' is related to the signified Tree and therefore creates the word TREE. But this is random because in other languages the signified tree would have a different signifier...

because for Saussure this structure is detached from socio-history it is profoundly opposed to Marxism, but a Russian Marxist linguist named Valentin Voroshilov took it up in a study called 'Marxism and the Study of Language' (1929). He accepted the concept of the 'sign':

> 'The entire reality of a word is absorbed in being a 'sign'.
> - Voroshilov.

However, ideology which here means both ideas and 'false consciousness' (Marx) is transmitted through language:

> 'everything ideological possesses semiotic (sign) value'.
> - ibid.

So, for Voroshilov the false dichotomy between the material base and ideological superstructure of classical Marxism is resolved through language or 'signs'. However, he recognizes the limitations of the 'sign'

> 'Signs only arise...they become material only socially, they comprise a group and only then do they take (real) shape.'
> -ibid.

But it is when 'sign' or words become what Saussure had called 'parole' or 'utterances' that they become significant i.e. both material and socially interactive. Language is as Engels had argued a defining human characteristic. Voroshilov enhances this position:

> 'In point of fact, the word is a two-sided act. It is determined equally by whose word it is and for whom it is meant.'

The 'word' therefore introduces not monologue but dialogue...we communicate with others, he concludes:

> 'A word is the product of the reciprocal relationship between speaker and listener. Each word the 'one in relation to the other"
> - ibid.

I would now like to apply this theoretical construct to the journey taken by Jean-Paul Sartre from the existentialist 'dread' of his novel 'Nausea' (1938) to the concept of 'praxis' as a path to freedom in 'Critique of Dialectical Reason' (1960). A path through human creativity as social rather than merely individual which be the solution to 'absurdity' characterized as mental health issues. The central character in 'Nausea' says;

> 'The nausea has not left me, I think it will be some time before it does...it is no longer an illness or passing fit: it is I.'
> - Sartre (1938).

The words nausea or sickness appear in two other of Sartre's works; 1) 'The Psychology of the Imagination' (1940) 'are conscious of a nauseating sickness.' and 2) in his first major philosophical work 'Being and Nothingness' (1943) 'dullness...feeling of sickness.' Why? Sartre defines three modes of being a) 'Being-in- itself' this are objects which simply exist like a tree, b) 'Being-for-itself' this is humanity, because we have no pre-determined essence, there is no 'First Cause', for Sartre, we make ourselves, we create ourselves. It is the absurd contrast between these two forms of being which is one cause for Nausea, c) 'Being-for-Others', here Sartre says we only become aware of our 'being' when in the 'gaze' of another, when someone 'looks' at you. Thus:

> 'I find myself in a state of instability in relation to the Other.'
> - Sartre (1943).

This is where Sartre's infamous phrase 'Hell is other people' is derived from. Any belief in a system of ideas or faith was, according to Sartre currently, 'bad faith'. But Sartre discovered the analytical tools provided by Marx and Engels and renewed them to explain and transcend this existential dread or 'Nausea' in 'Critique of Dialectical Reason': 1) he embraced Marx's concept of conscious human activity as the dynamic of History, once this was established he had to explain his early position of 'Nausea', 2) to achieve this Sartre created the idea of the 'Practico-inert' which is when humans are active but not social like atoms whirling around in a system and 3) he provided the solution of 'praxis' or 'depasssement' (going beyond the existing situation). This is a refinement of Marx's concept of 'species-being' which was, he said, the essence of humans i.e. to act interact with the world and each other. For Sartre 'praxis' and 'activity' are at the heart of the solution. This 'praxis' is genuine social activity created and made two-way by language:

> 'We set off from the immediate, the individual fulfilling him/herself to the totality of bonds with others...absolute concrete people.'
> - Sartre (1960).

The social is creative, and the creative is social, they are only divided in a social system which has what Marx called the 'division of labour' between mental and manual labour and ultimately between those who are compelled to sell 'social labour', which is their creativity, and to those who buy and profit from it. But the only way to prevent the commoditization of art is to abolish commodity capitalism; one is dependent on the other. But maintaining an active dialogue between artists and writers is a key step in breaking the chains of mental ill health and aiding recovery. Pick up you pen and write, and the chains of illness will dissolve.

The Situationist International: then and now.

> 'The spectacle is the moment when the commodity has achieved the total occupation of social life.'
> - Guy Debord: 'The Society of the Spectacle.'

Who were the Situationist International (S.I.), what did they believe and how influential have their ideas been since their dissolution in 1972? These questions can be answered by examining:1) the avant-garde movements in art and literature that first inspired the S.I., 2) the founding of the S.I. in 1957 and the ideas that they fused at that moment, 3) the split in 1962 and the creation of the Second S.I., 4) the rise of Guy Debord and the revolutionary upheavals in Paris in 1968, 5) the impact of Situationist ideas in the politico-cultural scene in the UK during the 1970's and 6) the positions of individual Situationists today.

Firstly, one of the avant-garde groups which influenced the Situationists was the Dadaists. They had complex sources for their radical art critiques which they vigorously applied to both their art and lives. Dada embraced the 'new' in his 1918 manifesto:

> 'I am writing a manifesto and there's nothing I want, and yet I'm saying certain things, and in I am against manifestos, as I am against principles...Liberty DADA, DADA; the roar of contorted pains, the interweaving of contraries and of all contradictions, freaks and irrelevances LIFE.'

And Arthur Rimbaud who had said:

> (the poet should) become a seer by a long, prodigious and rational disordering of all his senses (embracing all forms) of love, of suffering, of madness.'

- Arthur Rimbaud.

However, the avant-garde was inevitably linked to the oppressed and Dada's art had flourished in the working-class movement. Situationist writer Mustapha Khayati would later argue that:

> 'Dada had a chance for realization with the Spartacus's, with the revolutionary practice of the German proletariat, (their failure) made the failure of Dada inevitable.'

The S.I. formed itself at a small village in Italy on July 28th, 1957. Their intention was to reactivate radical art movements like Dada and Surrealism. However they came to the conclusion that Dada was the end of art in the West and that a new form of creativity was necessary:

> 'The modern artist does not paint but creates directly...Life and art are One.'
>
> - Tristan Tzara.

Emboldened the S.I. produced a journal called 'Internationale Situationist' in 1958 which contained an important insight into the direction the S.I. would move:

> 'A new form of mental illness has swept the planet: banalisation. Everyone is hypnotized, by work and comfort: by the...washing machine. The liberation of man from material cares (has) become a life-destroying obsession.'
>
> - Gilles Ivain. I.S. 1, 1958.

A key moment in the development of the S.I. came in 1962 when a split occurred and a Second S.I. created which was interested in what could be called pure art. The 'French Section' and its main theoretician Guy Debord became the dominant force and he began to apply the ideas of the S.I. to Marx's theory of alienation. Marx had said a worker under capitalism only:

> 'Feels himself outside his work, and in his work feels outside himself. He feels at home when he is not working, and when he is working does not feel at home.'
>
> - Karl Marx.

Alienated from their own labour (for Marx labour is the 'species being' of humanity) these relations of alienation are

Completely Fragmented:

reproduced throughout capitalism. Debord in his 1968 book 'The Society of the Spectacle' had refined these ideas into the concept of the 'spectacle':

1. 'The entire life of societies in which modern production heralds itself as an accumulation of spectacles.'

2. 'The spectacle is not an aggregate of images but a social relation among people, mediated by images.'

3. 'The spectacle is capital accumulated to such a degree it becomes an image.'

Debord quoted a letter to Marx from Ruge (1844) towards the conclusion: 'Shall we live long enough to see a social revolution.'
In May 1968 French students rioted, the workers occupied factories and a huge General Strike began, the S.I. was at a pinnacle. After the defeat of the revolution the S.I. collapsed into endless theoretical debate and personal animosity dissolving itself in 1972. However the ideas of the S.I. were sown in the underground scene of the UK and influenced groups like the 'Angry Brigade' who spoke with a fist and the 'Sex Pistols' who howled with music.
An unorthodox Situationist UK terrorist group called the 'Angry Brigade' carried out activities 1969-1973. Most of their operations were against property, but this did not prevent the state from giving them very long prison sentences. However they carried out a number of symbolic attacks:1) Minister of Employment, Richard Carr, had his house bombed during the strikes against the Industrial Relations Act and 2) An attack on Miss World contest in 1970 showed solidarity with the Women's Movement. The Brigade hoped that the spontaneity of the 'autonomous working class' would be triggered and the 'spectacle' broken. However the S.I. had been critical of terrorist tactics in 1969:

> 'From the strategical perspective of social struggles it must first be said we should never play with terrorism.'
> - Internationale Situationiste 1969.

The Angry Brigade was imprisoned in 1973, some for 30 years.
Malcolm McLaren had been acquainted with the pro-Situationist group 'King Mob' in the early 1970's and he was therefore aware of Situationist texts. Later he set up a shop called 'Sex' which became a 'hang-out' for those interested in cultural rebellion; he formed from the circle that grew around him there the punk-rock band 'The Sex Pistols.'

> 'a tide of nihilistic refusal of the spectacle was initiated.'
> - Sadie Plant.

A pamphlet called 'The End of Music' produced in 1978 was circulated around the scene; it described 'punk' as a movement with:

> 'no desire to negate music...merely to make it free.'

But after a brief blooming of creativity, individualism and some solidarity the 'punk' movement was assimilated back into the 'spectacle'. But McLaren had before that injected fresh life into the Situationist critique for a new generation. Punk had claimed as DADA did that anybody could be a poet and that art was radical. Punk, a major working-class movement, had drowned in commercialism and hedonism. The decline of Sid Vicious into heroin addiction and the death of both Sid and his partner Nancy were like bells toiling, ringing out the end of punk. However we can see how the fundamental concepts of the S.I. continued and were metamorphosed in the UK.

What are the Situationists saying now? One of the leading French intellectuals from previous struggles, Raoul Vaneigem, is tuning into a tendency within Situationist thought that can be traced back to the first issue of 'Internationale Situationiste' in 1958 (see above). He argued in 2000 that:

1. 'Time spent working is time lost...time which you would otherwise be free to spend however one wished.'

2. 'In the commodity system the aim of obligatory work is to churn out commodities...Commodities have no purpose other than to sustain the profits and power of the ruling class.'

3. 'By accumulating and replacing commodities with your obligatory work you are merely boosting the power of the bosses.'

Therefore, the argument is 'don't do obligatory work' as a method of breaking the 'spectacle'. This is similar to the first recorded piece of Situationist graffiti which was on the 'Left Bank' in Paris in 1957; it reads 'never work.'
A final solution to the hegemony of the bourgeoisie can only lie in, as Marx argued, an active class-conscious proletariat. S.I. had said correctly in 1963:
> 'We don't claim to be developing a new revolutionary
> programme all by ourselves.'

Nigel Pearce

On the revolutionary poetry of Bertolt Brecht.

' The poet has watched the people's mouth.' - Bertolt Brecht.

Bertolt Brecht is probably best known for his experimental plays and the dramatic theory he developed around them. But he was also one of the most important poets of the 20th century and arguably the most significant Marxist poet of this epoch, he wrote 1,500 poems. But he also entered into debates over the nature of 'Socialist Realism', which he deplored, with Lukacs in the 1920s/30s, a polemic which divided Marxist aesthetics into the 1960's and beyond. Therefore this analysis will address these issues: 1) what were the conditions and circumstances that moulded Brecht's creative work and aesthetics 2) the debate between Brecht and Lukacs on the nature of socialist writing 3) the content and nature of Brecht's Marxist poetry and 4) Brecht's great error of not actively supporting a worker's uprising in East Berlin in 1953 which was crushed by Russian military power and his subsequent withdrawal from the field of Marxist poetry and aesthetics and 6) Brecht's impact on the Situationist International.

Brecht was born in 1898 and would therefore experience all the major events which shaped the 20th century until 1956. Of course the first crisis was the First World War which Lenin had correctly analysed as the result of competing Capitals exporting 'finance capital' in an attempt to stabilize and expand their own capitalist economies and the inevitable conflict which would ensue i.e. World War 1. Brecht was a military orderly towards the end of the war and this experience of imperialist war and its bloody results were an important developmental factor for the young Brecht. No longer would the tradition of Goethe and Romanticism dominate German literature; the world had been objectively changed. An early poem by Brecht captures his horror of and the hypocrisy of the war (Brecht had not had access to Marxist of Leninist writing at this time) called: 'The Legend of the Dead soldier' 'And when the war was four springs old And of peace there was not a breath The soldier took the logical step And died a hero's death The war however was not yet done So the Kaiser was displeased to be sure That the soldier had given up like that To him it seemed premature.

Completely Fragmented:

The soldier is then dug up and pronounced fit for active service. Accompanied by an army Chaplin and draped in a German flag he is escorted through cheering crowds on his way back to the front line. So many were dancing around him now That the soldier could hardly be seen You could only see him from the sky above And there only stars can gleam

...

The stars are not forever there. Daylight gives new breath.' - Bertolt Brecht.
The next significant stage was Brecht being introduced, by two women who were both committed communists and also lovers of Brecht named Helene Weigel and Elisabeth Huaptmann, too classical Marxist texts. Huaptmann noted in her workbook on 25th October 1926:
'Brecht obtains works on socialism and Marxism and asks for lists of the basic works to study first.' - Elisabeth Huaptmann.
By 1929 and the Wall Street Crash which was followed by the Great Depression of the 1930's Brecht had studied Marxist economics and philosophy, some Lenin and early Mao Tse-Tung on dialectics and the role of the artist in the revolutionary struggle. But fascism was on the rise throughout Europe; now Brecht was ideologically prepared for it and in this poem delineates what he believed should be the attitude of the poet towards it:
'Within me here is a conflict between delight in the blooming apple-tree And the horror of the painter's* speeches. But only the second Drives me to my desk.' - Bertolt Brecht
*Brecht always referred to Hitler as 'the painter' because he had been a house painter.
Therefore it is possible to discern four elements in the formation of Brecht's poetry: 1) imperialist war, 2) embracing Marxism as a world-view, 3) the inevitable decline of capitalism and 4) the rise of fascism. His aesthetic was rooted in the class-struggle; you can perceive his use of everyday language and form. Brecht's position became:
'For art to become "unpolitical" means only to ally itself with the 'ruling group" - Bertolt Brecht.
However during this period there was a debate within Marxism regarding the correct 'line' on literature. Lukacs argued, in the 1920/30's, that 19th century realist novels

reveal the true horrors of capitalism with 'typical' characters, hence the need for 'socialist realist' novels. Brecht disagreed and argued that the 19th century realist form is outdated and has no capacity to radicalize the oppressed and that new 'dialectical' forms were necessary. He argued in the 1930's against those who pursued the official Moscow 'line' of socialist realism:

'They are, to put it bluntly, enemies of production*. Production makes them feel uncomfortable. You never know where you are with production; production is unforeseeable. you never know what's going to come out. And they themselves don't want to produce. They want to play the apparatchik *and exercise control over other people.' - Bertolt Brecht

* For Brecht all 'production' is artistic 'production', a free 'collective act' (Brecht) * Apparatchik:Communist Party functionary in the former Soviet Union. Marx and Engels were against 'applied tendency' in literature and Marx described it as: 'The most wretched offal of socialist literature.' - Karl Marx.

Brecht used everyday language in his poetry but he poses a dialectical question, it demands a response. In the poem: 'The Sixteen-Year Old Seamstress Emma Ries before the Magistrate' Brecht exhibits two essential aspects of his poetry; 1) that it is worker centred and 2) that it incorporates a knowledge and application of Dialectical Materialism, the science of the proletariat. The poem is about a sixteen year old working class woman who has been caught distributing revolutionary leaflets. She is in a material situation, not in the vacuous spheres of bourgeois speculation. It is also the inevitable dialectical situation workers are objectively drawn into...she is in conflict with the oppressors. So here is the dialectical contradiction and how Brecht does resolve this contradiction, of course in the same manner the working class must ultimately resolve it, by revolutionary synthesis:

'As reply, she stood up and sang the Internationale When the magistrate shook his head She shouted: 'Stand up! This is the Internationale!' - Bertolt Brecht.

Therefore it is clear that in his poetry Brecht is creating a new tradition in German poetry, moving away from the

themes and methods of Goethe and the Romantics and towards the future of communism.
However once ensconced in the German Democratic Republic in the role of Staatsdicher (state poet), a role he was never comfortable in Brecht made the biggest mistake of his life. It was 1953 and a spontaneous workers uprising erupted in East Berlin, after hesitation he finally supported the Stalinist elite in calling for Russian tanks to crush the revolt. He never recovered from this error and retreated into rustic silence and a poetic wasteland. But Brecht was not entirely curbed by this error and in the aftermath of the rebellion wrote one of his best anti-Stalinist/anti-capitalist poems:
'The Solution.' ...Would it not be easier In that case for the government To dissolve the people And elect another.' - Bertolt Brecht.
Finally I would like to examine the relationship between Brecht and the Situationist International's concept of detournement 'anything can be used' (Guy Debord) to disrupt the alienation within the 'Society of the Spectacle.' To put it more abruptly: 'Plagiarism is necessary. Progress implies it.' (Debord). It is necessary to place this in the context that for the Situationists art was concluded when the Spartacus League failed to bring German dada to fruition in the workers revolution of 1919. They reflected with pleasure that Brecht had commented:
'That he had made some cuts in the classics of theatre in order to make the performances more educative...closer to the revolutionary orientation we are calling for.' - Debord/Wolman.
Brecht encapsulates his aesthetic in the poem:
'Hymn to Communism'. 'It is so simple which is so difficult.' - Bertolt Brecht

Nigel Pearce

On dialectics and Marxism: a philosophy for today.

> 'Dialectical materialism is more than a philosophical system it is a philosophy of action.'
>
> - George Plekhanov.

Here is an explanation of the philosophical concepts which inspired and re-enforced much of the confrontation which occurred between rightist members of staff and myself. The theoreticians of the bourgeoisie, in their many manifestations from the academic to that of the padre who condones imperialism, exhibit a single and constant intellectual position in their opposition to the philosophical system of the oppressed which is dialectical materialism. The bourgeoisie are compelled to do so by their objective position in the class system of 'late-capitalism'. They are obliged not only to accumulate Capital but must, therefore, also reproduce the system of ideas. This is because ideas are created by the reproduction of the economic or material life of capitalism. In the same way the proletariat are placed in opposition to capitalism and its dominant ideas because they are economically exploited and also oppressed by bourgeois ideology. The masses are therefore drawn into opposition against capitalism and, ultimately, they are the agents of its overthrow:

> 'The emancipation of the proletariat is the
> task of the proletariat.'
> - Karl Marx.

Hence the philosophy of the working class can only be forged in the furnace of the class struggle and its theoreticians must move with the motion of historical necessity which is the inevitability of proletarian revolution. So we can see how Marxist philosophy did not materialize in the minds of Marx, Engels, Plekhanov, Lenin and Trotsky spontaneously, but rather it was the consequence of the proletariat and its intellectuals learning the lessons of the class struggle.

Leon Trotsky (1879-1940), one of a vanguard of Marxist thinkers, maintained that in the process of the development of human ideas:

Completely Fragmented:

> 'Two systems of logic are worthy of attention; the logic of Aristotle (formal logic) and the logic of Hegel (dialectical logic).
> - Leon Trotsky.

More than 2,000 years ago Greek philosophers who were exploring the human mind and the natural world discovered the dialectic:

> 'The ancient Greeks were all natural-born dialecticians and had already analyses the most essential forms of dialectical thought'.
> - Fredrick Engels.

This is clearly illustrated in the work of Heraclitus (540-480BC) who argued that:

> 'Everything is and is not, for everything
>
> is fluid, is constantly changing, constantly
>
> coming into being and passing away'.
>
> - Heraclitus..

We can locate the essence of dialectics, which is impermanence, here in the thought of Heraclitus.

The concept of 'logic' which is derived from the Greek 'logos' meaning 'word' or 'reason' formed the basis on which Aristotle (384-322 BC) constructed the model of formal logic. This became the dominant form for much human intellectual endeavour. He discerned three main laws in formal logic:

1) The Law of identity: A=A.

2) The Law of contradiction: A cannot be A and non-A.

3) The Law of the excluded middle: A is either A or non-A.

Aristotle

These three principles of logic are the foundation of modern science and mathematics. Aristotle's model of logic dominated Western thought intermittently for about 2, 000 years and appears to be 'common sense'. But 'common sense' does not look below the surface appearance of nature and the processes of History. We can begin to perceive the limitations of formal logic and to become aware of the scope of dialectical logic. As Trotsky commented:

> 'Dialectical understanding is not limited to the problems of daily life, but attempts to arrive at an understanding of a more complicated and drawn-our process. Dialectical and formal logic bear a relationship similar to that between higher and lower mathematics'.
> - Leon Trotsky..

The limitations of formal logic or what Trotsky sometimes called 'vulgar thought' became clear with the rise of modern science. An enormous blow to the bourgeoisie and their lackeys was Charles Darwin's theory of evolution. This theory proved that one species can be transformed into another and that therefore qualitative change outside the static categories of formal logic takes place. Trotsky commented:

> The fundamental flaw in vulgar thought lies in the fact that it wishes to content itself with motionless imprints of reality which consists of eternal motion.'
> - Leon Trotsky..

Therefore modern science needed a philosophical system to create a theoretical model to explain its discoveries, this theory is dialectical materialism.

The roots of modern dialectics lie in radical German philosophy which had been inspired by the French revolution of 1789 and the collapse of the old order. The major thinker of this progressive wave was George F. Hegel G (1770-1831). He studied the Greek dialecticians and combined their insight about the transitory and interconnected nature of reality with German naturphilosophie or 'Philosophy of Nature'. His orientation was essentially one of metaphysics i.e. he saw reality as 'ideas' or 'spirit' rather than 'matter in motion'. However Hegel's philosophy of dialectics challenged the mechanistic ideas about motion which had become dominant. For Hegel there were three stages in the dialectical process:

1) Simple unity, the object before any change.

2) The negation, this is when the object creates its opposite.

3) The negation of the negation when the opposites are reconciled in a higher synthesis.

Hegel believed everything existed in the mind of God. His whole system was to show how these three moments of the dialectic, described above, are acted out by the 'Absolute Spirit' or 'Absolute Idea', which are ultimately terms for God, in History. The three stages described above became:
1) The simple unity of God.
2) God creating his negation which is Nature.
3) The unification of God and Nature through the development of human
consciousness into a higher union.
To understand this it is necessary to see it in the context of Hegel's ideas about the progress of human consciousness:
1) The simple unity of the isolated human mind.

2) The separation of the human mind from nature which Hegel called alienation.

3) Unification of the human mind with nature in the higher synthesis with the
'Absolute Spirit' or God.

Interestingly Hegel believed that this higher synthesis of the human mind, Nature and the 'Absolute Spirit' was made possible by his philosophical system. So, we can see how Hegel, as a result of the rise of radical German philosophy which was influenced by revolutionary France, created a system of ideas which transcended the limitations of formal logic and 'vulgar thought', but:

> 'Hegel fell into the illusion of conceiving
> the real as the product of thought, the real
> subject retains its autonomous existence
> outside the head'.
> - Karl Marx.

This means that for Marx (1818-1883) reality did not reside in thought or spirit but in the world, we see around us i.e. 'outside the head'. Hegel had advanced the concept of the dialectic; however, it was with Marx's critique of Hegel that a major leap in philosophy took place. Marx said:

> 'The dialectic is standing on its head. It
> must be inverted in order to discover the
> rational kernel within the mystical shell'.
> - Karl Marx.

It was with this analysis that Marx created the flowering of ideas which is dialectical materialism. This is the philosophy that every class-conscious worker needs in his or her daily battle with bourgeois ideology and is the system of ideas that prepares the path for worker's revolution.

Three basic laws are at the core of dialectical materialism and as a whole they form a coherent system. They comprise of:

> 'The general laws of motion and development of nature, human society and though.'
> - Fredrick Engels

The Law of the Unity and Struggle of Opposites.
Lenin (1870-1924) summed this up:

Completely Fragmented:

> 'The condition for the knowledge
> of all processes of life of the world
> ...in their real life is the knowledge
> of them as a unity of opposites.'
> - V. I. Lenin.

Let us consider two consequences of this:

a) 'non-being' must contain its opposite 'being' within itself, in the same way 'being' must contain 'non-being'. Therefore, the bourgeois argument for the necessity of a 'First Cause' to set the clockwork of the universe in motion is unnecessary because 'non-being' or 'nothing' created its opposite 'being' or 'existence' at the beginning of Time.

b) In capitalism the bourgeois and the proletariat are bound together by the system, yet they also exist as material and antagonistic opposites which creates the class struggle.

2) The Law of the Transformation of Quantity into Quality. Engels (1820-1895) defines this law:

> 'We could express this by saying that
> in nature...qualitative changes can only
> happen with the quantitative addition or
> subtraction of motion'.
> - Fredrick Engels.

An example of this would be that when heat is applied to water and the temperature of the water changes a quantitative change takes place, but when the water becomes steam a qualitative transformation has taken place. Similarly we can see how a series of quantitative changes takes place in a capitalist society e.g. trade union struggles and how these inevitably lead to a 'dialectical leap' or qualitative change i.e. proletarian revolution. Learning from the lessons of History Lenin developed this position:

> 'Capitalism creates its own
> gravedigger, itself

> creates the elements for a new system...without
>
> a 'leap' these individual elements change nothing'.
>
> - V.I. Lenin.

Hence Lenin ascertained that there is no reformist path to socialism, there must be a 'leap', a revolution.

3) The Law of the Negation of the Negation.

In capitalism a process called the 'negation of the negation' takes place. This essentially means that the 'thesis' or first aspect of a dialectical contradiction is not destroyed by its opposite or 'antithesis' and some aspects of both the 'thesis' and the 'antitheses survive within a higher 'synthesis'. The 'negation' is in the class conflict between workers and bosses which creates the 'negation of the negation' that is proletarian revolution and socialism. The result of the 'negation of the negation' is a classless society, a society without contradictions. Marx examined the concept in Capital:

> 'The capitalist mode of appropriation is the first negation of individual private property based on one's labour. But capitalist production
> begets with the inevitability of a natural process its
> own negation. It is the negation of the negation.'
> - Karl Marx.

What tactics should revolutionaries pursue? Ulrike Meinhoff (1934-1975) argued in 1971:

> 'That a pre-requisite for progress and an eventual
> victory of revolutionary forces is the armed struggle.'
> - Ulrike Meinhoff

But today the conditions of the class struggle have changed, and we must again win the battle of ideas, an ideological hegemony, to prepare for the inevitable revolution. Today:

Completely Fragmented:

> 'Dialectics are our sharpest weapons'.
> - Fredrick Engels.

On Allen Ginsberg, 'Howl' and Trotsky.

My argument is stated succinctly and argued to its conclusion. I contest that Allen Ginsberg's Howl was, as some critics argue a popular, 'an over-simplification' of the poetry regarded by the Canon as high-quality literature. Rather, Howl formed a new genre which mirrored in its innovation other seminal moments in literature connected to changes of the 'mode of production' and had similar ramifications. The 'primitive accumulation of capital of English capitalism' that Caudwell (1937) Illusion and Reality associated with William Shakespeare, the 'bourgeois' revolutions that permeate the ideas of Wordsworth (1802) Preface to Lyrical Ballads and the shocks of Darwinism, Freud and imperialist war which informed Modernist literature, particularly the avant-garde pertinently T.S.Eliot (1922) The Waste Land. What was the problem of the writer in late-capitalism as High Modernism entered its death throes? Trotsky (1981) Art and Politics encapsulate it:

> "The decline of bourgeois society means an intolerable exacerbation of social contradictions, which are transformed inevitably into personal contradictions, art suffers most from the decline and decay of bourgeois society. Art cannot save itself...But precisely in this path history has set a formidable snare for the artist."
> - Trotsky

(1981). p 105.

Ginsberg's reply is Howl, this is not the howl of the deranged madman outside of History, it resonates within the conversation of literature, King Lear (1603):

> "Howl, howl, howl! O, you are men of stones;
> Had I your tongues and eyes, I'd use them so

>   That heaven's vault should crack."
>   - Shakespeare (1603)
(5.3.2.58-64).

Howl

For Carl Solomon

1

I saw the best minds of my generation destroyed by madness, starving hysterical naked, dragging themselves through the negro streets at dawn looking for an angry fix, angelheaded hipster burning for the ancient heavenly connection to the starry dynamo in the machinery of night

- Ginsberg (1956) p. 9

It is the howl of a post-WW 11 avant-garde that must inherently employ the poetic devices of literary tradition but in a different 'form'. A 'close reading' gives us several insights here. They are 'howls' of emotion, of intense emotion and resonate with William Wordsworth (1802) Preface to Lyrical Ballads:

> "Poetry is the spontaneous overflow of powerful feelings: it takes its origin from emotion recollected in tranquility."
> - William Wordsworth (1980) pp. 410-424.

In Shakespeare (1603) we have a reference to the howling of a man driven to madness seeking justice from 'heaven's vaults'. Ginsberg also seeks refuge in chants to the 'Holy' in Footnote to Howl. The thematic howl of a literate madness, seeking divine justice, but not locating it in a corrupted 'world' runs counterintuitive against the whole Enlightenment project. Surely Reason and empiricist science will hear the poet's words. For Americans like Ginsberg the world could not be explained in these neat confines and as a poet who had read widely, he certainly could not accept the text by text alone reductionism of the New Criticism after Hiroshima and McCarthyism, Auschwitz and Stalinism. But what differentiated Ginsberg from other 'Beat' writers in particular Kerouac was that he rejected Kerouac insistence on 'first thought, best thought'. Ginsberg was influenced by both Kerouac in terms of first impulse, but also poets like Eliot, indeed Howl' is an attempt at reproducing something of the literary magnitude of Eliot (1922) The Waste Land. I shall therefore argue against the perspective taken by advocates of Mass Culture Thesis such as the renegade ex-Trotskyist Dwight Macdonald, who argues in (1953) A Theory of Mass Culture and again (1962) Against the American Grain that the collective taste of the 'masses' was reflected in the degraded mass culture that they consumed and that, therefore, they had no 'interest' in 'High Culture'. Dwight Macdonald combined an ex-Trotskyist stance with cultural conservatism and elitism. Also, I argue against a rightist conservative position which is derived from Matthew Arnold (1869) Culture and Anarchy that has an inherent trepidation at the sound of the popular and its revolutionary proclivities. He maintained a 'secular religion' of

> "The best that has been thought and said in the world."
>
> - Arnold (1869) p 6.

Was needed to prevent the erosion of civilization. It is no accident that Arnold began his opus magnum in 1867 after a period of popular and vigorous discontent over suffrage rights. Ginsberg's reply here is the 20th century equivalent to an articulate and insurrectionary mob assailing Arnold:

> "who dreamt and made incarnate gaps in Time & Space through images juxtaposed, and trapped the archangel of the soul between 2 visual images and joined the elemental verbs and set the noun and dash of consciousness together jumping with sensation of Pater Omnipotens Aeterna Deus to recreate the syntax and measure of poor
>
> human prose..."
>
> - Ginsberg 1956 p 20.

Arnold and his Leavisities descendant would be battered and lost for words, their Weltanschauung challenged. Also, here we can perceive Ginsberg's specialist use of 'strophes' which he defines as 'a one speech breath thought' which was akin to the jazz improvisation of Miles Davis or Charlie Parker, the black man's 'beat'. 'Form' with a regard for socio-cultural factors would be engaged by the New Historicism of

Raymond Williams with his 1958 Forward to Culture and Society:

> We live in an expanding culture, yet we spend much of our energy regretting the fact, rather than seeking to understand its nature and conditions.
>
> - Lodge (1972) p. 580.

However, my position is not simply that Mass Culture Thesis and the New Criticism were erroneous, but they failed to understand the nuanced nature of 'proletarian literature' which as Trotsky illustrates is complexified:

> Having broken up human relations into atoms, bourgeois society, had a great aim for itself. Personal emancipation was its name. In reality, all modern literature has been nothing but an enlargement of this theme.
>
> - Trotsky (1981) pp. 61-62.

My position is that only the proletariat has the creative potential and socially universal nature which allowed Marx to say 'communism has solved the riddle of history' can transcend the limitations of the bourgeois intelligentsia when the social and economic conditions are ripe, that is, in a Socialist society because as Marx argued they are the 'universal class'. For the first time in history was there a social collectivity in whose interest it was to dismantle class society, because 'class' fetters on the workers of the world are their 'chains and it is in there interest 'collectively' to break those chains freeing the whole of society.

Some Marxists misunderstood the nature of the relationship between the popular and the high cultures. Adorno and Horkheimer in Dialectic of Enlightenment saw an implied analogy between Marx's concept of his fetishized 'exchange value' as a commodity and 'use-value' a 'material object'. Then they extrapolated this analogy to the relationship between popular and high culture to the detriment of the popular. Walter Benjamin is better here, seeing the potential for mechanized reproduction to free the poet from the 'aura' from his or her primitivism and allow an engaged mass readership. Also, I will draw a parallel with Maxim Gorky,

Lower Depths (see Raskin 2004 p.82) and Ginsberg Howl, thus Trotsky:

> "At the beginning, Gorky was imbued with the romantic individualism of the tramp. Nevertheless, he fed the early spring revolutionism of the proletariat on the eve of 1905, because he helped to awaken individuality in that class in which individuality, once awakened, seeks contact with other awakened individualities"
> - Trotsky (1981) p 58-59.

For Trotsky the solution to the dichotomy of oversimplification and complexity in literature is resolved in the synthesis of revolution. Ginsberg, unlike Gorky would not be involved in a social revolution (as he may have wished) but a cultural revolution, a revolution of superstructure rather that of social base which left American capitalism weakened but intact. Louis Althusser (2006) Lenin on Philosophy and Other Essays commenting on the novels of Solzhenitsyn in (Althusser pp.153-153, 2006) makes the point of the difference between art and knowledge. Literature like Solzhenitsyn's, he argues, may have helped the reader 'feel' , 'perceive' the 'cult of personality' in the Soviet Union but doesn't provide the scientific knowledge to understand it. Althusser said art:

> In the language of Spinoza art puts the conclusions   before the premises.
> -
> Althusser (2010) p 153.

Ginsberg achieves this by employing and developing poetic devices, Walt Whitman's 'long-line' which is a non-metrical line of poetry of length which usually employs enjambment, anaphora which is a 'figure of repetition' in which the same word is repeated as in Part 1 'Who' usually at the beginning successive 'lines, clauses or sentences' , cauda or the tail-rhyme stanza and a surrealist juxtaposition of images such as 'helium jukebox' (1956).Also Ginsberg aspired to create: 'Certain combinations of words and rhythms actually have:

an electrochemical reaction on the body, which could catalyze specific states of consciousness.

Ginsberg (2001) p.31.

Brain Jackson (2010) argues: 'the most compelling example of reading "Howl" -specially out loud – is the sene of time shifting from the prosaic to the mythical. Lines such as:
> who walked all night with their shoes full of blood on the snow deck docks waiting for a door in the East River to open to a room full of steamheat opium,
> - Ginsberg (1956) p. 15

He continues:

> the rhythmic and trouping artifice of Howl constitute...a suspension of time in which the natural laws occur'.
> - Jackson (2010) pp 312-313).

Therefore, I maintain that Ginsberg poetry contradicted the ideas of thinkers such as Mathew Arnold, T. S. Eliot, and William Empson's Seven Types of Ambiguity on the Right and renegade Trotskyists like Dwight MacDonald and neo-Marxists Adorno and Horkheimer. I suggest that the neo-Marxism of Louis Althusser enhanced my general understanding of the positioning of the debates regarding the poetry of Ginsberg, particularly Howl and that in this context it is possible to comprehend him in a lineage of literati, Finally I argue that Ginsberg created not a simplified poetry for mass consumption and 'narcotization' of literary consciousness, but formed the matrix for a new genre of second wave of 20th century avant-garde writers who took and added to the High Modernism of 1910-39 and created a wedge into the monotonous conformity of 1950's poetry. Even poets like Sylvia Plath and Anne Sexton who were writing confessional verse which was challenging some conventions in terms of gender and 'content' i.e. mental illness Plath ([1963] 2004) Ariel and Sexton's (1960) 'To Bedlam and part way back' were not really contesting the terrain of bourgeois hegemony. Ginsberg did shift the aesthetics of the hegemonic superstructure cultural construct in favour of the 'progressive', he unlocks much in this poem, but he was unable to create a social revolution. I conclude that the task can only be brought to fruition by the self-emancipation of the proletariat as Leon Trotsky argues in Literature and Revolution:

> "Under Socialism, Literature and art will be tuned to a different key such as disinterested friendship, this will be the mighty ringing chords of Socialist poetry. However, does not an excess of solidarity, as the Nietzscheans fear, threaten to degenerate man into a sentimental, passive, herd animal? No, not at all. The powerful force of competition this, in bourgeois society, has the character of market competition, will not disappear in a Socialist society, but, to use the language of psycho-analysis, will be sublimated, Art then will become the most perfect ethos for progressive life-building of life in every field."
> - Leon Trotsky
> (1981). p 60.

The Beats could not vanquish 'Moloch' (essentially, 'Capitalism') but they did undermine, disrupted what Lyotard calls it 'meta-narrative' creating the conditions for minority narratives. Nevertheless, only socialist transformation as understood in the aesthetic writings of Trotsky can create authentic liberation for all of humanity. We may read Ginsberg as a disappointed, reincarnated Maxim Gorky lapsing into a hope for Nirvana with a juxtaposition of the social and questioning 'Who' of Part 1, with the devastation of Moloch only relieved with the introspection of fifteen iambs in two sentences, one 'long-line' without punctuation except the repeated and insistent exclamation marks after each Holy! Footnote to Howl pp 27-8. Ginsberg did provide hope in a new 'beatification' of language within Historical Materialism's philosophy, a new Communist International to resurrect Trotsky's Fourth International...

'holy the Fifth International!' (ibid).

Bibliography.

Adorno, T and Horkheimer, M. ([1944] 1979) Dialectic of Enlightenment, trans. by Cumming, London: New Left Books.

Althusser, L (2006) Lenin and Philosophy and other essays, Dahl: Aakar Books.

Arnold, M ([1869] 1993) Culture and Anarchy and Other Writings, ed. by S.Collini, Cambridge: Cambridge University Press.

Caudwell, C ([1937]1977) Illusion and Reality, London: Lawrence & Wishart.

Eliot, T.S. ([1920] 1960) The Sacred Wood, London: Macmillan.

Empson, W ([1936] 1966) Seven types of Ambiguity, New York: New Directions.

Ginsberg, A ([1956] 2002) Howl and Other Poems, San Francisco: City Lights.

Ginsberg, A (2001) Spontaneous Mind: Selected Interviews 1958-1996. New York: HarperCollins.

Jackson, A, Modernist Looking: Surreal Impressions in the Poetry of Allen Ginsberg Texas Studies in Literature and Language, Vol. 52, No. 3, Fall 2010.

Lodge, J (1972) 20th Century Literary Criticism: A Reader, London: Longman.

Lyotard, J.F. (1984) The Postmodern Condition: A Report on Knowledge, trans, by G. Bennington and B. Massumi, Manchester, Manchester University Press.

MacDonald, D (1953) A Theory of Mass Culture, Rosenberg, R. and White D.W (1957) (eds), Mass Culture: The popular arts in America, New York: MacMillan.

MacDonald, D (1962) Against the American Grain, New York: A Da Capo Paperback.

Plath, S (2004) Ariel: The Restored Edition, London: Faber and Faber.

Ruskin, J (2004) American Scream: Allen Ginsberg's Howl and the making of the Beat Generation, Berkley, University of California Press.

Sexton, A (1960) To Bedlam and part way back, Boston: Houghton Mifflin Company.

Shakespeare, W (1603) King Lear. Pugh, T and Johnston, Margret R. (2014) Literary Studies A Practical Guide, New York: Routledge.

Trotsky, L (1981) On Literature and Art, New York Pathfinder Press.

Wordsworth W (1980) Selected Poetry and Prose of William Wordsworth, New York: Meriden Books.

"This thing of darkness I acknowledge mine" : Jungian analysis of The Tempest (Prospero and Caliban).

> "Tumult and peace, the darkness and light -
> Were all the workings of one mind"
> - Wordsworth.

This analysis will argue that Shakespeare's "The Tempest" functions on many levels:
1) the tempest as an allegory 2) that the play can be understood, persuasively, by applying a model of Jungian psychology to it 3) in this context Caliban is a projection of Prospero's unconscious and, finally 4) that Prospero's achieves "individualization" by accepting his "darkness"."(by individualization I mean) becoming a single homogenous being...Becoming one's own sel...Coming into selfhood"- Jung). .

Firstly, the backdrop to the drama is conflict: a storm rages. The idea of a tempest is embedded in the Western cultural tradition which emanates, to an extent, from the Judeo-Christian perspective of which Shakespeare would have been aware. This is manifest in the Old Testament where a storm is perceived as the consequence of repression of natural forces or a birth trauma:

> or who shut up the sea with doors, when it brake forth, as if it had issued out of the womb.
> - The Bible.

However, Shakespeare enhances the traditional image to give it an egalitarian orientation:

> "What cares these roarers for the name of King?"
> - Shakespeare.

This storm is a symptom of inner conflict within Prospero and is therefore, in turn, his allegorical reality.

> The Tempest) is an example of allegory the leading characters are not merely typical but symbolic.
> - Lowell.

The world of symbols is significant in psychology; Freud believed that they existed in the "unconscious" and were repressed material expelled from the "ego". However, Jung developed this concept to embrace a "collective

Completely Fragmented:

unconscious"; a world of primal images which occur consistently in humanity's mythology and religions. These recurring or primal symbols he called "archetypes." The philosophical dimension of Jung's psychology can be located in Plato's „Theory of Forms" ‚here the "Idea" exists in a pure "Form" beyond the material world in the same way that Jung's symbols exist beyond consciousness. But Jung expanded his theory of symbols to describe a more precise element of the unconscious:

> "a symbol was a particular manifestation of something unknown".
>
> - McLynn.

One of these "particular" symbols, for this analysis, is the island where the drama is enacted which is a "projection" (Jung) of inner worlds:

> .... the isle is full of noises
> … Sometimes a thousand twanging instruments
>   Will hang about my ears.
>
> - Shakespeare.

The onomatopoeia of "twanging" enforces this sense.

On the island the relationship between Prospero and Caliban was an exploitative one. Prospero treats Caliban as a slave by day and torments him at night. I would like to examine their relationship in the context of contemporary cultural sources. Firstly, Caliban is an anagram of "cannibal", spelt "canibal" in Shakespeare's era, secondly that Shakespeare would have been aware of, in particular, Montaigne's essay: „Of the Cannibals" in which "primitive" societies are seen as natural until tainted by civilization:

> " Montaigne is saying that the life of the South American Indians proves that mankind is capable of living peacefully, happily and humanly without the constraint of law, or the institution of private property".
> - Middleton Murry.

> This is reflected by Gonzalo"s speech on utopia:

> I'll the commonwealth... I would admit; no name of magistrate ...
> ... Riches, poverty, service none. No occupation, all men idle.
>
> - Shakespeare.

Hence Caliban can be perceived as a member of a, potentially, utopian community and Prospero as the corrupting force of civilization. Thus, Caliban is perceived as the "primitive" (unconscious) and Prospero as civilization (conscious). This idea can be developed by applying Jung's conception of the feminine perspective which he believed to emanate from the "Great Mother" archetype:

> She has always been connected with the moon and the earth...
> she was and is the matrix from which all is born.
> - Von der Heydt.

This analysis maintains that, following Jung, the feminine is the source of creativity {See Robert Graves (1961) for a theory of the feminine as Lunar Muse"}. Therefore it is possible to argue that Caliban is in tune with his, to use Jung's term, Anima (the unconscious feminine) i.e. the creative/primitive (Earth) aspect of his psyche:

> " . .Caliban! Thou (being of the) Earth speak
> ...
> - Shakespeare.

Caliban can therefore be comprehended as the source of the play's creativity. This is stressed, by Shakespeare, as Caliban speaks in poetry and Prospero in prose. Caliban's role as a vehicle for creative energy and of his being, therefore, in tune with nature and poetry is illustrated in the following passage:

> ....in dreaming, methought the clouds would open ...
> Ready to drop on me; when I wak"d, I cried to dream again.
> - Shakespeare.

This passage is beautiful in its poetic innocence. Coleridge elaborated on this aspect of Caliban's being:

Completely Fragmented:

> Caliban…is a sort of creature of the
> earth…He is a man i
> n the sense of imagination.
> - Coleridge.

However, Prospero's attitude towards Caliban could have been influenced by the attempted rape, by Caliban, of his daughter Miranda.

> In mine own cell till thou dast seek to violate the honour of my child.

- Shakespeare.

But some Jungian theorists have maintained that this was itself a projection by Prospero of incestuous feelings onto Caliban:

> "Incest; the molestation and rape of one's daughter. Miranda had reached womanhood with herself and her father as the only two humans in their world".
> - Beck.

Why then is Caliban defined as "other" or "dark". in the play? The Jungian concept of "The Shadow" provides an explanation. Jung explains his concept:

> The shadow personifies everything the subject refuses
> to acknowledge about himself.
> - Jung.

The ideas that are not accepted become repressed into an unconscious complex: the shadow. There are, essentially, two methods which Jung thought people employ to address their "Shadow": 1) projection i.e. projecting your "shadow "onto another person. or 2) "integration", i.e. the accepting your "shadow" as part of the "Self." Jung thought the latter lead to selfhood and "individualization". Prospero has repressed his "shadow", his moon and Earth dimensions, the Anima which is the source of creativity. The consequences of this were 1) becoming introspective and interested in using manipulation (magic):

> And to my state grew stranger, being transported
> And rapt in secret studies.
> - Shakespeare

2) projecting his "shadow" onto Caliban and using abusive language to describe him: "Thou most lying slave...
> Filth thou art
> - Shakespeare.

This is the generalized "tempest".

Caliban can be seen as a projection of Prospero's "shadow", his unconscious complex which is both creative and destructive.

> Prospero is afraid of Caliban. He is afraid because he knows that his encounter with Caliban is largely his encounter with himself.
> - Singh.

Prospero has a choice: either his unconscious will overwhelm him and he will descend into madness or he can integrate his "shadow", Caliban, into himself. Prospero chooses the path of self-integration:

> This thing of darkness I acknowledge mine.
> - Shakespeare.

Completely Fragmented:

An encounter between Virginia Woolf and some Poets.

> Communism in the truer sense is an effort to think,
> and think into action, human society as an organism
> (not a machine which is too static a metaphor).
> - Louis MacNeice

I shall argue that a dialectical tension existed between Woolf's understanding of the aesthetic nature of poetry which as she articulated it in *The Leaning Tower* (1940) was essentially a *Victorian poetic* which I argue is flawed as it was an Aestheticist view and was contradicted by the complexified literary method presented by many writers of W. H. Auden's generation as illustrated in Christopher Caudwell *Illusion and Reality* (1937), which I favour, and Auden *Introduction to The Oxford Book of Light Verse* (1938) who developed to a greater and lesser degree respectively a dialectical materialist view of British poetry. I shall show that in Skelton's anthology *Poetry of The Thirties* (2000) Auden *Spain* (c. 1937) wrote a complexified poetics consistent with this literary methodology. However, this cannot as Woolf argues be separated from the work of T.S. Eliot. Indeed, it is contextualized by the Modernist poetry of Eliot (1919) *Prufrock and Other Observations* and also in his masterpiece The Wasteland in 1922. I also maintain that because of the material contradictions of Modernity and the 'reflection' of this in literature created in the iconic writer of modernist poetry, T.S. Eliot, a contradictory consciousness in his literary output. This can be perceived in the tensions between his revolutionary stylistic innovations and his 'conservative' literary criticism even before his shift to Anglo-Catholicism. These can be comprehended in the context of contradictory and contending Modernisms reflected by the material contradictions into the ideological 'superstructure'. This contestation between the old and new productive forces in a period of social transformation can be manifested as fragmentation of the consciousness which can be seen in Eliot which mirrored the crisis of post WW1 European capitalism. The revolutionary and the reactionary forces which emanated from the material conditions contented for hegemonic cultural dominance.

The methodology I employ in this analysis was encapsulated initially by Marx in the Preface to *A Contribution to the Critique of Political Economy* (1859):

> In the social production of their life, men enter into definite relations that are indispensable and independent of their will, relations of production which correspond to a definite stage of development of their material forces... The mode of production conditions the social, political and intellectual life process in general.
> - Marx

The creation of a new mode of production which developed into finance capitalism unleashing yet more competing social and economic classes but also contending models of literary production. This upheaval was characterized in Lenin (1916) *Imperialism, The Highest Stage of Capitalism* as 'moribund capitalism'. It is the crisis of modern in which he also described as 'late capitalism'. Ernst Fischer in *The Necessity of Art: a Marxist Approach* (1978) applies this pertinently to art:

> In a decaying society, art, if it is to be truthful, must also reflect decay. And unless it wants to break faith with its social function, art must show the world as changeable.
> - Fischer

The European 'Mind' was not the homogenised entity claimed by Eliot in *Tradition and Individual Talent* (1919) with its individual traditions, it was a system torn by war and crisis:

> The whole of the literature of Europe from Homer and within it the whole of the literature of his own country has a simultaneous order. This historical sense which is timeless as well as temporal.
> - T.S. Eliot

Completely Fragmented:

The revolutionary nature of *Prufrock and Other Observations* (1917) which in there form and content challenged the hegemony of the bourgeoisie which he was paradoxically defending in his conservative criticism. T.S. Eliot was the personification of the contradiction of literature in 'late-capitalism': both avant-garde yet reactionary. The writers of the 1930's where caught between these opposing forces. However many did not sit on or lean against an ivory tower as Woolf had argued, but volunteered with the International Brigades or the more independent P.O.U.M. to fight Fascism in the Spanish Civil War as Orwell in *Homage to Catalonia* (1938) illustrates vividly. Some of the writers Woolf critiques in *The Leaning Tower* (1940) did as she points out:

> They feel compelled to preach, if not by their living, at least by their writing, the creation of a society in which everyone is equal and everyone is free. It explains the pedagogic, the didactic, the loud-speaker strain of their poetry.
> - Woolf.

Auden had articulated in these words the milieu which many of these writers inhabited included a belief that it was necessary to transform the 'means of production' in order to solve the malady of the estrangement of literary production, in particular that of the poet:

> In such a society it, and, in such alone, will it be possible for the poet, without sacrificing any of the subtleties or his integrity, to write poetry which is simple, clear and gay. For poetry which is at the same time light and adult can only be written in a society which is both integrated and free
> - Auden.

Eliot had maintained in *The Perfect Critic* (1920) that:
> The creative writer and citric should frequently be the4 same person.
> - T.S. Eliot.

Here Eliot is undermining the very position he articulated as the theory of the 'depersonalized poet', the poet cannot, I would maintain, be both an anonymous 'poet persona' and then self-consciously create a body of criticism about this work. These inconsistencies in Eliot are at the heart of his project for creating a *modern classicist poetics*. The conflicts, contestation and ambiguities are thus evident in Woolf's essay *The Leaning Tower* for three reasons, firstly Woolf's understanding of Romanticism is flawed in that she does not comprehend the revolutionary nature of *Preface* to Lyrical Ballads written by Wordsworth in 1802 which rather than positing the solitary aesthete of Woolf's essay he wrote:

> The principal object, then, which I proposed to myself in
> these poems were to choose incidents and situations from common
> life, and to relate or describe them, throughout, as far as was possible,
> in a selection of language really used by men.
> - Wordsworth.

In its context at a time of revolutionary tumult by contesting Classicism as the dominant verse form is was radical as opposed to conservative. Secondly when she wrote *The Leaning Tower* the USSR were not supporting Britain at the beginning of WW11, they only did so later in 1941. In that context I would argue some of the comments about Leftist poet 'winning' and 'bleating' against the system that educated them is unbecoming of a great woman of letters and finally she does not anticipate David Hume's philosophical critique of her version of the why do you stay argument, 'a society which would like to kick them off its back' Virginia Woolf where Hume likened dissenters to captives on a ship who were unable to get off (Hume 1748). In opposition to Auden who in *Memory of W.B. Yeats* (1939) wrote 'poetry makes nothing happen'. I would argue following Bertolt Brecht:

> Art is not a mirror to reflect reality,
> Rather it is a hammer to shape it.
> Brecht.

Completely Fragmented:

I shall use a 'close reading' of Auden, Spain to make my argument. I agree with Christopher Caudwell in his exposition of the essential feature regarding the social nature of Art:

> Art has social functions. This is not a Marxist demand but arises
> from the very way art forms are defined. Only those things that
> are recognized as art forms which have a conscious social function.
> Caudwell.

My 'close-reading' which illustrates my thesis is Auden, *Spain* (c. 1937), I adhere to Caudwell's insight regarding the general writing of poetry, Auden and the Audenesque in in the 1930's when he wrote:

> But a prerequisite is to attain a world-view that will become general... This Auden, Spender and Lewis have so far failed to do.
> - Caudwell.

That is they didn't embrace and understand the methodology of dialectical materialism and hence their later Rightward turn. Auden *Spain* (c, 1937) of which he Auden would in 1965 refer to this poem 'as a bad influence' thus retrospectively editing his work, at least in ideological term. But Auden is not here writing a simplistic didactic poem. The 'force' of his 'foregrounding' of the signifiers 'yesterday', 'today' and 'tomorrow' for the 'signified' 'History'. He uses these refrains in a particular synaptic pattern throughout the poem to create a sense both the immediacy of the Spanish Civil War and the larger overarching context of human history. He juxtaposes the old 'Yesterday' in which Medieval and Romantic are represented by two troupes as follows and contrasted with the urgency of Spain during the Spanish Civil War and revolution:

> Yesterday the prayer at sunset And the adoration of the madman. But today the struggle.
> - Auden.

We can also see his use of assonance to stress both the contrast but also paradoxically the continuity of paradigmatic model: with the 'ya' of 'Yesterday' and ay of 'prayer' and the 'ae' of 'Sunset'.

The controversial nature of phrases like:

> ...the young poets exploding like bombs.
> - Auden.

Is to an extent overemphasised as it is a simile used as a poetic device and therefore means 'exploding with ideas' as well as an encouragement to join the International Brigades and:

> The conscious acceptance of guilt in the necessary murder.
> - Auden.

Here Auden is writing as much the Freudian psychoanalytical poet as the recruiting sergeant. So here he makes 'conscious' the 'necessary' Oedipus or Elektra Complex as a poetic Bildungsroman or 'coming of age'. Orwell is missing the point in regard of poetry here, I would suggest:

> so much of this sort of left-wing thought of playing with fire by
> people who don't even know the fire is hot.
> - George Orwell.

It is apparent from this couplet which forms the end of a quatrain and his use of alliteration and metaphor. The 'o's reinforce the agency and 'world-historic mission' to coin Fredrick Engels phrase of the proletariat with the poetic mode of the post-revolutionary 'refreshing river.' However, the enjambment: the/Organizer is a little dissonant and suggests a wariness of the 'Party organizer.' We can understand Auden's poem not as a crude piece of didactic writing, but a complicated and well-constructed piece of verse. Obviously, he was in favour of the International Brigades, but this is poetry not sloganizing. Indeed, it is only by with the proletariat acting as the agent of social transformation that we have a 'new' poetry:

Completely Fragmented:

> The social revolution... cannot draw poetry
> from the past, only the future.
> - Marx.

Miscellaneous Poetry
On hearing of the death of a hippy.

That herd were thronging to and through,
While I rolled along the old academic slot,
Not unaware of a lime green undercurrent,
The radar is still fine-tuned, clean thirty odd
Years, street woman flies on crystal crutches,
She stops dead 'Arthur is dead morphine OD',
Those buttresses of ice melt and we embrace,
'I am going to see him in the chapel I am now',
She is skimming heaven on crystal meth how
Long has she got, I shake for they are blessed.

He was gentle shadow of a man always said
The same lines about some Nirvana, I-Ching.
Each death is etched on my heart that bleeds.

in memoriam.
Many would not survive the medicines,
Our beauty was like the circling vulture,
A creature swirling above golden sands,
We had that look like the stoned idolater,
An outcast stumbling across a wasteland,
Now Stelazine is best said the ward sister.

It was just a ritual to cleanse misfits' carrion,
A corpse is pecked raw with hooded beaks,
Then we smile with toothless gums barren,
On Sunday's visitors come to visit us freaks.

Nigel Pearce

I am the lost child of Simone de Beauvoir.

I was made for another planet altogether. I mistook the way.
— Simone de Beauvoir, The Woman Destroyed, 1969.

An Icarus had flown in those currents that whirl around the disc of frenzy and Truth, You were mother half crazed with that music of Beethoven which caressed minds,And where else could that Appassionata Sonata be played but bliss in our heavens, A wandering Aphrodite chained to a cruel cross, our love was crucified and bleeds, Neither of us was of this world, but we were made of the stuff dreams are shaped by.

We celebrated our love of poetry and philosophy, you Muse of past and the present, My wings had whipped up some tempest as contorted limbs can towards time terribly, Until no longer your butterfly heartbeat for me, but drowned in a sea of golden coins, An ornate veil hid a petrified perfection, that brute had finally bought and formed you, Mind melts and blood runs sour since there is no sacred milk to nourish nor heroin hit.

I, amphibian without wings, gliding, sliding through endless pages of waves and books, Solitary creature shunned by a world, hermit in a watery wasteland of thesis and writing.
.

Autumnal.

This season of mellow fruitfulness the apples were teeming with termites, That Tree which held a fruit of temptation called knowledge is now rotten, An earth where its roots clasp and grasp is frozen like leaden bronze sky.

Completely Fragmented:

A howler of hurricanes tossed the loose leaves; laughter was lost so soon, This woman who kicks her way through the shades of brown and crimson, Until she flees in a flurry of rustling colour, Eve escapes the Garden gladly.

An Adam lies in depths of a cider vat; he had waved, drunk and drowned, The leeches replace manacles on his mind and his body is now wormed.

So, in a Universe where time grinds with the motion of mortar and pestle, The divine is shrunk into tedium of day and the humane was hammered In a mould which was made of clay cracked and so broken melted away.

A teenage political prisoner is detained on wards x and y during the 1970s.

An older monk on a secure ward also talked of Tim Leary and Che so we colluded, The nurse without eyes just a film covered One presumed in purveyor of darker art, A poet wrote in metaphor not grasped by those who had embalmed patients' minds,

Children are born in a bell-jar of discontent but do not worry doctor has the thorium, But the clientele spat sputum into cardboard spittoons not emptied but flung in rage,
So we were hidden on wards with sycophants, faces like brick and mortar monotone,

A nurse wanted patients to be aborted cherubs of heaven, some were like banshees, No one commented until the ritual burial of a demon because things are hot in a hell,
Just play bingo pleads Janus therapist while he winks towards some wincing nurses,

No take over the asylum and make it your campus howls that interned revolutionary, The patients rise-up like tigers but then the panzer squad prepare a chemical Cosh,

As electro-convulsive therapy was had by all in the aftermath, the wires just buzzed,

Not forgotten were those whose deaths in Stammheim Prison left us with bitter taste, Bitter is the taste of lemon, lemon is yellow that will colour us if cancer strikes in liver, But red will be funeral shroud as jaundiced eyes never glazed by cowardice of heart.

Poem to lost love.
An intellectual is someone whose mind watches itself.
I am happy to be both halves, the watcher and the watched.
-   Albert Camus, Notebooks 1935-1951, (1998).

The worms are in her hair and creep like crazy symmetry of slurred syllogisms, Her black and translucent pupils are the corridor back into the infinity of inferno, The nymphets were left broken like alabaster dolls sacrificed to a dumb phallus, Some gathered their skirts and stole the microdots hidden in haste but now lost, Camus stands alone a pillar of stone and utters his words of wisdom but weeps, Back in Sputnik I spin trying to keep the letters of R. D. Laing's Knots on a page, Tumble into a purple zone through a rose garlanded window etched in her mind, Put the harpsichord concertos on again please I love them much Hermes sighs, The statue of Camus vaporized, Hermes levitated and we went weaving waves.

I write these words about those days of dreams and wish my love not died in vain,

Completely Fragmented:

We were children of ether who were not of this world, entombed within its bounds.

A light-bulb.
(prose-poem)

He sits in a luxurious sea of crimson cushions observing a solitary light-bulb.
It is suspended, like his mind, by a single cord. This is pulsating slightly, or so it seems; no, it is the bulb flickering. The room, it is like being in a cube of pure
white, is caressed by fingers of light and shadow. The darkness is merging into the dawn which is peeping through green curtains, they are hung on steel wires suspended between two hooks, the Alpha and the Omega. He finds his feet and glides around the bulb to discover a yellowing square of plastic, here is the switch, he clicks it off, the bulb is extinguished and so is his mind, it's cast into an ocean of crawling patterns that dissolves into mirrors of soft wax. He locates the switch again, pushes the button on and the knowledge of electricity envelopes his awareness, but the dawn lurks outside, there is the world.
In that place lurk purple serpents with eyes composed of composite deceptions, ice which burns like the Sulphur of hell, flee knowing I am both ice and in this purgatory perhaps That torn and twisted red heart you see before is not cold or black, it beat too much.

Nigel Pearce

A portrait of my dead mother.

You were confined in this
sorrow,

Standing quietly entrapped by a
drama,

Whose ivy script slowly bound you.

This actress performed before an
audience,

until weeping,

Her tattered mask dissolved onto
a stage of dust with whispers of infinity.

Our mime was like an ancient memory, A text with those
tears that burnt.

I light a candle,
it flickers in this night of cobweb.

'What a shame'.

(In a physical heath Medical Centre waiting room)

Ex-psyche nurse wanders in with an inane grin like he is on
gin says 'what a shame',
You are lucky your enamel is still in place for the Herr
Dentist had gouged out mine,

Completely Fragmented:

Pull your own daisy but you try that one again and any plastic flower poetry is gone.

Refresh memory on a ward a decade past: 'you will never study philosophy', I have.
Whoops, the phlebotomist says they cannot take that vial of blood you handed her,
You clown minus powder and paint; I am not insane say some in Latin and Sanskrit,

Poor nurse is absent of mind a shame; he is no more than a pain in a patient's brain.

A poem for William Burroughs.

I saw the best minds of my generation destroyed by madness, starving hysterical naked, dragging themselves through the streets at dawn looking for a fix.
                              - Allen Ginsberg, Howl, 1956
Staring streets reflect the voids in your eyes which are mirrors of the squares, they exist without the pricking needle easing chaos; you found the mainline again,
an embrace like an orgasm burning through a vein, Zen with and without the hassle,
this Light strikes those chemical cells calling calmly to the soul like the whispered welcome of nothingness,
The Absurdity is not in these oceans where weeping tranquility tumbles into dreams
for you were dancing into the masquerades of non-being.
High womb-like peace sleeps, wake, write, weep, fix again.
You survived, died at 83 because being you; you always 'went first'.

.

Lines in praise of Sappho.

Your heart is aflame like beauty;
With these flowers you garland sacred Helen
Drifting with your bodies and stroking a sultry air of love
flowing between senses, your imaginations of flowers
wander in groves with humming Aphrodite of tears, your
voices are sweet as flutes at dawn the music wrapping your
beloved's body, in her white linen robes of purity and desire,
on Lesbos the Muses sang with joy, to wake a verse of bliss
and lyres do play, but night still wails the song of Rhea. Then
Eros had glanced at them and gasped,
I genuflected dumb before this muse who fragmented.

Mother, it is not Maxim Gorky.

Unlike Gorky the flower of proletarian authorial voice this
poem will not be a novel
Mother,
It is 4.30 a.m. again; and descent into Hades has begun
because my aged Eurydice is
entrapped,
The Russian dolls within dolls within a mind must be
unscrewed given a little personal autonomy, Orpheus and
his double Oedipus must descend and cross the river of the
Acheron, a river of woe, Gorky saw 1917 blossom, so
revolutionaries waited for the winds howl, the crisis came it
was calm, Mother is bewildered in Hades   proletariat   is
dazzled by reflections of commodities in mirrors,

Completely Fragmented:

Not writing Mother and no revolution is the Sisyphean
burden for those also expelled from a heaven.

The ferryman, Charon, undying boatman charges each of us
Orpheus and Oedipus fee:
it is insanity,
The depths swirl in a twist of whirlpools which are typhoons
of the mind, but he has navigated across,
Madness possess some incarnations of Orpheus as children
they were hurled   out in blizzards of acid, Metamorphosis
from Orpheus into Oedipus is ancient like gnawed wormed
apple bitten by a Serpent, The poet Ovid writes Orpheus
abstains from love of women because things went badly for
him 'no',
The pen is numb and weary of the struggle with double-
demonization of the mind and body,
Reality tears like shoals of Paraná fish devour a pair of
lovers, I weep and the sea, the sea
is crimson.

Two Traditional Haiku.

\# 01
Sun is the fragrance
Of love breathe that sweet scent choke
And live in moonlight.
-
\# 02
Cherry blossom burns
Bright for those it praises weep
We sleep in the frost.

The Day I realized René Descartes was wrong.

You were an 'I' who could not pass through the eye of a needle too wealthy in ideas, That Doubt of dream games of molten wax, but you were not an explorer of Psyche,
An ideologue who would never doubt Cogito Ergo Sum along his preordained Way, Conjured an Evil Genius to deceive all, the thought of deception without a hesitation,
Squares become triangles in a Cartesian circle, round and round you were just dizzy, Baseline was always going to be Saint Anselm, the proof of perfection by God alone.

René the rabbits were all in a bag the one you pulled out was Carroll's White Rabbit, That day my doubt became an epiphany was when the lie of Cartesian Doubt died,
An awaking of a lotus flower in the moonlight, rebirth in the mists of lunacy and love.

Lines for 'J' (down and up in London).

You, most precious saint of the sacrament from beyond enlightenment, we had stalked along the pavements of dust that billowed into our minds, Core like mine was pure Zen Void tied to the sacred vein in knots, A dazed Dionysus with tongue of fire roaring love for our tribe, Contempt for those swarms of ants that crawl in rhythmic conformity, Squares within squares, pulsations of electrical energy
Who preyed on us, prayed for us blind to their encrusted corruption;
Beloved jive junkie whose crimson sedition is still shouting from misty eyes, Down and up in London, still defying that recurring Obelisk of glinting black stone,
I hope…

Completely Fragmented:

The poet's tasks: a blessing or curse.

Still hard at heel, those steel bonds don't bind his mind like blinkers,
 The fire is not to be quenched within his mind and body: a vocation?
 Those flames which lick like lovers probing tongues cocoon, wrap Him,
 But they just burn and erode the being, this is the poet's grained Fate,
 No choice almost like a sort of pre-destination of despair, myopic mass

Six haiku.
#1.
Rust burnt in a mind
It was acid,
now teardrops Explode euphoric.

#2.
Corn stood strong golden
Ready for harvest, the rain
You brought left famine.

#3.
A heart was made of
Blue glass and beat,
But it broke Smashed like smithereens.

#4.
Madness exhales breath
To lift veils, there the sane gasp
For they have no air.

#5.
Vampire bat poets
Had sucked your veins, gave them blight
The depths they needed.

#6.
Love was spat out like
Spittle, a flute is silent
For it has no reed.

The Blood-Jet.

Poetry is like the blood-jet, it just keeps on flowing.
- Sylvia Plath, Kindness Collected Poems, 1981
An Apple was offered by that delightful serpent, she snakes into a syringe as the vein is hit,
Or gushes from the severed artery of a child when hit by shrapnel, seeps from that cut wrist,
Her brilliance is in the ability to transform any piece of cloth from pure white to a darkest red,
She flows through every syllable this severed finger slides across tyranny of the blank page,
She is dripping from the poet's pen in splendid crimson as from vampire's satiated mouth,

Completely Fragmented:

A poet's ink blood is deeper red being contaminated by crazy cells which is cancer,
He had bitten the Apple offered, gorged upon it but it was not in the Garden of Eden but Hell,
The Invisible Gardener had forgotten to give him entry to Eden, the poet fell before the Fall,
Poetry is blood-jet, then anemia leaves these poets prostrate before the death time wink.

Two Classes, Two Poetics.

A hair and the width of it is all that matters on the scalp because it is seething like greed,
You need trophies because of all those lost like any myopic vulture searching for carrion,
That bejewelled pen you posture with run dry before any ink oozed to awake blunted nibs.

The nib of the masses is forged with both steel and blood, it has the sound of thunder clap,
It writes on papyrus, parchment and paper, the internet and is flexible like a   willow in wind,
We have many pens, you know not all who hold them, some scribes, sleepers and workers.

One History, two classes, two poetics and a single struggle: clash of revolution and reaction.

Poem of a redeemed suicide.

An angel had fallen into Grace,
this is the damnation at the antechamber of despair,
Now beyond tepid temptations
he stumbles through the scrub of tangled blind stares
Of willful unseeing eyes no, blind stares and jealous glares
of those who claim to spare,
This baptism is of sand, a font
of dust just like those who are sieves, nothing there but
Barbed wire and head holes,
the fruitless bites of those rotten apples make me puke into
an abyss which is home
I know it well, here the lotus flower blossoms at 5.00 a.m.
A poet was persecuted by the magicians of modernity the
priest purveyors of psychiatry,
His persuasions are portrayed in patterns of ink which we
call words not smeared turds.
Their wands are broken on a philosopher's stone which is
where the poet learn craft.

Her Book of Cold Spells.
Moonbeams awake again as the White Goddess has
crackled into his mind like electricity,
This morning the pen scribbles because a poet's thighs are
bound in tight bondage of blue,
A witch had locked the belt some barren desert drifting time
ago with her brass prison key,
She peddled tears and fears from a pious silence, her book
of charms only cast cold spells,
The bell had rung at birth to exorcize desire from her body
that perished in pure purgatory,
Curses were cast in her casket; she gouged out hearts with
a lunar crazed cardiac surgery.
To tickle love again would not be my metaphor,
But a rook woman who writes with dark thread.

The Transformation.

That saint of sanity is trapped in a glass menagerie of sanctimonious deceit,
Until a flea has penetrated the dome and flies around in search of dog dung,
The master of platitudes swipes the irritant into apparent oblivion with a fist,
A metamorphosis takes places and the black dot mutates into a fluttering bat,
Hideous beauty is born it crawls leaving a trail of crimson slime on the floor.
Being blessed with a sound mind the saint books a check-up with Doctor Sane,
The shrink with a grin and a wink says you have found your vocation Narcissus,
To be generous I will diagnose you with schizophrenia, so you better play a role,
Go and roll into the foetal position because it is medication time says that nurse,
Insanity's martyr lives in an asylum but it is dwarfed by the shrine of Absurdity

A latter-day leper

A bug was bagged just for moral sanctimony in a shop of a holy sacred music faith,
It was a case of contagion danger so he is to be pillared as he must be on the fiddle.
No nothing to do with appearance for they know not yes, they do he has the plague.
I have the flu so have this rather large of box of tissues I bought at Boots just now,
We do not want any of that here they say in a jerked horror which is spattered out,
A leper is not in a colony it is clear but is from an asylum, prison or infections unit.
They are so pleased until the parasite speaks and is sprinkling holy water on them,

Exchange complete, money for folk, manna for Mammon, art thou holy hypocrite,
All are children of the bourgeois so germ smiles and says good-bye and they reply.
This poet in amber begins to weep with ink these words for people cut like knifes.

Another Adonis (upon the suicide of a friend).

Looked in those eyes and saw a galaxy of stars like death's untameable love,
Not beloved Cohen's 'Bird on the Wire' but your words with syllables unstained,
Tigers glancing out of the shadows but always they would purr perfect pulses,
Asymmetry maybe but who wants to be a square, disequilibrium of pure tides,
They would wash us both away into torrents of tremendous terror but tenderly,
Always the day dawned danced its words across our minds, the cloud of light.

A scroll not rolled out for those staid sane pens with their soulless nib scratch,
Our pens etched souls of amber, but words will reverberate like love and loss.
Haiku.

The winter spirit
Smiles, mistletoe whispers but
Always breaks like ice.

Haiku.

This sun shimmered stalks
Of corn pieces wounded flesh
And shed icy blood.

Completely Fragmented:

In the temple of Aphrodite.

Shoot
white light in a rush
to entwine in pulsations with the ivy of death,

drown in that heaving tissue
with our shadows of poetic nothingness, we are cast into hollows

Here banshees
awake us from from
dreaminess with their folds of white silk, they sooth our cries

In
temples where those melting molecules are vibrating, it is here that
                    we weep with Aphrodite.
No more will the creatures of Prometheus fail in their tasks.
A spark zigzags then you put a hand to cool the heat into this lake and your fingers,
Became frost bitten and they just clawed us cruelly, the reaction we pose does not
Require refrigeration rather a transformation from victims of timidity into blacksmiths
Of molten metal, we fashion steel into objects of collective
Nemesis, instruments of Retribution; once buried and lost until the new vanguard of Spartacus performs acts,

To lance a swollen abscess of pus, it must be drained, the bare-foot doctors Inflict
A necessary pain an incision, a wound with History's scalpel, poets don't just wear
The masks of Dantesque masquerade, no; our dreadful dream is a relentless beam.

The chess board consists of 64 squares, are you one?

The chipped chess pieces, the pawns, chant their
abhorrence at the Smooth and uninterrupted movement of
both a Rook and the Queen, At the fatal power of the King's
demise which terminates their game, He was checkmated
because of impotence and ineptitude, you didn't Avoid being
mated: the Grand Master who is reincarnated as a flea
Studies the game, metamorphosis's himself into sticky
brown slime, He then oozes onto the board, only godless
like the inexorable tides, The tacky mucus seeps its way into
the pristine checkered surface. Did you lead a checkered life
or as cramped as the pawns, chipped and clipped, never
raced from A8 to R8, only P-K4*, an anticipated Opening
and so is everything else, just predictable like the ticking of A
chess clock, you 'play by the rules', 'stay on the board';
secure, its Death-in-life because the brown snot is caustic, it
will erode you until Deranged the only option is to plead for
checkmate, you 64 squares.

Conception in the desert.

Jab
a silver
pin into any

Poet and see
sand pours out,

It
flows into
a scratched hourglass

Which
leaks particles through dream's prism

Into
desert, here
poetry is conceived

With
those relentless sandstorms, they blind.

Winter Haiku.

Ice has formed across
A lone pool, words are crying
Beneath its smooth face.

Haiku written in memory of Edie Sedgwick (1943-1971).

Bliss was fixing fire
In shadows, flower of flame
You wilted to bloom.

Haiku on poets
Cut that mind of coils
And it bleeds an ink of joy
That is caught by stars.

Haiku No. 4.
A pillar of stone
Has a cloak of golden
It wraps itself in.

A poet becomes catatonic.

A
heart of dust
is fleeing the square of black onto white?

The
silken veils are drifting into a river of mirrors,
here baptism is transience trapped in a house of tears

With
the Dead, they kiss with burning words
like bubbling acid which blisters until poetry is left mute.

A priest realizes God is dead and mourns.

A chill
chasm of coldness is beating this heart

Where
once lover's warmth had ridden like dawn,

He
had celebrated
a mass, a libation,

Now
standing stunned in torn vestments

Night
has enfolded
his soul, the sacrificial

Rite
of Winter frost
has frozen his tears into rivers of ice.

Completely Fragmented:

Lines on the loss of love.
The poet had gazed into a sky of lime green clouds carved in crystal,
his mind Embraced a sun of white linen,
but her Sun sunk and spiralled before him into a World without those who love to roam the lunarscape,
there poets fix into dream, that stratosphere is where the fallen angels who touch mind
And body perform their undying ballet of love and lamentation.

The poet's moistened eyes can see only her drama of pain,
He genuflects before her bejewelled chalice,
but its wine has seeped into luminous gutters, here the drunken poets tumble.

Metamorphosed.

A crown of thorns is encircled by a ring of rose petals,
Its rays are piercing his eyes of confusion, she sits still
And listens to the foaming breath which winds around Her head like a black serpent, it is contracting, she is suffocating but pulls at the coils of this twisting snake and begins to heave and then breathes again, he pulls at the cord and drags it down around his waist in silence,
He's waiting until the black-backed beetles have scuttled Across their dappled floor, she now begins her chant, a Dirge to gods of dust and lace good-byes, an exorcism of Insects, she is metamorphosing and flies out of a window.

Narcissi and Red Roses.

Gusts of wind are howling around this white cube, our bare room;
I pluck the veils of silver cobwebs from these shrouded, stinging an
d bloodshot eyes, a globe of green satin is rolling around the floor in a mist of purple, at its burning core is a priestess of Aphrodite,
one of those who serve the cult of love on Lesbos, t

the isle where Sappho sings her spells.

She begins to celebrate mass, I genuflect before her altar of withered narcissi, an aroma of sandalwood is weaving like dust blown across a calm sea, this scent intoxicates our senses, my supplicant's hands are cupped in the form of a chalice before her, she is peeling the petals from a red rose, they flutter gently into a porcelain cup, it shatters into jagged fragments.

Our Lady of Sorrows in Notting Hill Gate (1973).
That green-scaled goddess of grief how she is wailing from her brown soil grave,
it is here that those recently resurrected Dead Exchange their laughter without lament, but you, who are skeletal With yellow skin pulled tight in a smile of delight, you, a beatified Courtesan who roams these connected and tuned-in grids, a heart Wrapped in the sackcloth which is worn by an incipient lover of Chaos, here a frozen embryo begins to pulsate, it breaths and stings The bitter pulp of that apple bitten in the Garden of Pleasure, ice folds Into our eyes until lost we're born into this spectrum of zoned silence, I embrace you, you are took the crucifixion from my yes we weep.
.

Oedipus is expelled from Eden.
Her tears of crystal are an unbound metaphor dripping from those silent Pools of his mother's ocean of eyes, Oedipus glances away, blinded with Pain, picks up a Syringe and finds his mainline to a tranquillity of night. In These depths there is a shadow dance of desire and Oedipus is tied to the mast for this voyage into a zero, Sirens, lovers, mothers and the Madonna are the poetry,
Their nectar is sweet to taste, his tongue touches moist Petals and caresses with the relish of finite whispering.

But the Inquisitor gazes down spewing us from an Eden, we were beatified with a band of light around our heads, but a bond of thorns is formed which pierces both mother and son, so now roam an interminable lunar wasteland.

Completely Fragmented:

Hymn to the Mortality of the Nazarene.

The Void beckons like graves welcome the dead, she
weaves barbed Threads of wire, dark mystery, to coronate
the poet who paces forward to glance into an infinity of
broken glass, her eyes of smiles
In circles of black staring from a bed of rippling folds, here
she washes the blood from sheets, these stains Are bled in
a cycle of betrayal and love, sunset and Sunrise, he wipes
the tears of mortality from his eyes and steps to look beyond
the edge, a taunting precipice, He howls 'Father, Abba, why
did you leave my corpse to Hang among unclean men and
these anemic women?' 'Mother, why wasn't it your blood
which mingled with the Blood flowing from my wounds in
hands, feet and side? You blessed the wisdom of fools, that
myopia of deserts',
This infant, the Lamb, is a man tuned into those pulsations
Of Alpha,
He leaps into the Void to dance with the damned.

Psalm to the poetry of joy.

The moon rises like mist distilled from a burnt river to whirl
with her humming until the bonds unravel, now she is
caressing her smile into radiant morning, her dust is
lingering it sprinkles onto dormant souls of night awaking our
song of love to a golden dawn, the poet's pen is dipping into
this chalice of nectar, we wander across pages with infinity
and innocence a dance with the light and shadows of sacred
ritual, Psalm of joy to a pristine
        moon and the drowsy sun.

She is the bridge across the river of Death.

A vulture sweeps on hidden currents seeking carrion. We cuddled death and squeezed it
out of a rock; the vibes began gliding around a hill of lush green grass overshadowed by
A Gold Phallus,
The phallus ejaculated the words of the dull with a force that shot them high into the
sky where glazed eyes are blind, drilled them into the side of the head where dilated
pupils are gobbling madness into their depths and then a pink fish gulped their dirge.

Flying beyond the cruel clasp of fire and reaching the icy shady spheres where there
was a river of sparkling glass which was fluid and flowed fast, a woman clothed with black robes approached, her face was deathly pale and her eyes dark and sad, she said: 'take my hand', we floated on and skimmed across the surface of the river that sparks,
her whisper is melody: 'this is your end, dissolve atom by atom in my tunnel of night'.

(a journey into the subconscious of the poet.)

Those eyes of a mistress at dawn cloaked in silence, staring into the hollow vision of his sight like night, the poet, ancient like crazed Oedipus cast in marble, burn with those licking flames melting these colour,

Sucked into this still lake of mirrors, wind blows the butterflies in this star gazed flight, now we are ebbing

into tactile darkness soothed by dusty lunar wandering.

This mirror is shattered by the incessant beating with hail, Frost clad poetry swallows glass, we're stumbling Adams.

Dreaming of the Muse.

On Poetry
sweetest tears are wept,
Caressing the shadows of silence this Muse is ancient as Electra;

She whispers breath onto a tissue psyche,
Which vibrates like a web of gossamer:

Dream with shifting sands like a vortex of voids.

Doves with broken wings who fly from a cage,
Scribe those poems of Night which ache with love's sorrow.

Prometheus lives just outside of Babylon.

Babylon dreamer,
in her

groover drowsy
bound silken

baby demon

Prometheus

lemon

echo
fixing with

robe.

The writing of verse with night.

The poet of night's desert begins to scribe
like waves into an ocean whose mist is without dawn,

Drifting across these fields with wonder,
like the touch into swaying seas of corn and sun,
 sigh with the lovers

Like oceans, their caress is dripping like wax and breath
onto paper flowers, s
swirling into an endless spiral of clouds.

Moonshine weeps into this ocean of nothingness, the dust is
like a masquerade which is dissolving into white and zero,

Their masks melt, softening into visions like the oblivion with
eyes shining, shadows like insomnia with dreaming.

Spring's dancers wander across the virgin page with its
sighing, this is a word beginning to form into a wave, a
whisper of sand,

The cloaked pen weaves into this morning shimmer of
cobwebs in which the Muse hangs suspended like eternity
caught in ivy.

Poem without a title.
No existence
without language no journeys
without those words to
Prepare self for
this trip in
imagination
 A
voyage deep below dive into
the Abyss that underworld
it is here that we write with our demons.

Completely Fragmented:

The Steppenwolf.

A wolf wanders the Steppes in a dance of solitude,
The deserts of snow stretch interminably, glistening
Expanses without a horizon, his eyes are burnt by rays
Of sun which burrow into a heart woven of silk, freedom is
the price Paid for his emancipation, this Escape into a
wasteland is Anonymous, tracks left Soon melt for he leaves
no mark, the only Mark is the one that cuts his heart and
from which there can be
no escape.

Two poets contemplate Salvador Dali: The Persistence of Memory.

Her mind is opening like a lotus flower stung

By a spear of steel,
her breath drifts in lemon

Globules, pupils are fixed on the door which is woven

From willow branches, he opens an aperture to discover

A zone which interacts
with her black eyes, leaden

By the mist of lunar storms, they embrace, bodies are like

Cotton pages blown across a sea covered in silver scales,
until wrapped

In a ball of silk, they exhale rhythmically
with the pulse of the Earth, the clock faces have melted.

To Oblivion.

That mistress with melancholia is sitting like a consumed Buddha
in my prison cell,

Holy tears are wept dry here descending into a fathomless verse,
Feel the breath

but never the caress of her soul,
Intimate with the finite of vacuums whispered like night.

The Inquisitor pierces this haven
with voids melting our eyes

of glass which are pristine with weeping, footprints in the sand are swept away in waves of oblivion like spirals of hollow.

To Art.

The Void, its cloud has rain, a spring to quench our sight, to damn and pierce the pain,
        But art is fire in flight.
Lines written in melancholy.

Sweetest death
you are the goddess of summer nectar,
The honey for the poet to drown in unconsciousness, verse is prostrated before you, both in mind and body: Holy One, Holy Oblivion, Holy Death.

We, the children of the soul's catacombs scribe our ink onto virgin paper,
The white page glances shyly, trembles a little, anticipating the pen,

Completely Fragmented:

A nib begins to weave tapestries of willow meaning,
these are cloaked in the shrouds of images floating along a stream,

we are wandering through this labyrinth of poetry.

Dylan and Caitlin Thomas drink themselves into oblivion.

Let us dance with our dream of death,
Grasp tightly together, tumble in tunnels,
Chanting to nil, to cloaked zero, to chaos,
Until freed from this frenzy of whirling fire
We're stroked into sleep, a slumber of solitude.

Introduction to Experimental Poems No 1-6.

Poetry, 'stream of consciousness' writing and 'Beat' culture spontaneity.

This introduction examines the historical and theoretical context in which these Experimental Poems: No 1-6 were written.
A method of writing which was developed with Freud's theory of the unconscious became known as 'stream of consciousness.' It was an attempt to penetrate the great subterranean ocean of the unconscious. This writing was characterized by an inner monologue which was:
The direct introduction into the interior life of the character. - Edouard Dujardin.
Hence the reader would, by a free flow of language, gain access to the unconscious world. James Joyce and Virginia Woolf are examples of 20th century writers who combined 'stream of consciousness' techniques with realism. They wove complex patterns of language which were inspired, to a considerable extent, by Freud's discoveries regarding the nature of the psyche. The relationship between ego and id was of interest to those who would explore the mind for the raw material of literature.

Like all 'stream of consciousness' writing, these poems are an attempt to 'tune in' to twilight areas of awareness which are inaccessible through conventional forms and, therefore, to illuminate the id, the unconscious.

In an essay written by Allen Ginsberg, a 'Beat' poet entitled: 'Abstraction in Poetry' (1959) he suggests that the poet:
Reduces the artistic medium to its essential properties.
~ Allen Ginsberg.

This could, he argued, be the poetry of 'pure sound' (Ginsberg) like some of the Dadaist poets. However, for Ginsberg, writers such as William S. Burroughs created an abstraction not merely of 'pure sound' but, also, with the energy of an 'altered state of awareness', the vibrant condition of 'pure mind' (Ginsberg). Their work exhibited the negation of a consciousness which is enslaved to the perceptions of the ego:

The sensation of self-elimination of all being into the unconscious is the experience of pure poetry.
~Allen Ginsberg.

In his 1959 essay, mentioned above, Ginsberg describes William Burroughs' writing as:

A noncommittal transcript into words of a succession of visual images passing in front of his mental eye.
~ Allen Ginsberg.

However, the most significant aspect of writing, for the 'Beat' authors, was not their opiate induced dreaming, but the technique of spontaneous expression which was inspired by listening to improvised jazz:
To sketch the flow that already exists intact in the mind.
~ Jack Kerouac (Ginsberg, 1959)

So, in conclusion, these poems are an attempt to transcend ego awareness and swim in a sea of unconsciousness by employing the techniques of experimental poetry to open the doors of perception.

Experimental poem: number 1.

Caressed
the echo of a void embraces' reverberation,

Ache
descends in a river breaking the clasp of mind.

We are engulfed in this swimming of the id being tuned for a birthing of primal mother, She wept with the stroking of acid droplets those have been caught in a leaking chalice.

These eyes are dissolved with a flickering of colours that is a still pool in the twilight.

Experimental poem: number 2.

Poetry
lives in a crystal teardrop,

It
is here that worms burrow

Spewing
like the earth retching lava,

Clasped
by the mind manacles slicing

the body into daylight and the darkness, night is whispering with her misty breath.

Experimental poem: number 3.

Sand just flows
through a honeycomb mind,

Ideas
are blown
across an iridescent wasteland

dissolving into an ocean of beats, we throb, a pulse with this blood

wept
in eyes
cried for wandering poetry,

Descend into swarms
of crawling echoes

like the dissonant rhythm of chaos.

Experimental poem: number 4.

Tied
to a stake,
this ravishing of fire

caresses
the free thought
of the shrouded solitary mind,

Heretics
burn in their emancipation, the purity of our conflagration

Caresses
the cruel laughter
of a celebrant who is mocking

us, we sing in the finitude of our damnation, visionaries, we are incarcerated in the flames.

Experimental poem: number 5.

White light
licks into an abyss
with the touch of totality,

the
tongue draws a kiss murmuring with redolence,

this is eternity with whispered dew, begin our sobbing like a
dried lake, the butterfly is caught in morning flight

wrapped in a veil, his temple of mediocrity, she is beginning
to scribe oceans of lemon, here night and its burning tears
are coaxed

into humming, the drowsiness is like twilight.

Experimental poem: number 6.

The lunar chasm of verse
free with association,

ivy acid
dissolving the page into running plagues of

caged rats,
wire trap-door is opening onto the desert

as masks are cast in rivers of clay,
the smile of a bemused mystic at night,
she is writing with those caustic tears of fire

to be entranced in the cloudy liquid of dreams, spike is
eased into the mainline as infinity beckons.

She said: 'love is not enough'.

Stole
a ticket
to her theatre

Danced with this
ballerina of hurricanes.

Dropped words into
her bronze head

That
sparked, enflamed and revolutionized

Her
nails dug into taut skin

Leaving rivulets of
tingling red liquid

Which flowed into
my bamboo pen.

I
wrote lines
of love welcoming

Her
lunar landscape, Here we wandered

Completely Fragmented:

With
Molotov cocktails primed and ready

For
encounters with fascists or renegades.

But she became a reactionary, interrogating consciousness,
examining my arms like a drug-squad officer.

She said: 'You've got a needle-mark...a needle-mark from last night.'
I replied: 'That was the only opportunity to visit my friends, the only chance to get away from your tight tangle. Yes, there is a needle-mark, we shoot bliss it's called white light white heat.'

So, lost in
wastelands of ice.

Here
is where
poets and artists

Freeze
their colours into brittle webs

Of

nerves and
then sever them.

The tragedy
is acted out

we are tossed away on howls of orange wind into a welcome green trance.

'Mainlining' whilst meditating on a broken icon

Solitary
the moon is weeping crystal,
Welcoming
grey clouds which are a caress

For her eyes
glazed like glass spheres,
The dialogue is with silk veils
like the nothingness which beckons death

into twilight, we are tossed into whirls of dust.

He rolls up a shirtsleeve
the needle marks are like stigmata,
Brown and purple bruises that glare
as shadows weep across the terrain of whispers.

Glancing heavenwards
our light is dancing into the voids of night,
Silhouettes are roaming around this room, the Word
is suspended on a cross of wood, emaciated bodies are
sacrificed to this fire which is never to be quenched by the
dew?

Lines on William Burroughs' concept of 'death-in-life'.

Square hearts had
stopped, they were

Just
rusty bilge
pumps, someone turned

Completely Fragmented:

The switch off,
what a turn-on

Never dug that
scene with America

And
atom bombs, chant with those

Of
us who
have a different
 sound

and

song

to the hooded-snake death dirge, breathe an autumn
wind
 pure

of
purgation,

howl
cathartic
baby   burnout buzz   madness.

He had placed enigma in caps.
opened that cap, cooked it, fixed it, again, again, hazy.
DECONDITIONED HIMSELF FROM
STATE SUBLIMNIAL MIND MANIPULATION,
He had the sweet-death golden flight of Icarus, also the
endless labour of Sisyphus.

Illusion, allusion and delusion.

Crimson crystals are burning

pulsating
embers
gobbling

Inferno,

is this a solitary illusion like blood?

or an academic allusion to a sanitized

stained

sacred
Sacrament

Dante,

Although this may not scold your flesh

mistaken
because

At your peril purgatory will not cleanse

forget us

Damned

you, Hell
is where
we weep wild like galloping horses, just snorting this chaos,
the delusion is that heaven existed, no haven or home for
us.

Speaking of viral poetry...

Language is a virus from outer space...The author is simply a node on a network, through which ideas pass.
- William Burroughs, The Ticket that Exploded, 1962

That fatigue can no longer frighten us like the ice sheets in the mind, it is beyond any vestige or manifestation of fear as glaring of sun drills eyes.
the black petals begin to fold inwards
when a gaze is or isn't fixed, tangles of twisted thorns of a tight thistle bush are forests of emptiness, viral poetry is written and formed into lakes of ice, from ice is refined the pure crystals that are polished into those old cold stars, they had imploded long ago creating the gulping black holes, babies' mouths who drink from a black nipple which oozes dark milk, its ancient not nectar, it is the ingestion of the 'Other', us as dark subject, objectification is unmade.

Promenaded people you wake up and don't think black holes are empty, scabby fingers are grasping the bourgeois hand and it shivers with revulsion, grey suited exorcists wail 'demon get out', but we existed for eons before Eden or logos; our word is an infectious virus. For you are totally helpless, we have convinced your best philosophers since Epicurus and inspired the poet Sappho, then lit the fuse around October 1917.
We are the Virus made word, made material in your universe, we are cellular.

Some variations on a theme of unrequited love inspired by reading William Carlos Williams.

a).
In autumn
wind blew golden leaves like her sorrow.

b).
Have drowned

in her lunar silhouette
to wander in our shadow.

Lines on Brigitte M:

(a leading member of the Socialist Patients' Collective)

A chill and steel grimace glares and stares from the
tarnished goblet from which she

Substitutions are easy in class struggle, she didn't substitute
emotions with zeros

Replace the proletariat with a vanguard? but never replace
authenticity with shit

Kill a revolutionist with a gun or tablets but they will rise like
your fear of death.

From this cup with Brigitte M, not china tea-services of the
oppressor; she smiled

That red wine of love, it intoxicated her with a fantastic
desire to destroy Daddy in all his manifestations.

She was an incarnation, a realization and beatification of
insurrection, her gun fired
lemon butterflies
of love.

Completely Fragmented:

Summer of love, 1967.
(a villanelle).

Time melts; we thawed a frosty reality to dissolve ice with our love,
Our eyes whose dilated pupils could swallow any hardened gaze,
 (You fell across this hallucinogenic Cosmos, these stars tumble).

We crucified the betrayal of damned love and stared to humble
That dark spark, we conceived this just like evaporating into haze,
Time melts; we thawed a frosty reality to dissolve ice with our love,

I touched with delicate fingers the clasp on your eyes to unbuckle
A stream, the purple fragrance of humming, a goddess was ablaze,
(You fell across this hallucinogenic Cosmos, these stars tumble).

You crumpled into a sphere of sighs encircled by white light, a dove Whose wings were caressed as we dived into the sun in a daze,
Time melts; we thawed a frosty reality to dissolve ice with our love.

Our song was vibrating into weeping trees, nectar dripping,
 suckle Each other's ancient milk which is a sacred libation with soft praise,
(You fell across this hallucinogenic Cosmos, these stars tumble).

Tangerine gasp intertwines in a frenzy of breath, it falls from above,
Then we lie exhausted in a grave, our bodies consumed, but raised.

Time melts; we thawed a frosty reality to dissolve ice with our love,
 (You fell across this hallucinogenic Cosmos, these stars tumble).

A creation myth of Purusha in the Satapatha Brahmana (c.800BC)

Our minds may try and cancel, attempt to blank, this switch was flicked 800 B.C.,
 he had over 1,000 eyes And heads, Purusha was total visual, complete sight, absolute cognition: dived into night without oblivion.

But a core of zero he only became a number through introspection, digging that nothingness until he floats Around a crown of Lotus flowers, here he discovered the warmth and softness which is Yoni, he luxuriated
'I am.'

But like poets at dawn without a pen and paper he had only desire, he tore himself with pure golden energy to Create 'Other', lover, she became a daughter,# they were black and white flaming water and running fire: joined.

This act created you and you and me, so says this myth. ashamed she ran like a gazelle fleeing a lion, he would Become a gazelle, again and again he deceived her until they had produced each and every animal on this Earth.

Your eyes are shining.
(a prose-poem)

Those eyes shine with emerald green in our trip again, it has the certainty with which a frost in winter will freeze a blade of grass and is sure as a decaying autumn leaf of gold is trampled under the boots of eternity. But, my goddess of the lunar wailing, your perfume intoxicates the psyche of this poet as he is falling into a labyrinth of dreams. Here shadows are like obscured glass splinters which pierce the

mind, we are cast into a fallibility of chained genes, they
hang like globules of honey draped on a derelict hive. It is
here we return step by step, through the honeycombs, past
the corpses of dead worker bees to the queen who nestles
her sterile eggs and beyond to the primordial swamp, there
our stunted fingers clutch each other in a grasp of love. Your
eyes are still as we come down again, so softly into our folds
of tissue.

She is the bridge across the river of Death.

A vulture sweeps on hidden currents seeking carrion.
We cuddled death and squeezed it out of a rock;
the vibes began gliding around a hill of lush green grass
overshadowed by
A Gold Phallus,
The phallus ejaculated the words of the dull with a force that
shot them high into the sky where glazed eyes are blind,
drilled them into the side of the head where dilated pupils
are gobbling madness into their depths and then a pink fish
gulped their dirge.

Flying beyond the cruel clasp of fire and reaching the icy
shady spheres where there was a river of sparkling glass
which was fluid and flowed fast, a woman clothed with black
robes approached, her face was deathly pale and her eyes
dark and sad, she said: 'take my hand', we floated on and
skimmed across the surface of the river that sparks,
her whisper is melody: 'this is your end, dissolve atom by
atom in my tunnel of night'.

A meditation on Andy Warhol's 'Factory'.

Many had entered this company of the joyful and mad
because they wrote and did speed enticed, they were
sucked into a dark-room, dragged in but
Spewed out when in pain; some fixed and wrote, others
painted after a hit,

There were those who wailed their ink or paint onto paper like orgasms of
A moon's second rising: some were green-eyed with their claws extended
Scratching each other in the desert and simultaneously drunk from an oasis.

Their profane families of distrust were crucified and sacrificed, coffined permitting poets to descend from their cross without that burnt stigmata.

Some wandered and wised their way out, went to labyrinths of communes as hashish somnambulists, but alert they kept a pen and paper within reach.

The barbiturate bard taught to fumble, stumble and mumble proclaims:
'I can recall and write about the verse they wrote in his Methedrine Ark'.

An incarnation of Sappho and her friend accidentally OD.

Some spit with spite and call it love, but not us,
 Not in a temple of Aphrodite, here Sappho tends,
 A flame which brushes her lips, they are burning
 And red…now purple as the heroin hits hard like
A hammer thumping its heat up the arm into
Galaxy of welcoming brain cells,
the hypodermic Hangs limp from her arm,
 I gently draw the spike
Out of the bruised vein, her arm flops diagonally
 Across an orange cotton shirt, I clean the syringe
By rhythmically flushing water in and out and
Finally squirt the crimson juice into blue china Bowl next prepare my hit,
 we uncurl in a temple
 Of Aphrodite which is where lovers can purr softly,
The floor opens like a gaping mouth and swallows.

Completely Fragmented:

A man became an egg;
(surrealist poem).

There was a spectral man who hid in a physical frame,
he roamed like a grounded vulture across anonymous plains
of concrete, there is no harvest of golden corn or pleasant
deer too inspire the poet here, only the arched
acridness of the hard, the junkies huddled in alleyways
wailing with junk sickness: once a thin and translucent
membrane formed herself around the man and he just
touched it tingling rebirth, she shyly encrusted herself
but
egg
shells
are
thin,
 egg boxes

never are quite right like papier-mâché disintegrating
in the rain, the shell shattered and she madly distorted
herself and became his yoke: both essence and burden.

An artist with eyes like black oceans painted the egg in
beautiful gold, blue and bright crimson: he ate the egg, yoke
flowed out dark as bitter blood into the pen of the poet who
writes as a serpent who has just been uncoiled.

The ice-box.
This is a box within a box, a world within a world, a house
which is typical of many found within suburbia. It is brown
bricked, anonymous and almost transmits hymns of praise to
some tarnished copper god of mediocrity. In the kitchen of
this house stands a fridge, it looks white and prosaic. Open
the fridge door and at the top on the right is a sky-blue ice-
box, it has three white stars to confirm the adequacy of its
freezing capacity. Inside the ice-box is a rectangular tray
which is divided into squares, each can be filled with water
and then frozen to produce the perfect ice-cube. This can
then be dropped into a frosted pink glass which wraps
around it, add fruit juice and there is the perfect chilled drink.

Nigel Pearce

A son frequently opens the fridge door and pulls down the sky-blue ice-box flap and peeps inside. He examines the frosted walls which, paradoxically, burn his fingers; they are almost burnt with the coldness. It is in this world of ice-cubes that he discovers another dimension which exists separately from, but is intrinsically attached, to the ebb and flow of everyday life. The son's mother had died some years ago and he had been left the house, he did not sell it because there wasn't anywhere else to go. The son had an unusual relationship with the ice-cubes in the fridge finding great comfort in popping two out from the tray and holding them in his hands until they were numb, and the ice-cubes dissolved into water. The living-room of this box within a box was bare, no carpet, no furnishings or pictures. However, glaring at him was a gas fire. It had short brown steel legs with one at each end to support it. A copper pipe stuck up through the floor boards and was connected to the fire. The fire itself was coloured in two tones of brown, light brown at the bottom and around the sides of the gas jets and above was dark brown. The shelf which was on top of the whole apparatus and rested against the wall had white plastic knobs at each end, one is to turn on and ignite the gas and the other is to control the flow of gas to regulate the temperature. This fire concerned the son greatly, it almost dominated him. He didn't like the hissing of the gas or the flickering flames and the brief smell of gas at ignition caused him much anxiety. He felt little or no choice but to constantly check and check again that the gas was burning correctly and there was no leak. With the certainty of the tides his life became enslaved to this gas fire. The only respite was allowing the ice-cubes to melt in his hands. Just as the season's motion is inevitable the gas fire developed a leak. Fortunately, the son was elsewhere when the explosion tore through the house destroying it and its anonymity. It no longer looked like all the other houses in the cul-de-sac. The fridge was badly damaged and thought to no longer fulfil any useful task; it was taken to the local tip. The ice-cubes turned into water, but a more profound metamorphosis took place: a voice said:
'My son, there is no longer any need to worry.'
The water had leaked from the ice-box and out of the fridge into the rubbish of the tip in which it germinated a seed

planted at the beginning of Time. The shoot will push its way up through the waste and bloom next spring, a snow-drop.

Psychiatric nurse try reading some Dostoevsky.
The psychiatric nurse wears a smile of roses,
But when he opens his mouth only the thorns Show,
They rip into us as mercury is rising up the Thermometer,
but we are like Mercury, we are
The messengers of words, of communication
Between mortality and the void, our emotional
Temperature is wrong, our perceptions are askew,
So chant the nurses as they prostrate themselves
Before an idol 'THE SELF' in its glory and feel one
Of the few, a mental health professional, we break the
Shackles on the nurse's ego and drag them from their
Shallows of grey bourgeois murk, then of course they
React and start behaving like enflamed flamingos,
Moments of insight here, incisive understanding there,
then in wonder a diagnosis:
nurse read Dostoevsky
And step into the weird world of us underground people.

n Anne Sexton and her fellow confessional poets.
(a Shakespearian sonnet).

Her hands began to write a page with dew,
Those hearts had shed the haunts and bonds of light,
She turned and smiled to cast a spell, this guru
So tense until her pen began to write
A verse of storms, angels of night that share
Her seas of lavender wept waves of wonder,
The sun had raised so red to kiss her hair,
She sat quite still and breathed like Buddha
Her wine could sweeten bitter potions
But doctors, priests of modernity,
Were glaring flames, her poems were emotions
They tossed to Hell with shocks of electricity,
This burnt into these hearts of love, the mind
Was numbed by barbiturate and lay blind.

Dreaming of Morpheus and William Burroughs.
(a Petrarchan sonnet.)

We groove along furrows to cut the wet pavement,
 This street reflects an inner web, this glassy maze,
 The path to oblivion, it melts like an echo of praise,
The temple begins to sing with awaking ferment,
 The dream-powder, its magic is like night's scent,
A garden of delight where sight and tears are glazed,
You spike the mainline again; this is not so crazed,
The cobweb is caught like a dream's finite content.
But Morpheus is a cruel god, in darkness confess
His bonds, we know his mellow, like a nocturne
We were naked, our mind's flow to be dissolved,
A cloud whose rain which beats us nails, Venus
Always burns away my colours in eyes not taciturn,
What remains, the riddles of thought, never told?

A poet is sedated in a mental ward whilst contemplating death.

Embrace lunar death
of the most Holy beatitude,
You're swirling
with particles of dust

in winds,
Darkness has sung
without light again like pacing seasons,
This lamb
is sacrificed on an alter

draped with staring eyes,
A chant of hollowness rises
from the pulsating mass of communicants,
Their empty eye sockets
where love has been condemned

Completely Fragmented:

By supplication,
they genuflect and weep with tears of ice
as the poet is prostrated and given an injection of chlorpromazine.

Lines in praise of Sappho

Your heart is aflame like beauty; with these flowers you garland sacred Helen,
 Drifting with your bodies and stroking a sultry air of love flowing between senses,
Your imaginations of flowers wander in groves with humming Aphrodite of tears,
Your voices are sweet as flutes at dawn the music wrapping your beloved's body
In her white linen robes of purity and desire, on Lesbos the Muses sang with joy,
To wake a verse of bliss and lyres do play, but night still wails the song of Rhea.

Then Eros had glanced at them and gasped,
I genuflected dumb before a 'straight' muse who fragmented, some only do 'falling apart'.

A psychiatric nurse gets writer's block.

The nurse tightens as his bow bends back to shoot arrows of poetry into folds of sky,

That vampire is sucking inspiration from us patients, he falsely claims the tradition

Of Dionysus as he roams the ward, a giant glaring into our dormitory, we have hidden

Our words and pens in the secret place, here

We also store stocks of medication, kept just

In case of emergency, the tablet is stealthily licked under the tongue, retrieved and then

Hidden in a crack behind my bed, the nurse's bow has snapped, and his arrows fall upon us.

H

H is for Hell,
H is for Heroin, H is for Heaven, H is for Helpless,
H is for Hopeless, H is for Homeless,

Should have been aborted and lived in the safety of a bell jar.

S is for Schizophrenia, S is for Solitude, S is for Suicide.

Fled fragrant suffocation in Eden for the bitter taste of brown sugar.

Completely Fragmented:

A priest realizes God is dead and mourns.
A chill

chasm of coldness is beating this heart

Where
once lover's warmth had ridden like dawn,

He
had celebrated
a mass, a libation,

Now
standing stunned in torn vestments

Night
has enfolded
his soul, the sacrificial

Rite
of Winter frost

has frozen his tears into rivers of rivers.

A poem for William Burroughs.
I saw the best minds of my generation destroyed by
madness, starving hysterical naked, dragging themselves
through the streets at dawn looking for a fix.
- Allen Ginsberg, Howl, 1956.

Staring streets reflect
the voids in your eyes
which are mirrors of the squares,
they exist without
the pricking needle easing
chaos,

you found the mainline again,
an embrace like an orgasm burning through a vein,
Zen without the hassle,
this Light strikes those chemical cells calling calmly
to the soul like the whispered welcome of nothingness,

The Absurdity is not in these
oceans where weeping tranquillity tumbles into dreams
for you were dancing into the masquerades of non-being.
High womb-like peace, sleep, wake, write, weep, fix again,

is this a critique on the art of the bourgeoisie,
or the only form for a poetry for the oppressed? No!

Laboratory Experiment No 2.

Red tentacles are gripping the wasted wail of a seething brain which writhes in
delirium with C 10 H 15 rush, white light; the formula for methamphetamine
Eyes hang loose attached only by yellow threads to grey sockets, they melted
milliseconds ago and now are dripping, dropping
by diamond drop into a culture dish, the doctor makes a smear, places the slide
beneath the lens of a microscope and peers in, a child yells into her eyes,
she jumps back too late as the laboratory rotates into concentric circles,
 it has become a phantasmagoria
It is the formula for methamphetamine (Methedrine).

Completely Fragmented:

For poets who lose their sanity because of unrequited love.

Love
had sweetened tongues
to caress in these dreams of bliss

Numbed, this night is
enclosed in a cell, the shadows of desired

Emptiness
gaze from the melancholy in her eyes,
the poet is cursed by his plague of blindness.

An itinerant poet and a lover celebrate Mass.
A shimmering of shadows is pulsating from his crown of lemon light
This has encircled with rays the waves of matted hair, slowly this exorcism
Of disbelief begins, he is stroking the gold bond of slavery from her finger,
A breeze is caressing the sands from a forlorn temple into the tints of mortality,
An electric shock shoots
Through their grid, he bows before her mass of black forest,
 genuflects like Adam before Eve's temptation,
 they dissolve into ascensions of dazzled love,
she is smiling and elevates the Host before him, they feast.

Abel gets paranoid?
(a psychological study of Cain and Abel.)
Abel is trying to run but clinging dreams enfold His mind,
Then caught without motion and maimed by darts of fatigue,
He sinks and screams out: 'No stop please':
tumbling like a dice down a lime Mountain,
He has lost those bleating sheep,
Dazzled by eyes of glowing ruby which spit like drops of a
Bloody reverie, tears cling to his fingers like Swords Of
Yahweh,
Whimpers: 'Cain?', who replies 'cool man,
It's alright now I've killed Dad; we are free as the birds'.

Blood and Water: the most ancient sacraments.

In oceans the waves can look choppy and boats seem
tossed like flotsam,
Do dive deep down into the depths of seas and there lurks a
rushing current,
Which can suck a person into a zero, drive you into insanity
like a mob devours
its victim who like themselves is a wept victim, vicissitudes
cruel as the sea,
so here in these black blind bloody depths are flows that can
only be revealed
by the poet; but psychiatrists claim a similar trade.

Oedipus had loved his mother, this is the way of oceans,
but when she was like a branch and snapped like her sea
son, t
hen damnation roared. Oedipus was never freed, love
cannot ice,
and the sea chains are ancient like tears and fears:
tranquillity was new,
not deeply grooved and a pyre fanned by prayers of St
John of the Cross,
fire howled by wind

Completely Fragmented:

It burnt Oedipus, so he returned to the familiar sea of zero where he lives as
 A shy amphibian, there is no blood of Clytemnestra and Electra in this water.
Song to the oppressed: 'never trust men in suits'.

A howl encrusted with sores and dressed in the persuasive vestments of
An abomination slips from those contracting grins, that is the priest enrobed
In the cloak of an abortionist greets the pleated wail of another cocktail Party,
Another nightmare, so let them cruise in their seas of dollars and excrement,
Beware you anachronisms as the lava of the oppressed is beginning to bubble,
We say: 'No shit you pigs we're going to sweep away the dust from your theatre',
You entombed bourgeois whose ballet of cardboard replicas is step, step, stepping
To the toiling of a Death Bell, it is beginnings to ring in their ears and they wince with
Fear, our hammer, the mallet of History is striking their sculls only to reveal a vacuum,
 Never trust that pinstriped suit smile; it's obscured with clouds and in terminal decay.

The cobra and the poet.

The
cobra didn't wear a uniform,

It
slowly lifted
a swollen neck
which
was ripened

with venom, yellow

Eyes darted and
smiting tongue flickered,

Jaundiced
fangs impregnated
a trembling troubadour

With the poison of conformity, the poet felt nausea then
stung revulsion: He roams across urban Steppes and lives
with wolves to howl their words.

Hippie woman in a North London squat, 1973.

A chick
is sitting in silence
within the broken shell of

An egg,
her radiance ripples
around the room sinking into

Beds
Of rose petals, now
her gaze begins to penetrate the wall, white light is flickering
out of his hollow sockets of nil,

His
murmurings are staring,
but she moulds that lava surge

Completely Fragmented:

Into a
river and is deflecting
energy into a collapsing circle, wrapping her breath in lace

Caliban is reincarnated as a snake.
A cobra lay dazed and coiled, with glassy fang,
He injected waves of electrification in waxen veins,
This serpent was sliding in a ocean of disinfectant
Around suburbia with hooded amber eyes that glow,
He hangs without the chains of slavery which burden,
That place is poisoned by toxicity of blown innocence.

We left the funeral in boxes,
could only free ourselves from the cemetery of echo by
escape

to LSD psychosis
to amphetamine dependency to heroin addiction
to organize the proletariat
to advocate the armed struggle
to celebrate the sacraments of schizophrenia.

Untitled.
Poets wonder at love that blows like ribbons into infinity,
But write in cauldrons where the pure of Hades are floating
Let us dissolve demons with poetry.
    (lines for poets trapped in a ferment of the Inferno).
They pierced icy thorn and said it was a crown of thorns,
No love, then write about it,
Blisters of fatigue burn minds with their claw of phosphorus,
 No love, then fright about it,
Comrades have been driven like cattle stumbling into an
abattoir,
No love, then fight about it,
Counter-culture dreams drifted into deep and dark well of
Narcissus,
No love, then cry about it,
Cannot adore because serpent had spat into sad eyes and
blinded,
No love, then die about it.

Let us dissolve the mocking demons WITH OUR POETRY NOW.

The spirit of Ulrike Meinhoff addresses the bourgeoisie in 2009.
Ulrike Meinhoff 1934-1976.

I am, I will be,
Our waves will wash away the sand into a sea,
Bourgeois fuckers your system is screwed
Ripped off the poor and the tenants,
A hot and dry summer will scorch with fire and now burn baby burn.

Think you are stable...no just sinking into an ocean of Narcissism which is not pretty,
You never learn bourgeois
 Now your houses are being repossessed and the mind Twangs:
Those robbed of their dreams awake you shake In your shoes as the ghettos buzz,
Start to tremble...you Have failed and now the revolutionary Nemesis waits.

The Angry Brigade is aware, and alert and the Red Army Faction has not forgotten, Socialist Patients' Collective flexes their minds and their trigger-fingers;
Do not think the Red Brigades are all banged-up inside.

Our waves will wash away the sand into a sea
Bourgeois fucker your system is screwed,
Ripped off the poor and the tenants
A hot and dry summer will scorch with fire and now burn baby burn.

Completely Fragmented:

Storm and Desert.

The fiery worms which burrowed into my mind,
Are like the maggots which are eating the soul,
Now they have died, drowned in a dark ocean,
Which raged until evaporated by the biting sun?
That tempest has lulled and my thirst has abated.

MIND CLOCK.

Integrating like the hands of a clock,
Pointing to the misty time of no hours,
Which passes its breath in the silence?
Slowly returning to the house of a self,
Here are shifting sands, a wilderness,
And the clock has melted with a heat,
Forget to tock in time with their Rhyme.

Morphine Love.

A morphine angel stroked my mind,
As a mother rocks her child to sleep,
And a lover touched the soft breast,
Like dew on the grass in mornings,
No chaos, just the gentlest whisper,
 Love between sheets of dark death.

Heroin.

I shot a dream up my aching arms,
 In a haze of mind just lost in a skull,
Calling names from my quivering lips,
 Pastel shades soothed weeping eyes,
Heaven strolls like floating lilac lilies,

In that caressed pool of emptiness,
Forgetting the anguish of our hunger,
 Go those thunderclaps in our minds,
We were at peace a dewy humming.

It is alright babe.

The needle pieces that loving vein,
 Like Love smoothing a lover's hair,
 The white-heat rushes up our arm,
Into welcoming minds like sunrise.

Cruising with sleep forgotten eyes,
 I watched 'the Man' as he grinned,
He had shaken-up into the kitchen,
Nobody else has clocked his move,
I just rise and stumble gaining focus,
 Walk with amphetamine confidence,
 A crookery-high piled shooting room,
 Gently approach and smiling, saying,
 'It's alright babe, give me that knife,
I have Valium in my pocket so relax,
 Swallow four of them with water, relax.'

I groove back into to the music room,
He finds my lost vein and another hit,
Tears have burnt farrows into my face,
It was alright babe, because of Valium.

SHE.

Woman is the manna on the breeze,
Woman is the wind that plays chimes,
The hands that play and stroke a harp,
They welcome like warmth, shy, sharp,
Respond with moonbeams on the lips,
The memories conjoined never separate,
She is the stream entering green oceans.

She mutilates the Temple of Her Body.

My body has become a twisted shrine,
Is a tube of paste that is oozing slime?
It must be cut to allow the pus to flow,
The knife straight blade purges wrath,
This is incense to be inhaled by them,
Intoxicate them like a cyanide pellet,
She, the ultimate soliloquist departs.

A warm woman and a cold girl.

Grooving along a cold pavement,
Taking poems to a warm woman,
Cold girl just leers across a street,
With her harsh stems of corn hair,
Her eyes are dead, she is an advert,
Those ruby lips, mouth something,
A shallowness of mass magazines,
Not like a flowing river-fire woman,
Who reads and writes lunar poetry.

Today.

The poets languish in the mental hospitals,
The criminals are running the government,
The poor live in concrete boxes or streets,
Mind-control priests celebrating the Mass,

We weep from bruised, blackened red eyes.

Before the Incense was lit.

Before they lit their choking Incense,

He was

Dammed before the beginning of Time,
Fated to shed tears like autumn leaves,
Cursed to be blown by the hurricane,
Doomed to be drenched in raged rain,
Blighted at birth to be a series of selves.

A temple has been desecrated by fools,
Even before incense was burning scent,
At the Farwell, let there be no lamentation.

Sleeplessness.

Walking through these cold nights of bitter sleeplessness,
My being slid down the dust pipe, a Way of Nothingness,
Images become distorted in a mirror of caustic Absurdity,
These are both within and without no escape they shout.

Will any kind of peace, wipe my clay body, feverish brow?
Will the whisky-bottle or the syringe be a cloth of comfort,
Just to hush, hush this chaos that burns like hell in mind,
 And dissolve the soul to stop the cancer eating my body.

This barrenness of spirit with the potency of emotions,
 They cut like a missed arrow of love pierces the heart,
Lead to a desired death or a wilted bed of rose petals.

Completely Fragmented:

No walls, no floor.

There were no walls of haven in a family,
 And certainly, there was no heaven ceiling,
  No solid earth floor to stand upon or walk,
  It was sub-terrain world of misty shadow,
It would with certainty of sunset explode,
 A fiendish and hellish land of like Inferno,
Where all were tormented by their demons,
A family where no family ever could coexist,
I was born no self, a Tabula rasa smashed.

On the Scene.

Look whose back on the Scene man,
Lay some dope on him, be cool man,
A little acid tunes him to the frequency,
Give some speed to wake-up a brain,
Do-him-up with smack to get a habit,
Look whose back on the Scene man,
O.D. Off the scene is blue he is dead.

Inside my Skull.

Within the cave of one mind,
The skull of Dante's disciple,
Roam two evil men, who shout,
They both accuse me of devilry,
One contorted group therapist,
One a policeman with a baton,
They are stones within a soul,
They are beyond an exorcism.

Angie Baby.

She has worn a blue wool dress besmirched with coffee stains. Buttressed against the cold and the World with jumpers and a belief in witchcraft. She hummed with delight and rose-coloured blushes when her breasts were caressed with holy lips of a prophet, Her heaven roamed across her flesh as his tongue darted and teeth nipped. Only to drown in a sea of esoteric sighs. I loved her with my soul, relished her body if not the mind, I had lost mine. We twinkled across the fields in the moonlight. Until consumed we lay and slept in reveries. The police found a poet in a graveyard one frosty night, he was insane and awaiting a Resurrection of the Dead.

For Sylvia Plath.

I am resting in your grave of nettles,
Your purple soul weaves entrances,
Like an enchanted violin it is played,
By the nectar breath of your mouth.

My living willow is in a sullen tomb,
It is alight with colour and matter,
It is animated by wandering sighs,
Flowing in a purple force, my blood.
So, you stroke like a lover, my pen,
I write on pages midsummer frost.

Elegy for Elise Cowen ('beat' poet: 1933-1962).

Your smile is bright with magic, it

draws in verse

Completely Fragmented:

To glimpse the "straights", their

vision is blurred

 And gazes inert, that form is

carried in a hearse,

But you who danced the naked

poetics preferred

The peace of wombs, the warmth, and "rush" induced seductress,

Our wastes are frozen with promises, caught and chosen

  This moth of candle and flame is burnt and
                         wingless,

  At dawn you're cupped in a wrinkled hand
                    and have written

  A dirge of deserts and biting

   sand which sings Into the

  syringe, enchantment of the

          finite "fix"

Lies with accusations on pages scribed

in blotted rings,

         This sacred insanity is

vibrating your soul, a matrix

  For jewels the wind whispered opiate kiss,
                  its

Nigel Pearce

In here where belief lies on the

periphery, the poetry Ascends in

grace with those from Auschwitz,

You stumble across the graveyards and weep in symmetry

www.ingramcontent.com/pod-product-compliance
Ingram Content Group UK Ltd.
Pitfield, Milton Keynes, MK11 3LW, UK
UKHW041410180426
11947UKWH00007B/32